IMAGES
of America

SHERMAN

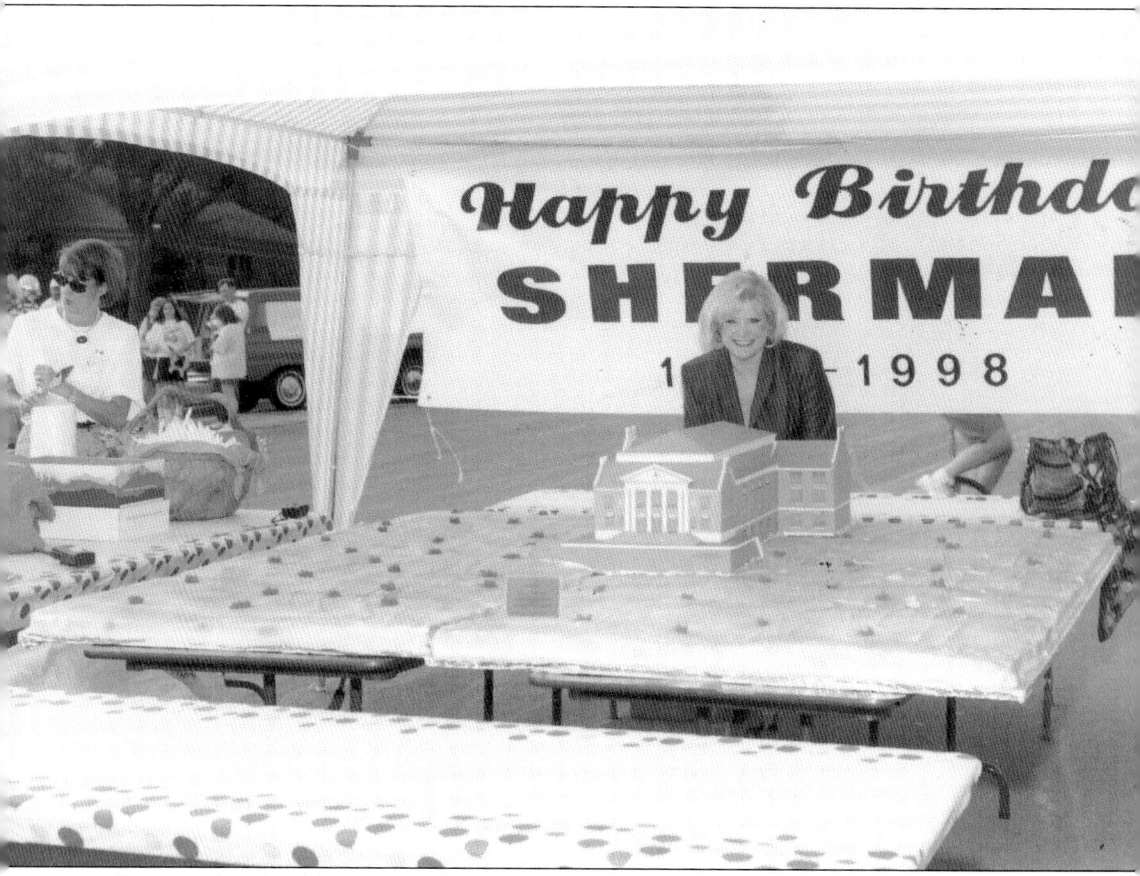

Sherman's 150th Birthday Celebration. Mayor Julie Ellis Starr shows off a cake with a replica of the municipal building for Sherman's 150th Birthday Celebration Encore! The event was held in September 1998 and featured period events displaying the town's history, a laser show in Bearcat Stadium, and a street dance featuring Dash Riprock and the Dragons. (Courtesy of Julie Ellis Starr.)

On the Cover: Sherman city employees meet around 1940 for a group photograph in front of the fleet and the new municipal building, which was completed in 1938 to house city offices. In 1940, the city manager was W. Morgan Works and the city clerk was J.C. Bryant. The estimated population of Sherman was 20,000, and the community covered 5.33 square miles. (Courtesy of the City of Sherman.)

IMAGES
of America

SHERMAN

Linda Ashby

ARCADIA
PUBLISHING

ISBN 978-0-7385-7983-2

Published by Arcadia Publishing
Charleston, South Carolina

Printed in the United States of America

Library of Congress Control Number: 2011920849

For all general information, please contact Arcadia Publishing:
Telephone 843-853-2070
Fax 843-853-0044
E-mail sales@arcadiapublishing.com
For customer service and orders:
Toll-Free 1-888-313-2665

Visit us on the Internet at www.arcadiapublishing.com

This book is dedicated to the men and women that have made Sherman the community it is today. Their dedication and perseverance have left a legacy for us all. It is also dedicated to my husband, Greg Ashby. Even though he was not born in Sherman, he has made Sherman his home. And to our daughter, Chelsea Ashby, who reminds us of the future generation of Shermanites.

Contents

ACKNOWLEDGMENTS

Many people helped and supported me during the writing of this book. First, I would like to thank the City of Sherman for allowing me to work every day at a job I truly love. Thanks to Robby Hefton for his support when I told him I wanted to write this book.

I would like to thank my mom and dad for instilling a love of community in me and for giving me the best childhood anyone could ever ask for. Also, thanks to Chelsea Ashby, our daughter. She keeps things real and keeps me grounded in today.

A big thank-you goes to the staff of the Red River Historical Museum (now the Sherman Museum), Marcia Rolbiecki and especially Chris Rumohr, who unselfishly worked to help me locate and scan photographs and information as I searched through Sherman's history.

Thanks to John Spears of Quin Studio, who often dropped everything he was doing and scanned photographs for me, even on New Year's Day.

I would also like to thank the employees of the Sherman Public Library, especially Jacqueline Banfield and Michael Miller. Jackie's keen eye and love for genealogy proved to be invaluable and Michael's knowledge of the historical documents housed in the library was especially appreciated.

Also thanks to the many people who offered me photographs from their collection including Ivert and Jeanette Mayhugh, Missy Sofey-Andrews, Julie Ellis Starr, Pat Dannel, Margaret Williams, Tom Watt, Jeff Jones, John Spears, Roger and Kay Goodwin, Waldo Funeral Home, and the Sherman Economic Development Corporation. Also thanks to the City of Sherman for allowing me to use their extensive collection of historical photographs.

Lastly, I would especially like to thank my husband, Greg Ashby. He was always supportive and willing to help during the writing of this book. He allowed me to use his collection of postcards and was invaluable as the research was done, the photographs were scanned, the layout was put together, and the final book took shape. Without his help, I could not have completed this task. He often took time away from his business to help me accomplish my dream, and for that I am forever grateful. This is his book, too!

INTRODUCTION

From the beginning, Sherman was a tenacious town with settlers that did not intend to compromise. They originally settled the town in 1846, four miles west of its present location, but by 1848, they had determined there was not enough water or wood, and they moved the town to its present site. They cleared the land, laid out some streets, and Sherman was on its way. T.J. Shannon earned the moniker "father of Sherman" after he donated land for the town site.

At first, Sherman consisted of muddy streets and a few buildings constructed out of logs or whatever else was nearby. By 1852, the population was 400, and the local newspaper described the town as "a row of clapboard houses, a few saloons, and a double log house with a few trees."

The Sherman Butterfield Stage Station opened in 1858, linking the community to St. Louis, Missouri, and San Francisco, California, on the 2,795-mile stage route. Sherman was six days from the eastern starting point, and the entire trip took about 25 days.

By 1872, the railroad was here, colleges were established, and industry began to grow. The population reached 6,000. In 1877, the City Street Railway Company began operating mule-drawn streetcars, and by 1901, the Interurban was the first electric railway line in Texas. People could ride the "Limited" to Dallas every hour and then continue on different routes to other Texas cities. Between the stage, the Interurban, and the railway system, Sherman was now connected.

Industry found a willing partner in the community as textile factories, grain mills, and food manufacturing plants opened—the cotton industry, grain mills, and food products, put Sherman on the industrial map. There was Washington Iron Works; Roberts, Sanford & Taylor Company; Burlington Industries; Birge-Forbes Cotton Brokers; Fant Milling Company; Hardwicke-Etter Company; Pool Manufacturing; and Anderson, Clayton & Company.

With the growth of industry, Sherman also saw a growth in culture. Hospitals, hotels, opera houses, and schools sprang up as the citizens demanded these amenities. Besides the public schools, there was Mary Nash College, Capt. LeTellier's Academy, North Texas Female Academy, Kidd-Key Conservatory of Music, Carr-Burdette College, and St. Joseph's Academy. Austin College, founded in 1849 in Huntsville, Texas, moved to Sherman in 1876, and is the oldest college in Texas operating under its original charter.

Then there was St. Vincent's Sanitarium, which opened in 1902 by the Daughters of Charity of St. Vincent de Paul and Sherman Hospital Company, which opened in 1913 and was later renamed Wilson N. Jones Hospital.

Hotels in Sherman included the Oriental, the Williams, the Binkley, and the Grayson. In 1929, the Grayson Hotel was touted as "the envy of the city." The Binkley Hotel saw such visitors as William Jennings Bryan and William Howard Taft.

But Sherman saw dark days, too. In the early 1860s, Sherman saw outlaw visitors when William Clarke Quantrill and his "Raiders" and members of the James and Younger gangs came through the area. On Christmas Eve 1863, a group of Quantrill's Raiders shot up the town.

Two fires in 1875 left the downtown in shambles. In February, a fire caused about $100,000 worth of damage and destroyed a major portion of the business district. Then, in October, another fire destroyed all the buildings on the south side of the square and all but two buildings on the east side of the square. The Binkley Hotel was destroyed by fire in 1887 but was rebuilt in the same location. It burned again in the mid-1890s and then for the final time in 1967, after it had been renamed the Texas Hotel.

Then there was "Black Friday," the deadly cyclone that cut a two-mile path through Sherman in May 1896, killing about 66 people and injuring countless others. The darkest day in Sherman's history happened on May 9, 1930, as an angry mob burned the Grayson County Courthouse. George Hughes, a black farm worker, was accused of assaulting a white woman. As the trial progressed, Hughes was put into a vault in the courthouse for his own protection.

The people outside grew restless, and a mob used dynamite and a blowtorch to get Hughes out of the vault. After his removal the mob drug him through the streets, hung him from a tree, and burned his body. Then they destroyed a portion of Sherman that was a thriving three-block black business district. Martial law was declared and the National Guard was sent in to protect the city from looters and further mob violence. Many of the rioters were said to be from out of town.

In October 1932, Clyde Barrow came to town and when he left, one more notch had been added to his belt. Barrow had been seen earlier in the day at the Grayson County Jail where his younger brother L.C. Barrow was being held on a car theft charge. Barrow later entered Sid Little's Grocery and Market on South Vaden Street and attempted to rob the cashier. Howard Hall, the meat market clerk, tried to stop the robbery but was shot four times by Barrow who left him to die within the hour.

During Sherman's history, two police officers have been killed in the line of duty. In 1880, city marshal Sam Ball was shot and killed while responding to a party of drunken "roughs" that were creating a disturbance. Then in December 1969, Sgt. D.C. Arnold was gunned down as he surprised two robbers in the Rocket Oil Company on West Houston Street. Sgt. Arnold had stopped by the station in the early morning hours to look in on his friend Omer L. "Rock" Chambers, a former Grayson County Sheriff's Deputy. Chambers was also killed during the robbery.

Also in 1969, seven-year-old Donna Marie Golish from Sherman was kidnapped as she walked home from school and was viciously murdered. Seven months later, 11-year-old Laurie Stevens from Denison was kidnapped and murdered. The bodies of both girls were found face down in ravines, one near Sherman and one in Denison. Life in Sherman changed for children after the murders. No longer would parents allow them to play outside after dark, and trips to and from school were a lot more closely guarded. A week after the second murder, 18-year-old Charles Dennis Easley was arrested and eventually received a life sentence for the Golish murder. Finally, citizens of the two communities could rest easier.

But as in every community, these dark times are far outweighed by the happier times. Both Pres. Theodore Roosevelt and Pres. William Howard Taft visited Sherman. Roosevelt visited in April 1905 on his way to a reunion with his Rough Riders in San Antonio. Taft visited Sherman twice, first in 1919 and again in 1920, after his term of office ended. During both visits, he spoke at Austin College.

In 1959, a contract was let for the first leg of a controlled access freeway through Sherman to be known as Highway 75. The 3.1-mile strip was completed from Houston Street south to the Old Dorchester Road intersection.

And industry, always the mainstay in Sherman, continued to grow, especially in the 1960s and 1970s. Companies locating in Sherman included International Business Machines; Johnson and Johnson; Olson Bodies—Grumman Allied Industries; Kaiser Aluminum; Miss King's Kitchens; Texas Instruments; Oscar Mayer; Fisher Controls; Folgers; and Libby-Owens-Ford.

In 1980, Sherman was designated an "All-America City" and in 1993 was ranked 33rd "most livable" city in the United States by *Money* magazine.

One

A New Town Called Sherman

In December 1845, Texas was annexed into the Union and the first State Legislature organized several new counties. One of these counties was Grayson County, authorized on November 17, 1846, and created from a part of Fannin County. Grayson County was named for Peter W. Grayson, attorney general of the Texas Republic in 1836 and 1837 and a candidate for president of the Texas Republic in 1838.

Sherman was founded in 1846 by the county commissioners and was located in the center of the county, approximately four miles west of the present site. Because of a lack of wood and water, in 1848, the town was moved to its present site. The site was marked by a large pecan tree on the southeast corner of what is now the town square. As Sherman grew, the pecan tree served as the bank, the post office, the place where court was held, the general meeting place for the community, and on Sunday mornings, a place for religious services.

The pecan tree continued to play a big part in the development of Sherman. T.J. Shannon began clearing the land for the community by hitching six yoke of oxen to a pecan tree and dragging it through the brush. After the town was laid out, Shannon's 12-year-old daughter, Julia Shannon, was allowed to name the streets using the names of Texas heroes and native trees. Thus Mulberry, Pecan, Elm, Walnut, Cherry, Crockett, Houston, Jones, Rusk, Lamar, and Travis Streets were born.

From the beginning, Sherman was known as an educational and religious center. The first school, founded in 1849, was a log cabin with a dirt floor and a hole in the roof to emit the smoke. Trinity United Presbyterian Church is the oldest congregation and was organized in 1851, as the "Sherman Society under the government and care of the Cumberland Presbyterian Church."

Sherman began its growth, and in 1857, the business section consisted of two or three little stores. The west side of the square was residential property. There was a store on the northwest corner, which was the first brick building in Sherman, and a six-room hotel on the north side. There was also a dry goods and general merchandise store. On the east side of the square, there was a long row of log cabins, one of which was used as a courthouse. Sherman was incorporated in 1858.

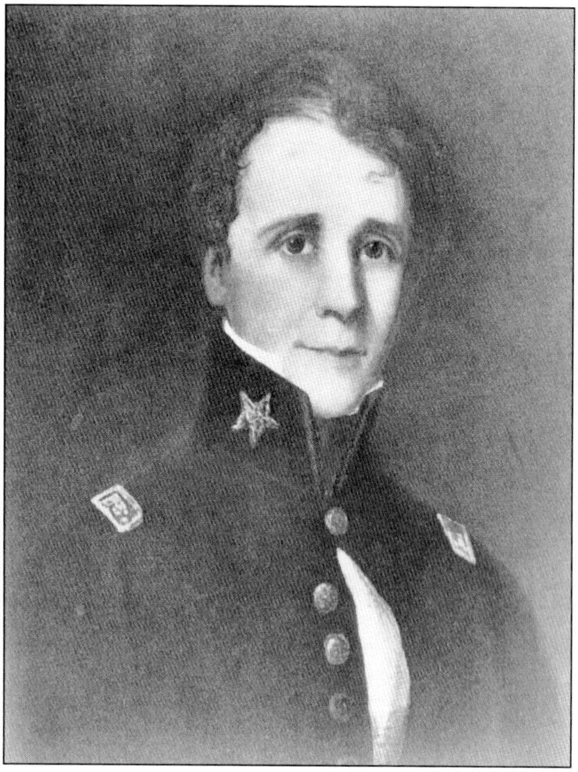

SIDNEY SHERMAN, 1805–1873. Sherman was named for Gen. Sidney Sherman, a hero of the Texas Revolution. On April 21, 1836, he led his regiment into the Battle of San Jacinto with the cry, "Remember the Alamo! Remember Goliad!" General Sherman was also the principal organizer of the Buffalo Bayou, Brazos, and Colorado Railway, the first railroad company in Texas. (Courtesy of the City of Sherman.)

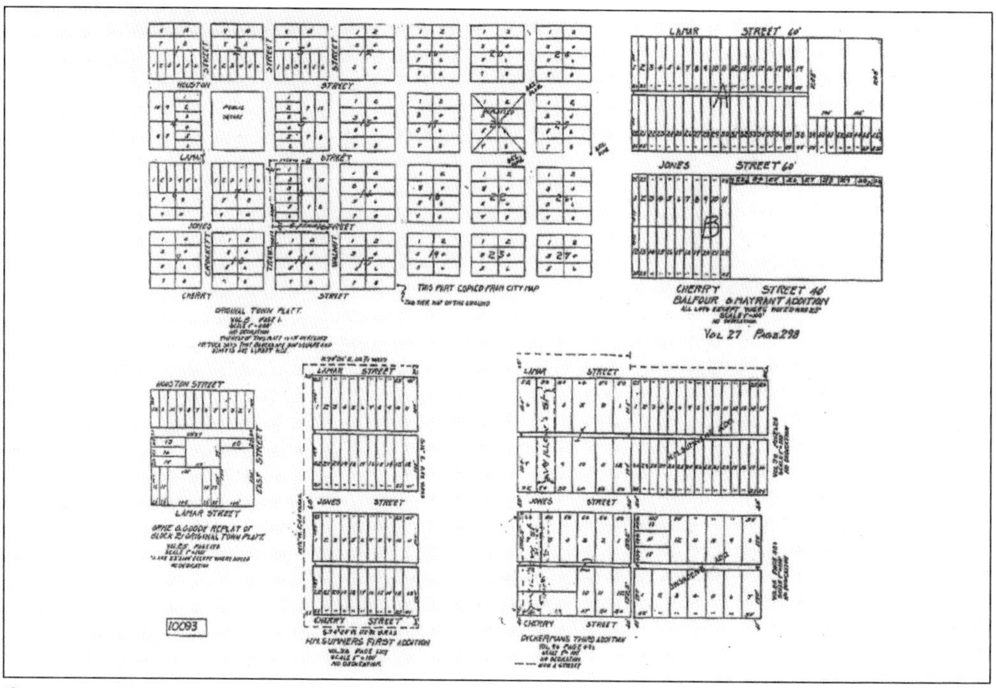

ORIGINAL TOWN PLAT. Samuel Blagg, a surveyor, deeded 80 acres to the Grayson County Commissioners for the present site of Sherman for $100. The sale is recorded in the Grayson County deed records in Volume A on November 23, 1848. (Courtesy of the City of Sherman.)

ORIGINAL ORDINANCES AND BY-LAWS. The city of Sherman was incorporated in 1858. This photograph shows a copy of the original set of ordinances that were approved January 27, 1858. They were revised and adopted by the board of alderman to "take effect and be in full force from and after the 4th day of August 1872." (Courtesy of the City of Sherman.)

ORDINANCES AND BY-LAWS
OF THE
CITY OF SHERMAN.

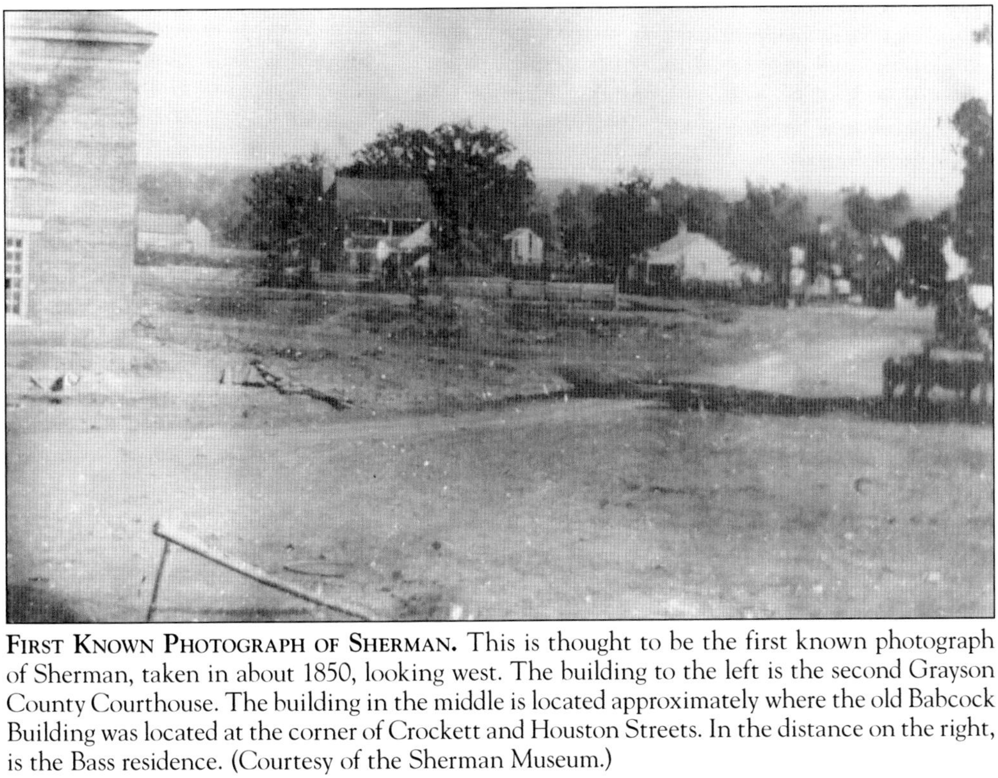

FIRST KNOWN PHOTOGRAPH OF SHERMAN. This is thought to be the first known photograph of Sherman, taken in about 1850, looking west. The building to the left is the second Grayson County Courthouse. The building in the middle is located approximately where the old Babcock Building was located at the corner of Crockett and Houston Streets. In the distance on the right, is the Bass residence. (Courtesy of the Sherman Museum.)

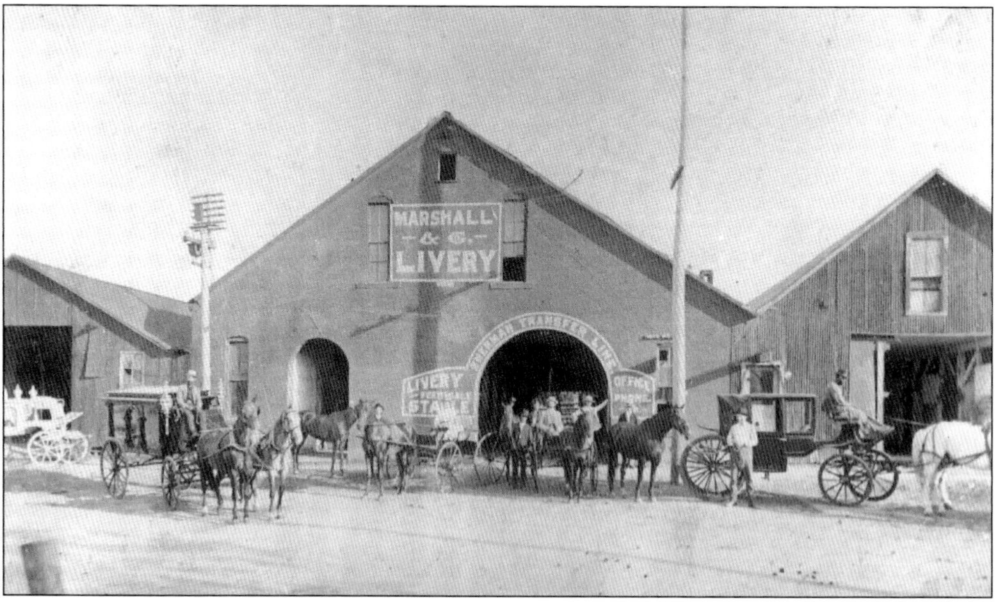

MARSHALL & CO. LIVERY STABLE. The Marshall & Co. Livery Stable was located at 118 East Pecan Street around 1901. It was part of the Sherman Transfer Company owned by Louis Sarazan. They advertised rubber-tired outfits, carriages and buggies for funerals, balls, and theater parties. They also offered a transfer service between hotels, residences, and train stations. Sarazan also operated a brewing distributor, a mineral water company, and sold cigars. (Courtesy of the Sherman Museum.)

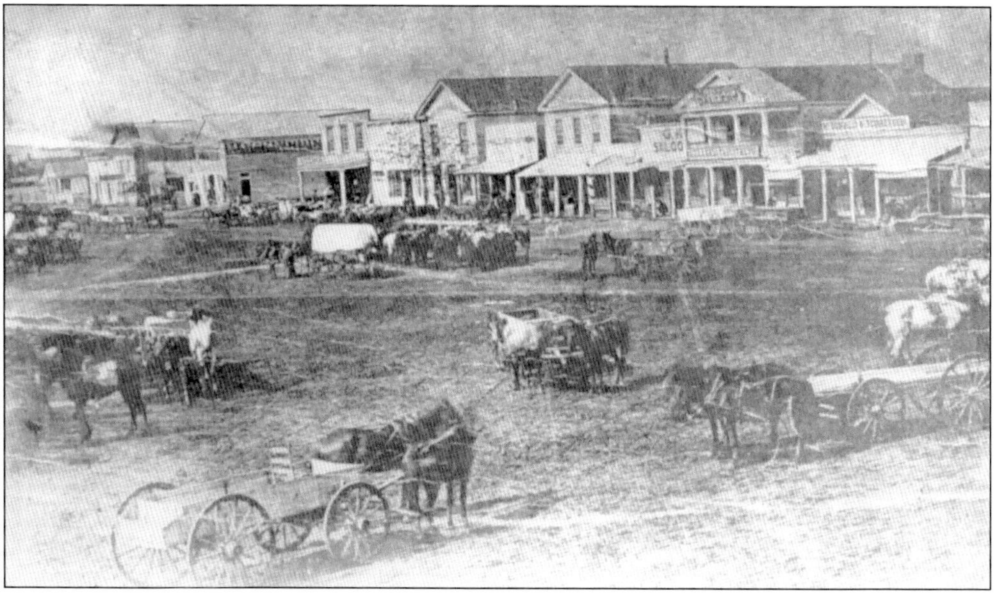

EAST SIDE OF THE SQUARE, 1868. This photograph shows the east side of the square, prior to the construction of the courthouse. M. Schneider Company (far left) was located at the corner of Houston and Travis Streets. To the south were Henry and Andrews, Dugan and Randolph general merchandise store, Hall and Chapman firm, John Shaw Barber Shop and the Iron Post Grocery, the OK Saloon, Eubank and Caruthers with a photography gallery upstairs, and McDonald and Roberts. (Courtesy of the Sherman Museum.)

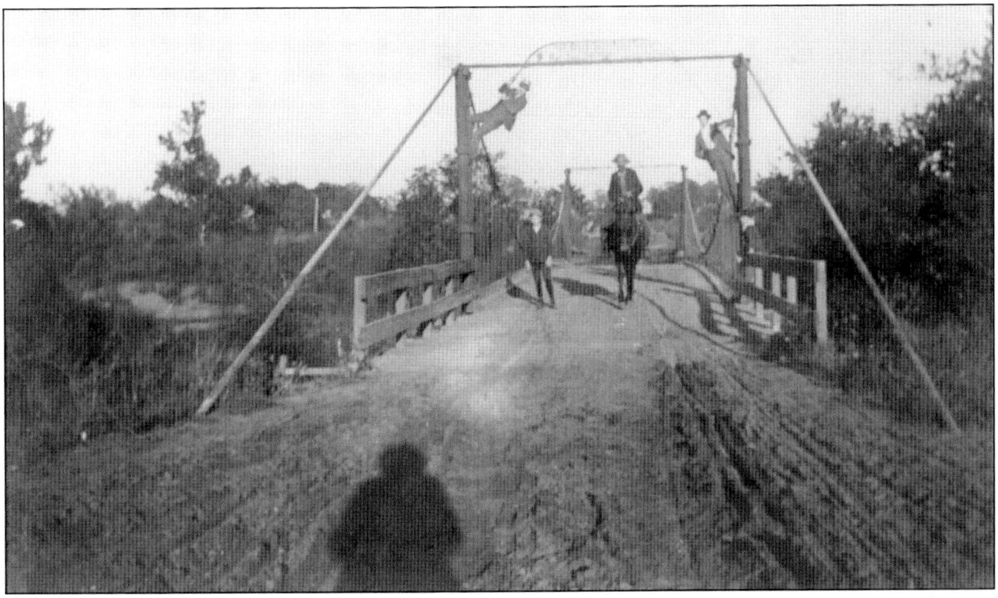

Suspension Bridges. Brothers Will Greer and "Uncle" Fate Greer built swinging bridges in the 1890s and early 1900s. The Greers operated under the name of Greer Bridge Company and held patents on the old swinging bridge and the system of suspension used nationwide. The bridges were built by the Knaur Foundry in Denison and installed by the Greer Brothers. The top photograph is an example of a Greer Suspension Bridge, and the bottom photograph shows a swinging bridge either on West Cherry Street or West Tennessee Street. (Both courtesy of the Sherman Museum.)

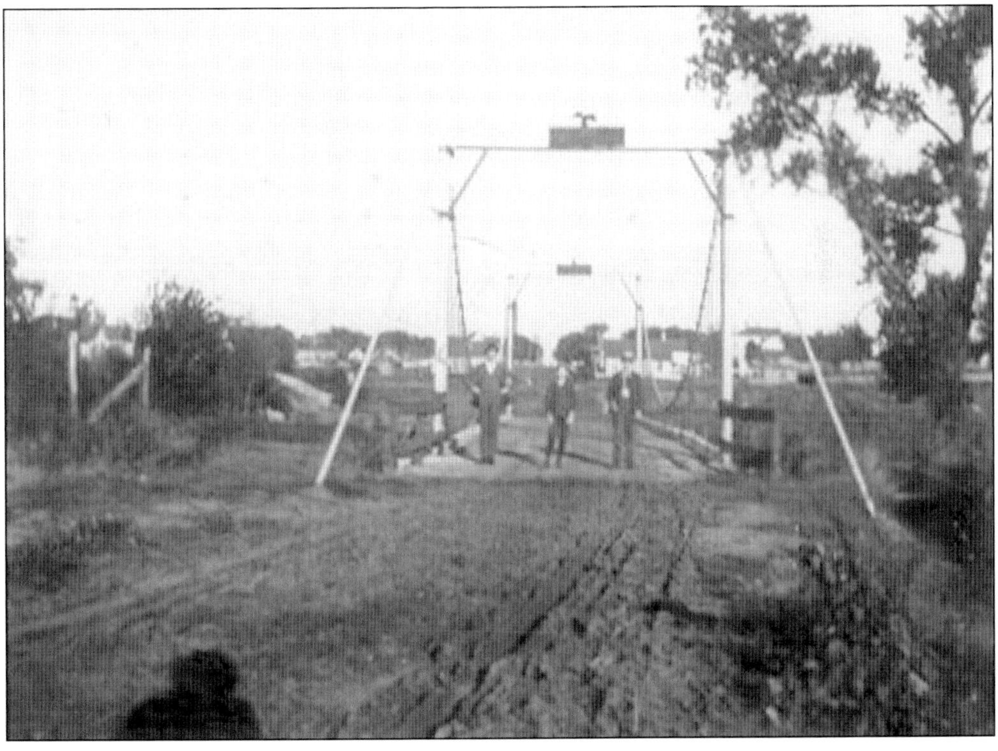

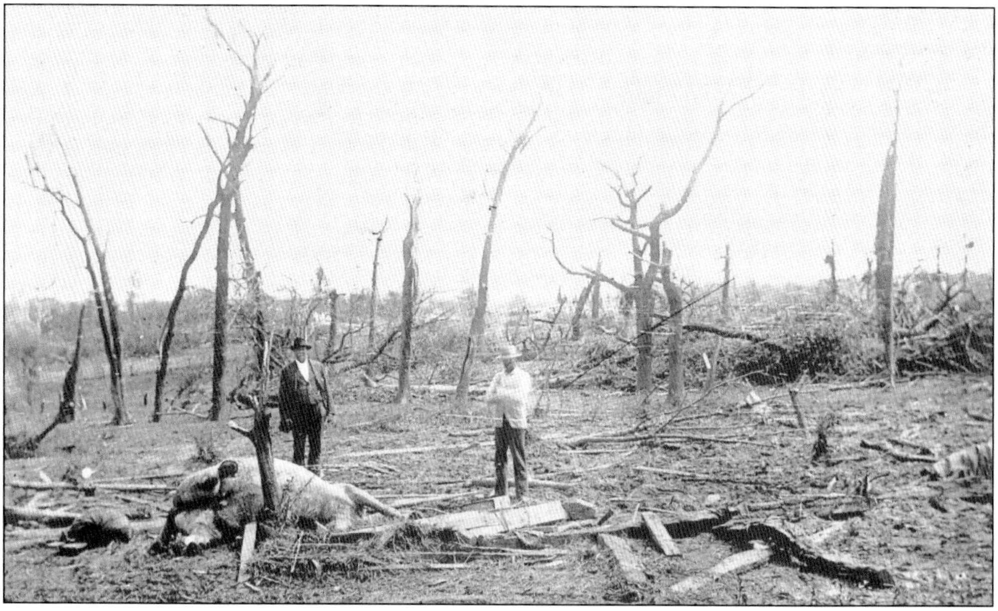

Sherman's Black Friday. The cyclone of 1896 was known as "Sherman's Black Friday" and devastated everything in its path. The cyclone was spotted at 4:45 p.m., southwest of Sherman. A weathervane at First Presbyterian Church pointed north, while the one on the oil mills, five blocks east of the church pointed south. The top photograph shows a landowner and a dead horse located in the remains of a grove on Gray's Hill, south of the ruins of Capt. L.F. Ely's home. The bottom photograph shows a man standing near the remnants of his buggy, north of the Ely residence. (Both courtesy of the City of Sherman.)

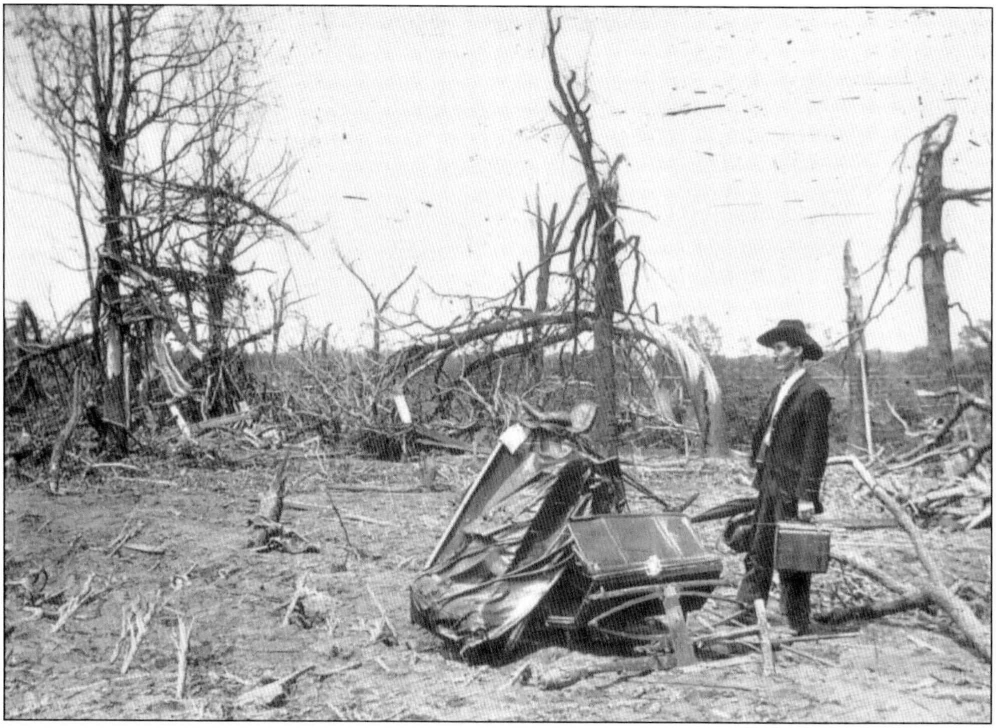

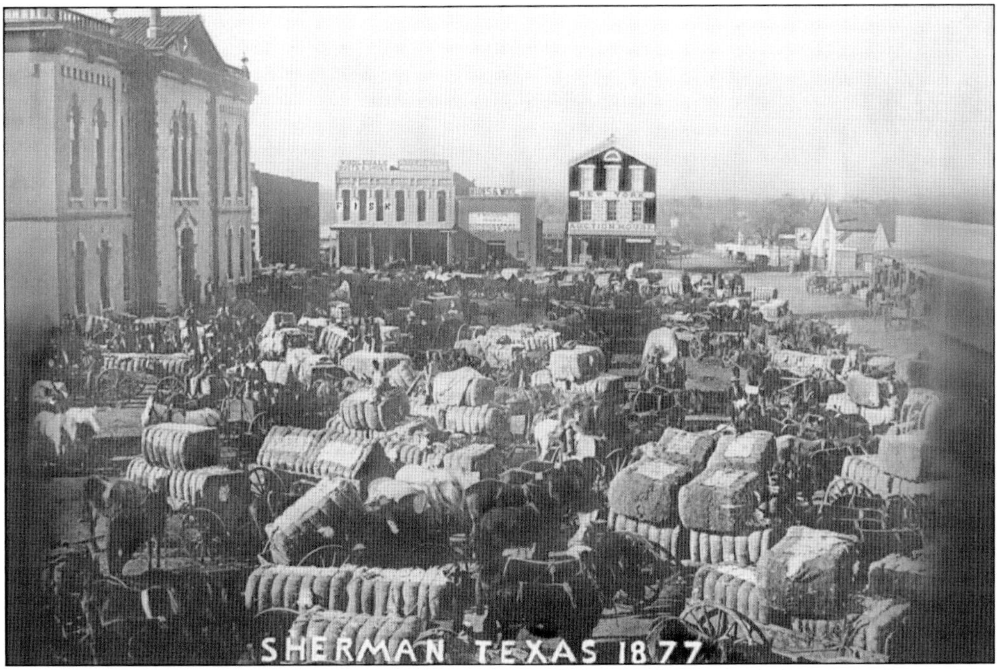

Cotton Sale Day on the Square, 1877. Wagons laden with cotton bales await the highest bidder on the courthouse square. The market scene looks west on Houston Street. Businesses seen in the distance are, left to right, the Fisk Building with wholesale boots and shoes, Patty Joiner and Company wholesale grocers, A. Wasson Hides and Wool, and the New York Auction House. (Courtesy of John Spears.)

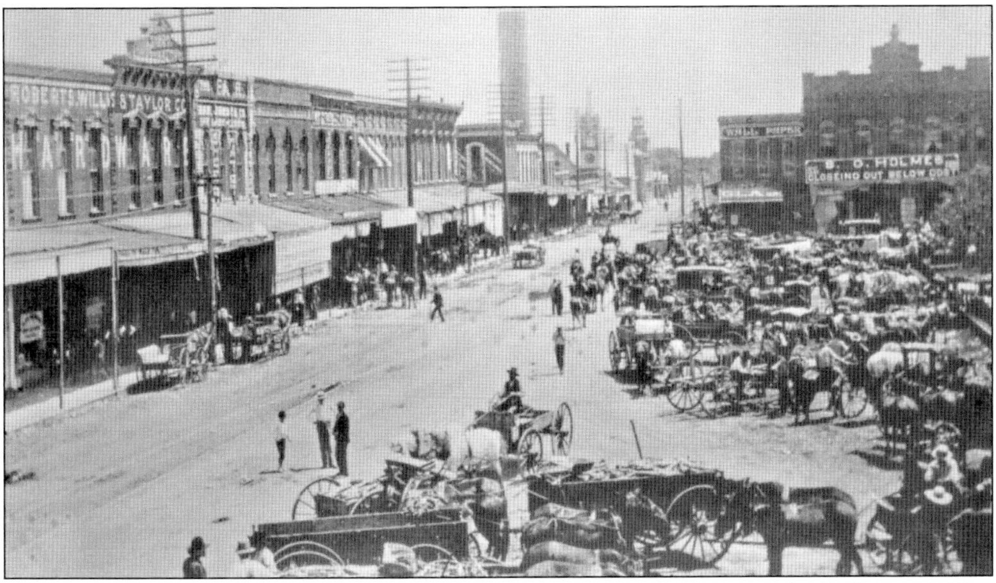

East Side of the Square, 1890. This photograph shows Travis Street as it looked in 1890. The horse-drawn wagons are parked at the courthouse. The identifiable buildings at left are Roberts, Hardwicke, and Taylor Company Hardware and Murphy, Joiner Company. In the background to the left, the fire department standpipe and the First Methodist Church are visible. (Courtesy of the City of Sherman.)

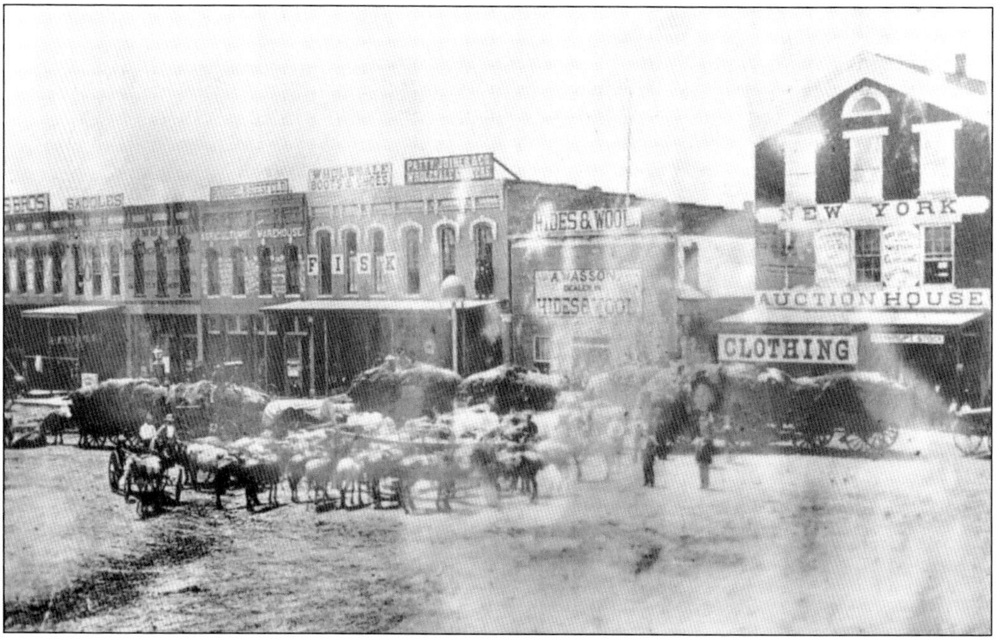

WEST SIDE OF THE SQUARE. In 1878, A. Wasson's Hides and Wool store received 2,500 bison hides. The New York Auction House is located at the corner of Crockett and Houston Streets. Other stores include, from left to right, Byres Brothers, dealers in agricultural implements; a harness shop; Roussel and Siesfeld; the Fisk Building; and the Patty Joiner Company. (Courtesy of the City of Sherman.)

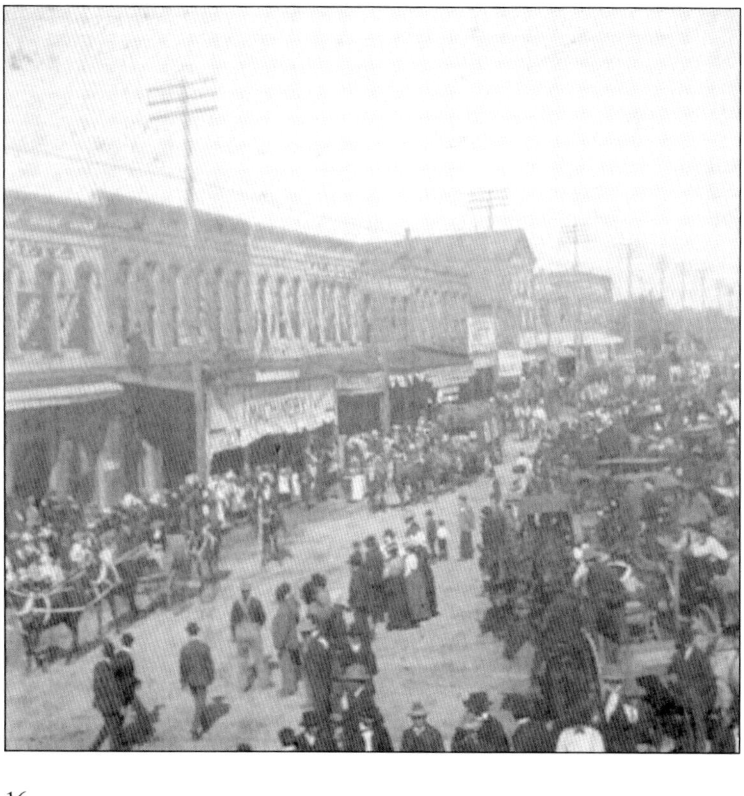

A BUSY DOWNTOWN. A bustling Sherman is seen in the late 1890s on the west side of the square on Crockett Street. Identifiable businesses include, from left to right, Metz, C.D. Hughes and Brothers Machinery, Dodson and Strong, Saloon, J.R. Cole Agent, and Misfit Clothing. (Courtesy of the Sherman Museum.)

OLIVE ANN OATMAN FAIRCHILD, 1837–1903. At the age of 13, Olive Ann Oatman was traveling west with her family when they were attacked by Yavapai Indians in Arizona. Six members of her family were massacred and she was sold to the Mojave Indians, who tattooed her chin with five blue lines, the mark of a slave. She was bought from the Mojave Indians by the Army in 1856 and reunited with her brother Lorenzo. (Courtesy of the Sherman Museum.)

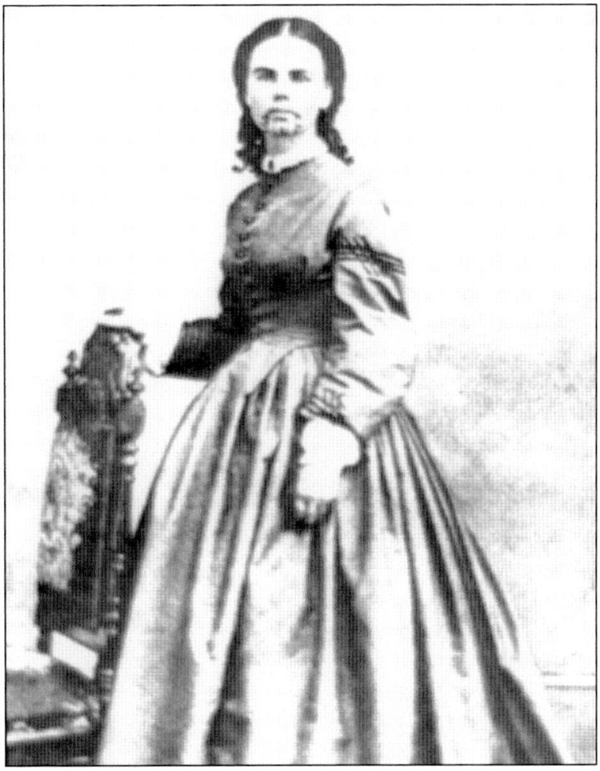

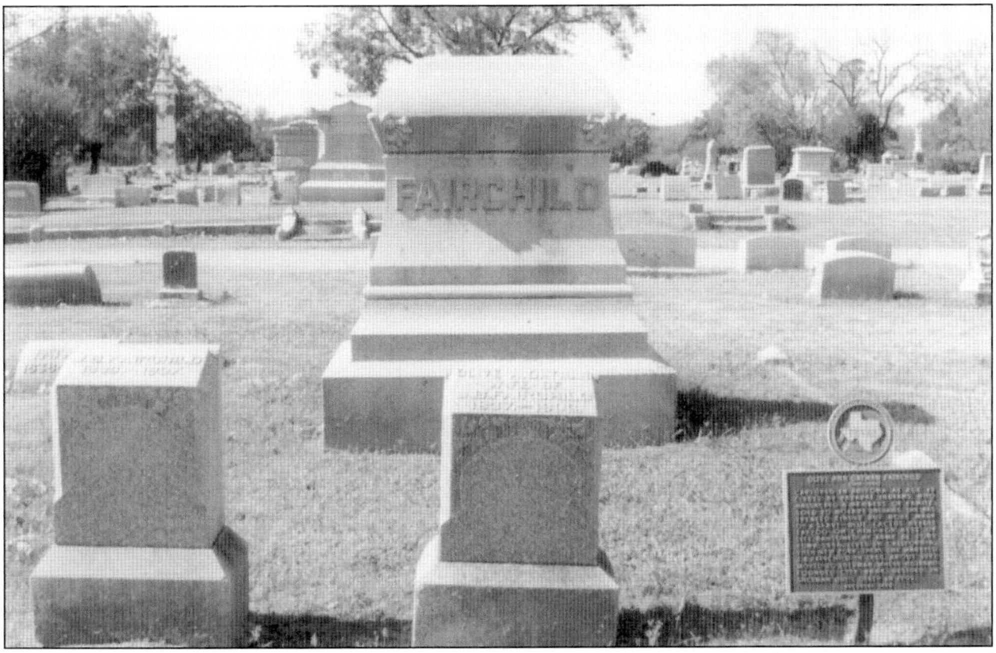

OLIVE OATMAN FAIRCHILD BURIED AT WEST HILL CEMETERY. In 1865, Olive Oatman married John Brant Fairchild and they moved to Texas in the 1870s. Maj. Fairchild founded City Bank of Sherman. In 1873, they adopted their only child, Mary Elizabeth "Mamie." Olive Fairchild died in 1903 and is buried at West Hill Cemetery. (Courtesy of the Sherman Museum.)

OLD COURTHOUSE, 1876. Capt. L.F. Ely constructed the old courthouse in 1876. In 1919, an explosion caused an estimated $100,000 in damages when gas accumulated overnight in the airtight vault. An electric fan was left in the vault to speed the drying of a newly laid asphaltic floor and a spark from the fan ignited the gas. After remodeling, the tower of the courthouse was removed. (Courtesy of the Sherman Museum.)

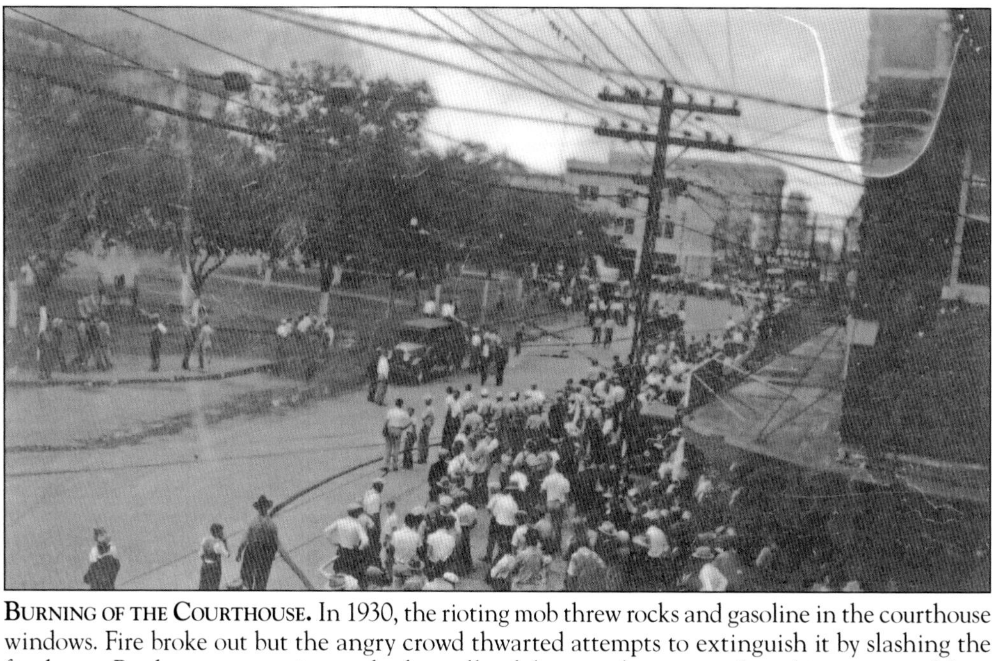

BURNING OF THE COURTHOUSE. In 1930, the rioting mob threw rocks and gasoline in the courthouse windows. Fire broke out but the angry crowd thwarted attempts to extinguish it by slashing the fire hoses. By the next morning, only the walls of the courthouse stood, and it was a total loss. The crowd was estimated at 2,000 people, but many rioters were reportedly from outside the county. (Courtesy of John Spears.)

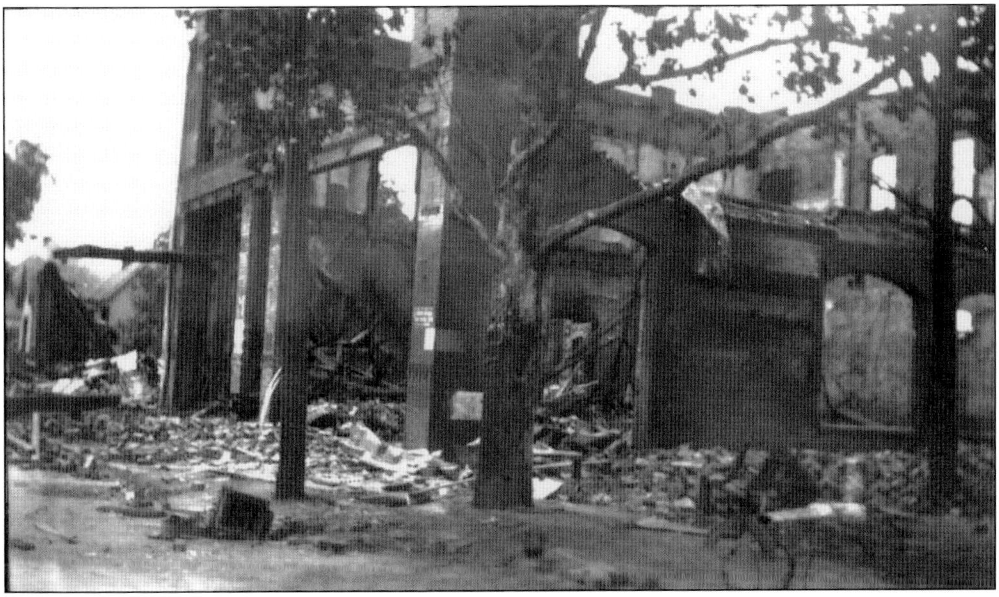

Grayson County Courthouse. Only some walls remained of the Grayson County Courthouse after it burned during the riot of 1930. A maddened crowd torched the building to get George Hughes, a black man who had been accused of assaulting a white woman. Officials put Hughes in the vault for his safety. The crowd cut the fire hoses to keep firemen from extinguishing the fire. (Courtesy of the Sherman Museum.)

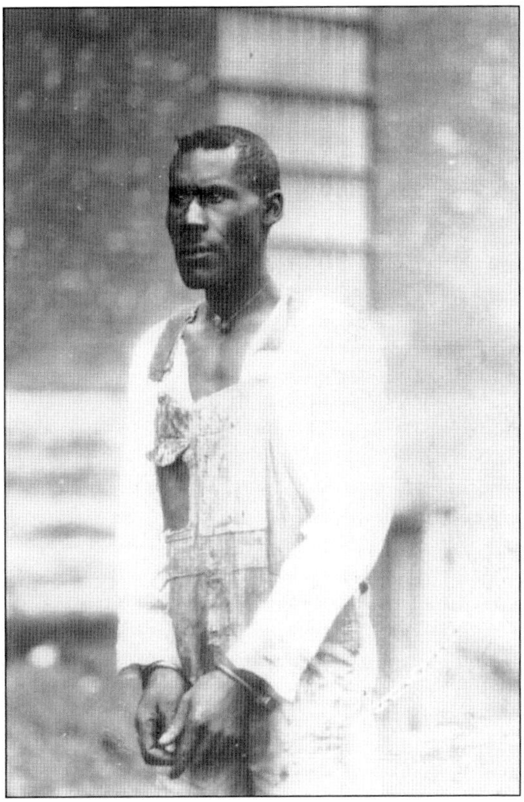

George Hughes, Riot of 1930. George Hughes, shown here handcuffed, went to trial in May 1930 for assaulting the wife of a prominent white farmer. During the trial, Hughes was placed in a two-story, fireproof vault in the Grayson County Courthouse for his own protection. An angry mob used dynamite to break into the vault, and he was killed. His body was dragged through town, then hung, and finally burned. (Courtesy of the Sherman Museum.)

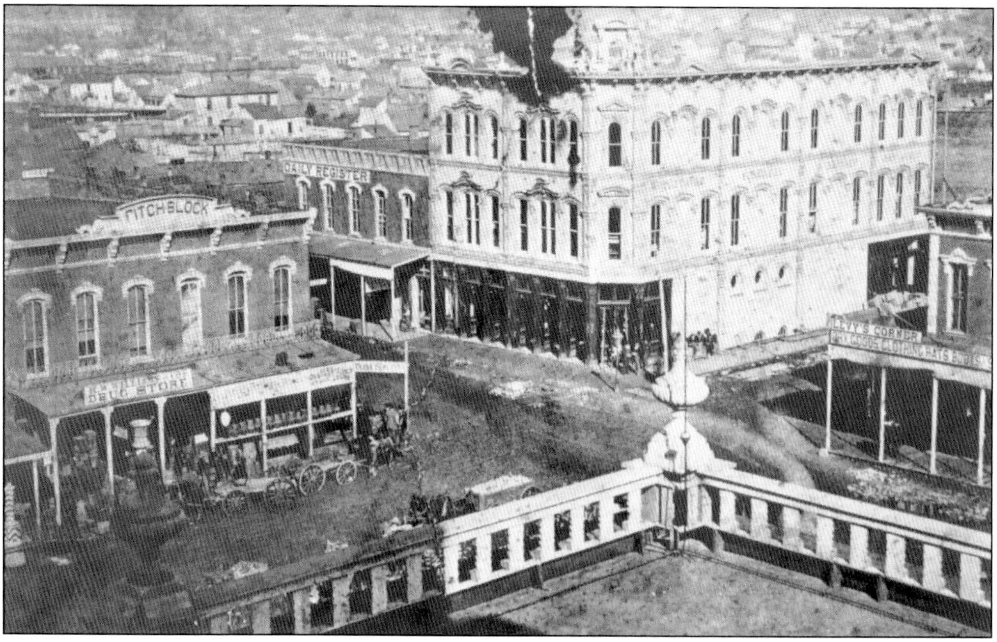

Northeast Corner of Travis and Houston Streets. This photograph was taken from the roof shortly after the second brick courthouse was completed around 1876. This courthouse was destroyed in the 1930 riot. Schneider's Department Store is located in the center of the photograph. It later housed Murphy's, Bass-Parrish-Taylor, Taylor-Vaughan, Price's, and Mitchell's Department Stores. (Courtesy of the City of Sherman.)

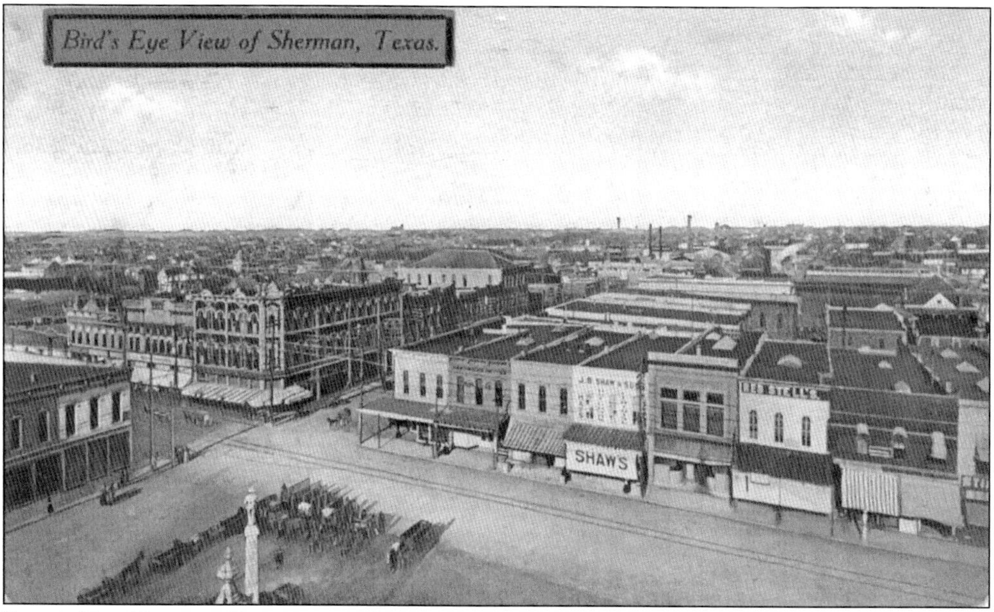

Bird's Eye View of Downtown Sherman, c. 1903. The photograph shows Travis Street on the east side of the square. J.B. Shaw and Sons was a dry goods store, and Reb Stell's was a confectioner. Murphy's Dry Goods is located at the northeast corner of Houston and Travis Streets. The Interurban tracks are visible in the street. The Confederate Monument on the courthouse grounds is at bottom left. (Courtesy of Greg Ashby.)

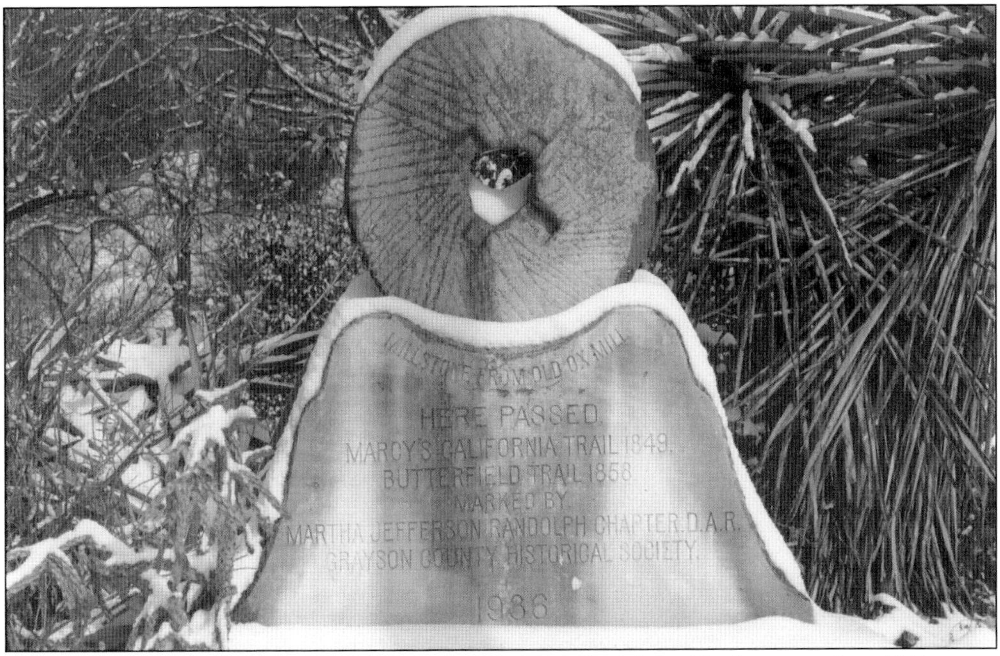

MARCY TRAIL AND BUTTERFIELD TRAIL MONUMENT. The Marcy Trail, surveyed in 1843, was a trail for immigrants to California. The Butterfield Trail of 1858 was an overland mail route. Both trails passed the same location in Sherman, near Washington Park. The monument was erected in 1936 by the Martha Jefferson Randolph Chapter of the Daughters of the American Revolution. (Courtesy of the Sherman Museum.)

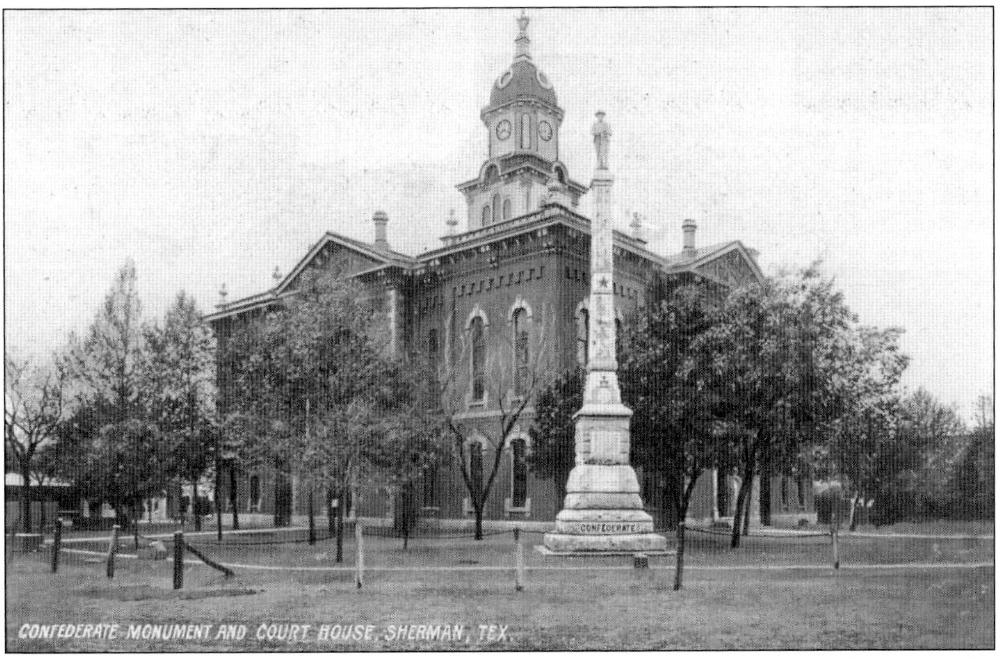

CONFEDERATE MONUMENT. The first Confederate Monument erected in Texas was located on the Grayson County Courthouse Square in 1896. The courthouse was constructed in 1876 and is the same one destroyed by fire during the riot of 1930. (Courtesy of the Sherman Museum.)

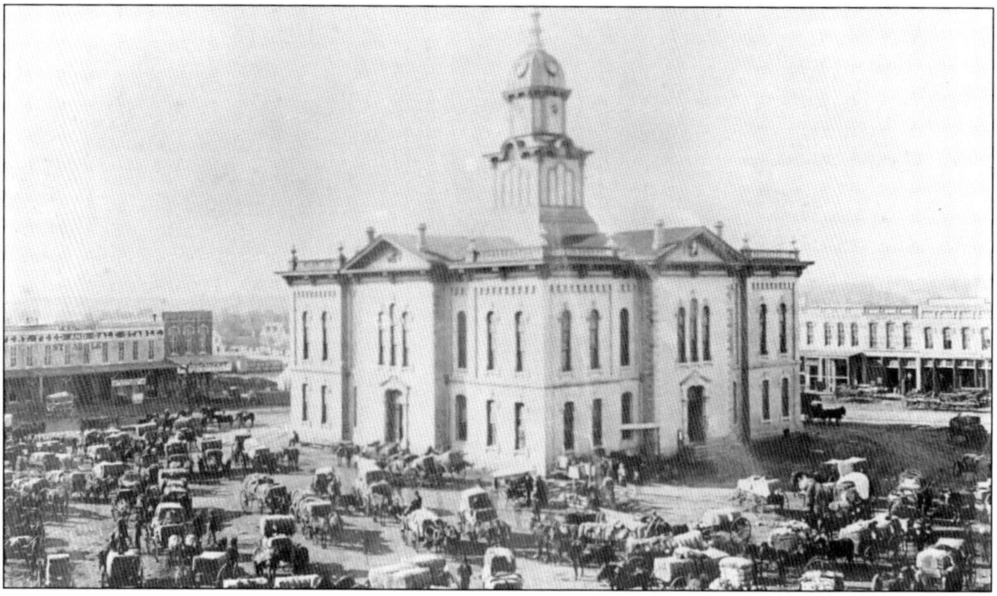

COTTON HARVEST AND THE RED BRICK COURTHOUSE, 1876. Farmers brought their cotton bales to the courthouse square to be auctioned off. The Red Brick Courthouse was constructed by Capt. L.F. Ely, who described it as a "majestic building." There was so much extra space in the building that the county rented rooms to the *Sherman Courier* and to various lawyers. During 1906, the streets around the courthouse were paved and the old cisterns covered. (Courtesy of the City of Sherman.)

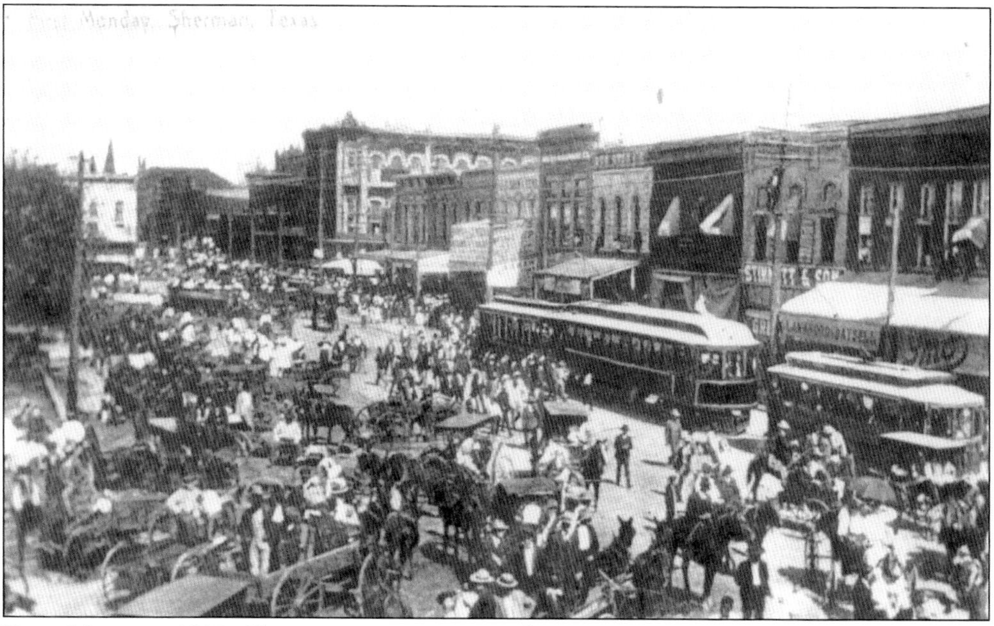

FIRST MONDAY, 1908. Sherman was a major market town in North Texas on First Mondays. Farmers from Montague to Lamar Counties came to sell their wares on the courthouse square, where customers could buy everything from potatoes to cotton to venison. These trade days eventually grew into the Red River Valley Fair. This photograph shows the east side of the square looking north on Travis Street. (Courtesy of the Sherman Museum.)

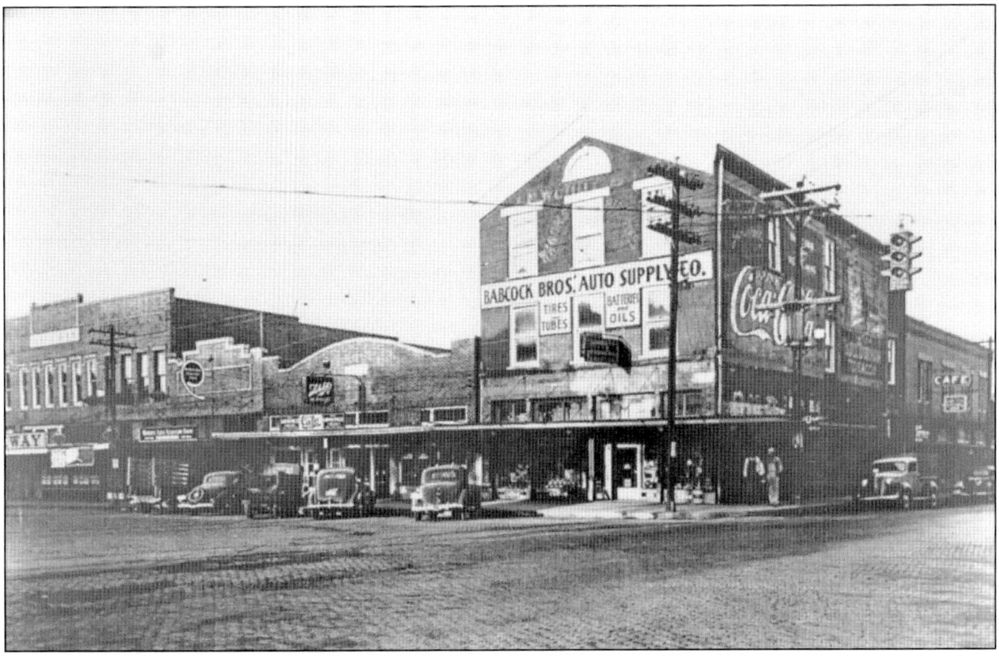

SOUTHWEST CORNER OF CROCKETT AND HOUSTON STREETS. This photograph shows Crockett Street as it looked in the 1930s. Hestand's Pharmacy was located in the Safeway Building. The Babcock Brothers Auto Supply Company building was built in 1856 and is the oldest building in Sherman. (Courtesy of the City of Sherman.)

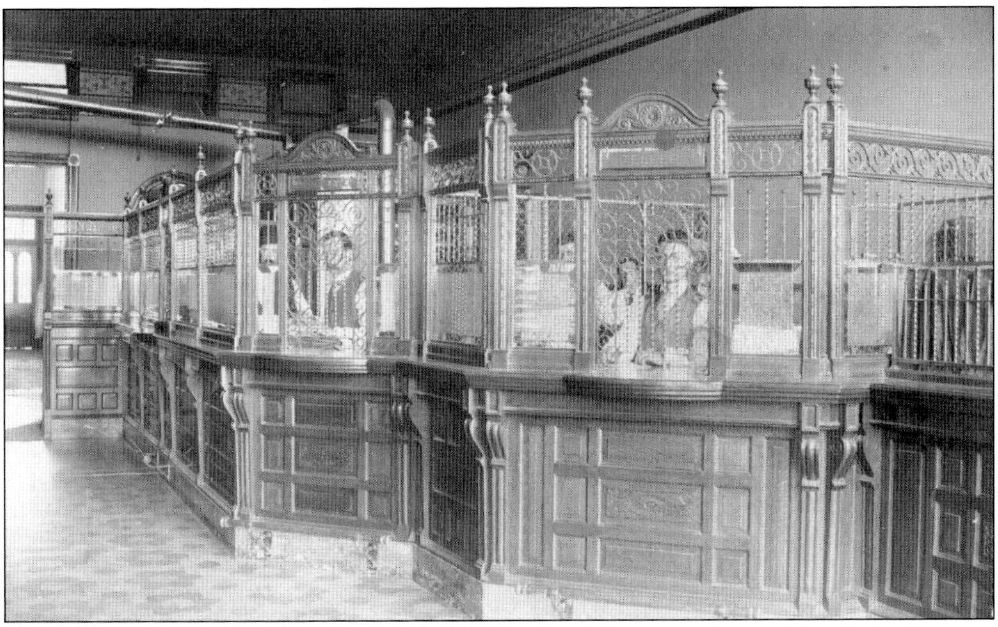

OLD CITY BANK. Old City Bank was founded by Maj. John Brant Fairchild in 1872, the same year as the Merchant and Planters Bank. One of the organizers of the bank was Judge Joseph Bledsoe, who also served as president. Major Fairchild was the husband of Olive Oatman Fairchild. Old City Bank was located at 118 North Travis Street and closed around 1900. (Courtesy of the Sherman Museum.)

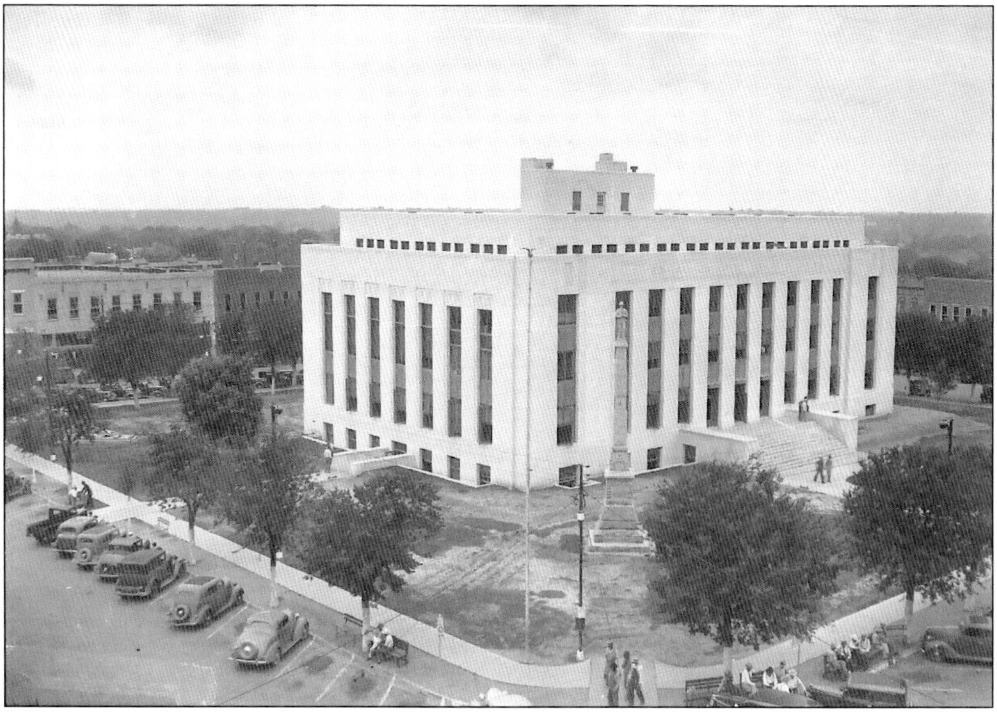

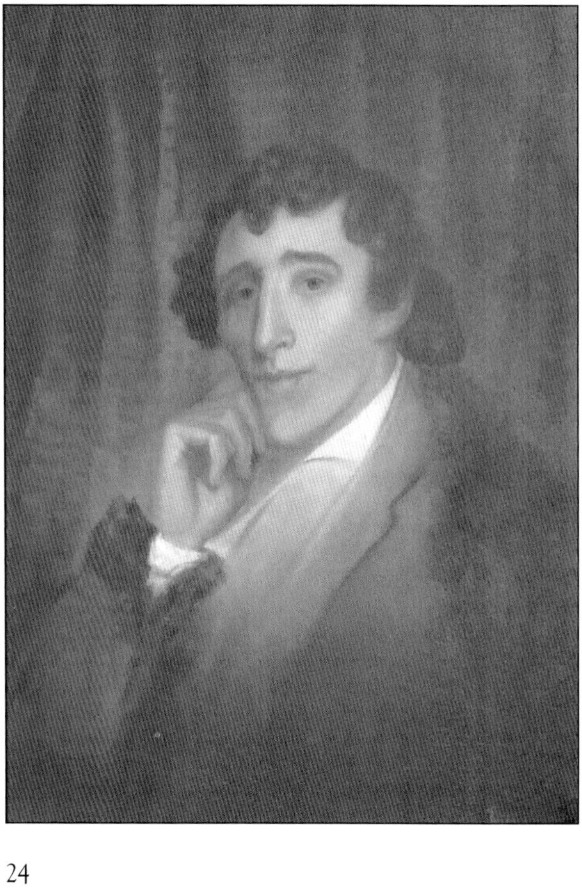

GRAYSON COUNTY COURTHOUSE. The current courthouse was completed in 1936 at a cost of $307,580 and featured Italian marble in the corridors and staircases. There was also a four-color map of Grayson County embedded in the floor of the main lobby. The fifth floor was used as a jail and could accommodate 60 prisoners. A new wing was added in 1963. (Courtesy of the Sherman Museum.)

PETER W. GRAYSON. Grayson County was named for Peter W. Grayson, who served as attorney general of the Texas Republic in 1836 and 1837. He was also a candidate for president of the Texas Republic in 1838. After Texas was annexed to the United States in 1846, the Texas Legislature created Grayson County, naming it for the Texas patriot. (Courtesy of the Sherman Museum.)

Two

The Birth of Commerce

From the beginning, Sherman maintained an industrial foundation that was diversified with textile factories, grain mills, food manufacturing plants, and the manufacturing of heavy machinery and machine tools. From a population of 400 in the 1850s, when the downtown consisted of a few log saloons and a log hotel, to the 1870s when Sherman boasted five large flour mills, growth was phenomenal.

The first railroad reached Sherman in 1872, and by the following year the town had a population of 6,000. Industry sprang up including Washington Iron Works which grew out of Totten Brothers Blacksmiths; Robert, Sanford and Taylor Hardware; and the Sherman Seamless Bag Company, which later became Burlington Industries. By 1891 Sherman Oil and Cotton Company was the largest cottonseed oil mill in the world and by 1896 Birge-Forbes Cotton Company was the largest cotton brokerage in the south.

Growth continued with Fant Milling Company (Gladiola), Hardwicke-Etter Company, Coca-Cola Bottling Company, and Pool Manufacturing Company. By the 1920s Sherman was called the "Fifth Industrial City of Texas" and by the 1930s the population was over 15,000.

Between the cotton market, the arrival of the railroad, and the 1927 vote that created US Highway 75, Sherman industry took off and never looked back.

In 1928, the *Sherman Daily Democrat* touted Sherman's favorable factors as, low taxes, an abundance of lumber, electric power, and transportation facilities for every need. It also had a favorable year round climate, opportunities for work or for play, and a progressive citizenship. As a city of manufacturing, the surrounding area furnished raw materials and provided a market for the products.

By 1948, Sherman industries featured Mrs. Tucker's Foods with approximately 425 employees, Quaker Oats Company with about 450 employees, Hardwicke-Etter Company with between 350 to 450 employees, Sherman Manufacturing Company with 300 employees, and Pool Manufacturing Company with 325 employees. These industries alone had an annual payroll of over $4 million, and manufactured everything from cornmeal and flour to shortening and margarine to overalls and workpants.

Along with the industries, Sherman also featured elegant hotels such as the Binkley and the Grayson, an opera house, and the Interurban, the first electric railway line in Texas. Other Sherman businesses included Chapin Title Company, an abstract service; Lewie and Lavender Company, selling wholesale groceries to retail stores; Locke the Tinner; and Ashburn's Ice Cream Parlor.

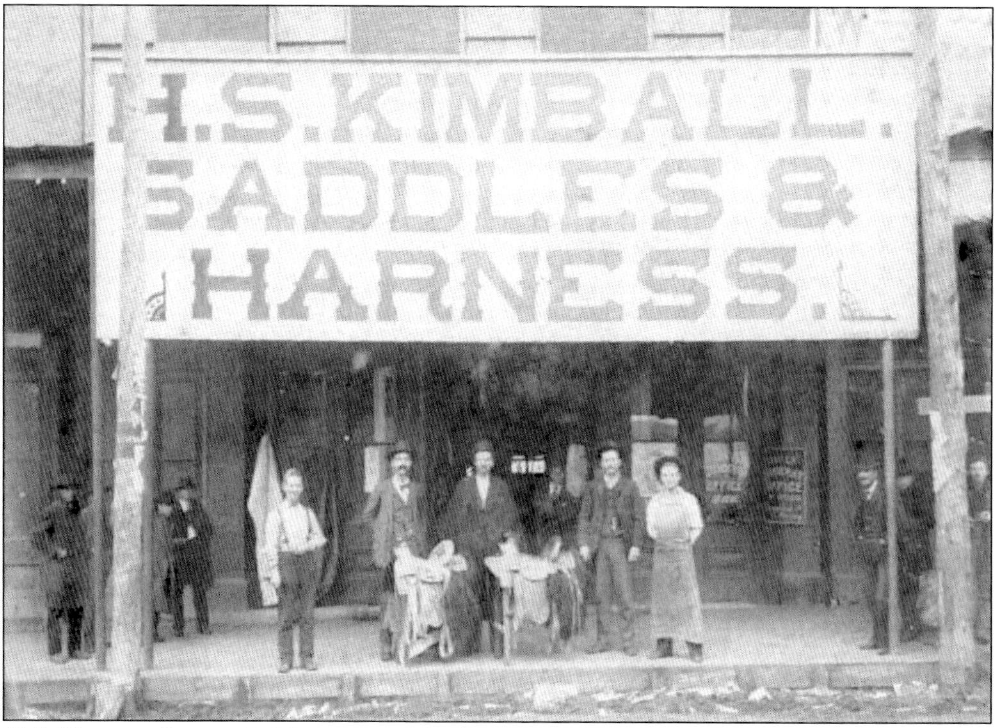

H.S. KIMBALL SADDLE & HARNESS. In the late 1880s and early 1900s, H.S. Kimball Saddle & Harness was located on the west side of the square on Crockett Street. Many harness shops and livery stables were located in Sherman, since the main mode of transportation was either by horse or wagon. (Courtesy of the Sherman Museum.)

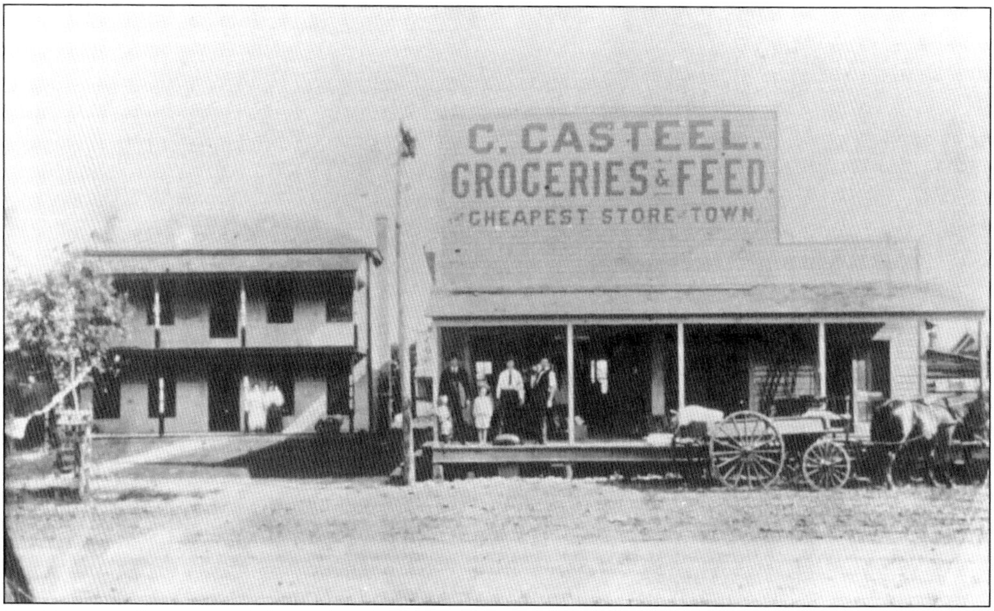

C. CASTEEL GROCERY & FEED. In the 1890s, C. Casteel Grocery & Feed was located on West Houston Street near Rusk Street. The store was purchased in the 1920s by Marvin Reid and continued as Reid Grocery Store until about 1945. (Courtesy of the Sherman Museum.)

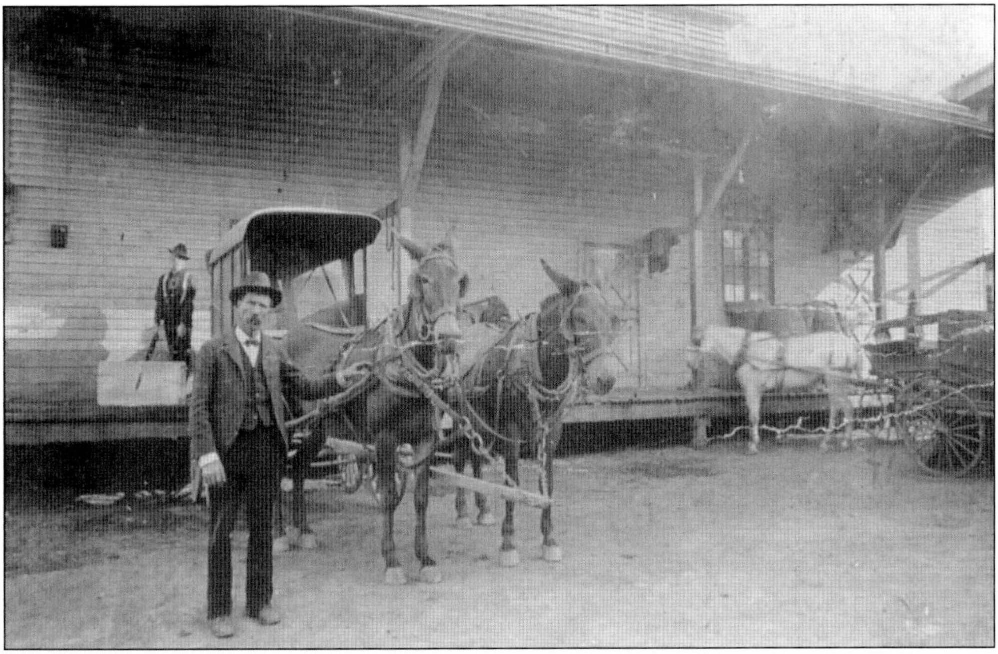

SHERMAN ICE COMPANY, C. 1885. The Sherman Ice Company was located at 413 East Houston Street and was managed by Ernest Arnoldi from 1889 until his death in 1916. The plant was rebuilt in 1919 by the Sherman Ice Company, and in 1925 it was sold to the Southern Ice Company. They advertised that the ice was "made from Sherman's Famous Artesian Water." The photograph above is of the Sherman Ice Company building, and the photograph below is of their horse-drawn delivery wagon. (Above, courtesy of the Sherman Museum; below, courtesy of A Touch of Class Antique Mall.)

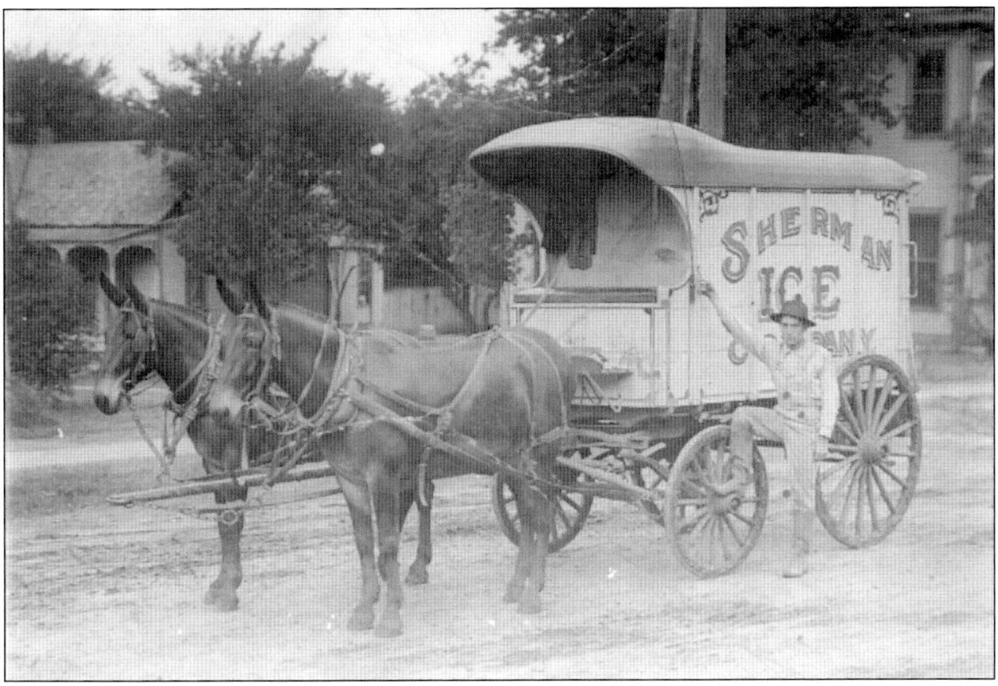

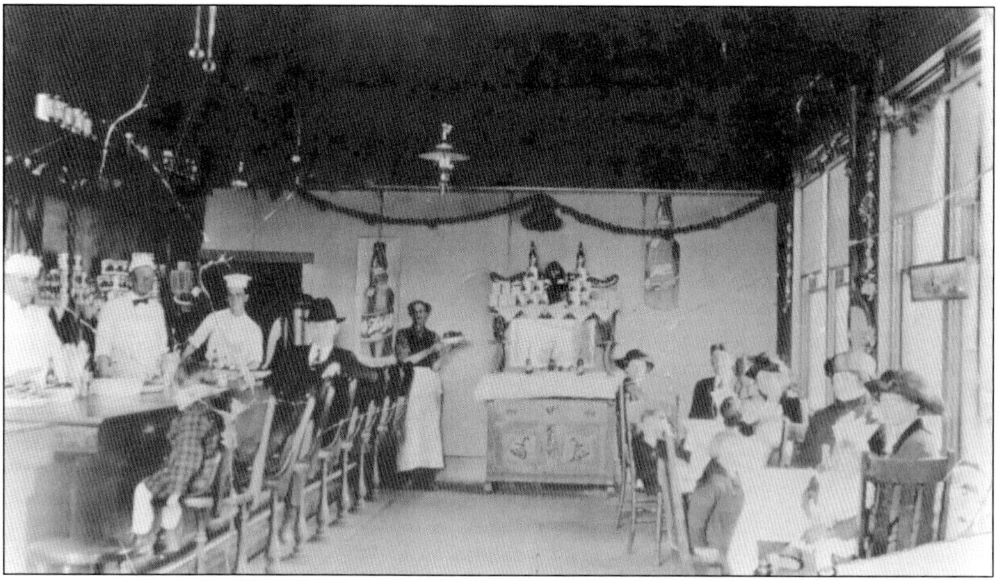

RAILROAD DEPOT CAFE. In the early 1900s, Union Depot was located at the corner of Railroad Avenue and Broughton Street. There was also a Union Depot Hotel with a café. The Frisco Railroad closed the last passenger train in 1948 in Sherman. (Courtesy of the Sherman Museum.)

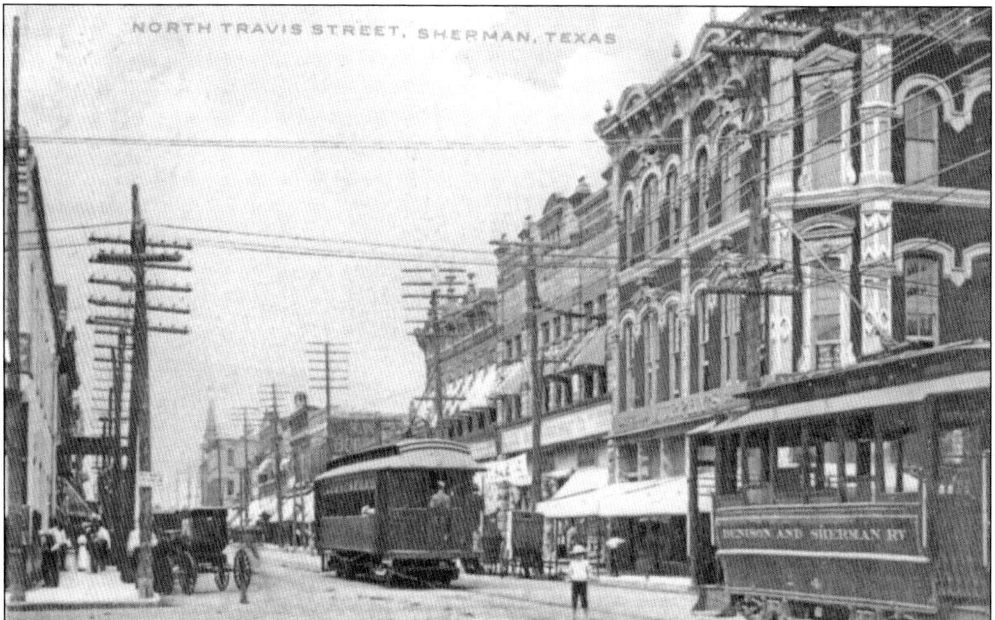

NORTH TRAVIS STREET, 1909. The Interurban travels along North Travis Street on a rail line that operated between Denison and Dallas. Murphy's Dry Goods is located on the right at the corner of Travis and Houston Street, looking north. The last Interurban train ran on December 31, 1948, 47 years after the service began in 1901. (Courtesy of Greg Ashby.)

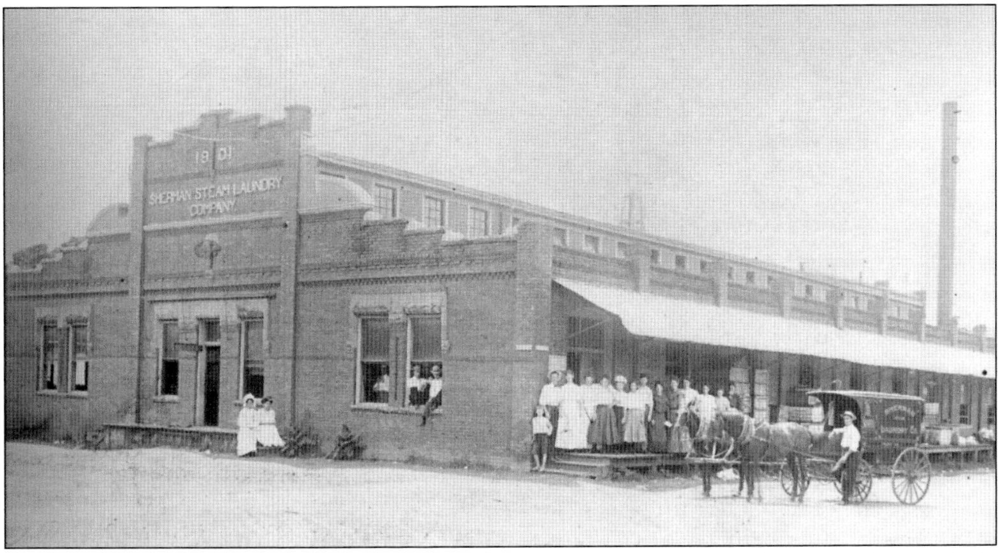

SHERMAN STEAM LAUNDRY. The Sherman Steam Laundry was originally established in 1884 and located near the Binkley Hotel on Travis Street. In 1901, the new facility was built at the corner of Rusk and Lamar Streets. Sherman Steam Laundry was recognized as the second oldest laundry in Texas. The horse and buggy were used for the pick up and delivery service. (Courtesy of the City of Sherman.)

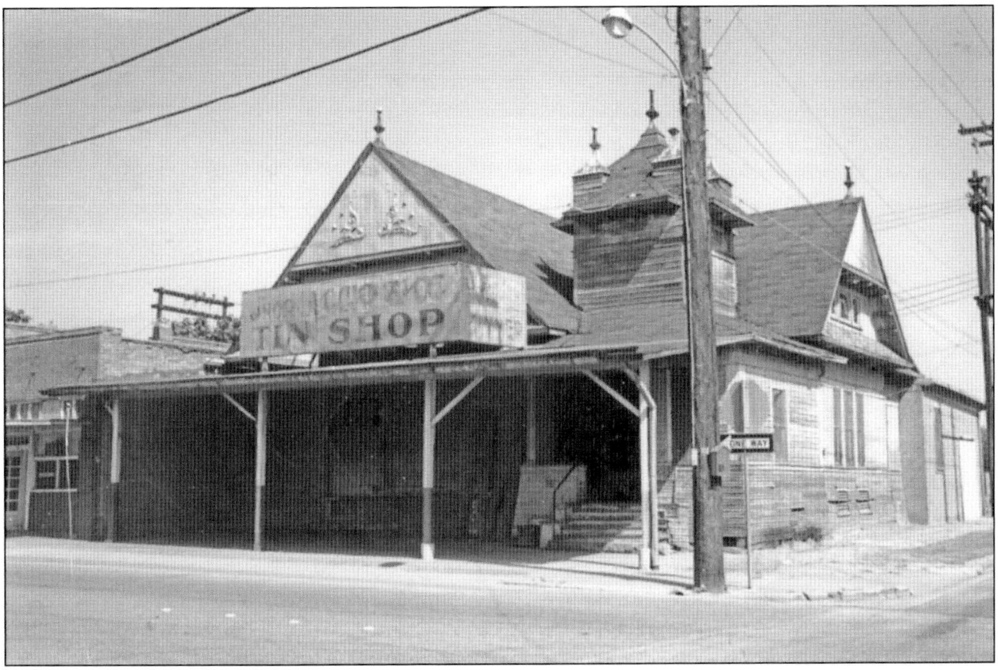

LOCKE THE TINNER. The Locke the Tinner building was the original site of the first Church of Christ building in Sherman, constructed in 1874. In 1882, a group from the church left and formed the Central Christian Church. This building was constructed in 1905 or 1907 and replaced the first church building. Locke the Tinner purchased it in 1920; it finally burned in 1998 while housing a private business. (Courtesy of Missy Sofey-Andrews.)

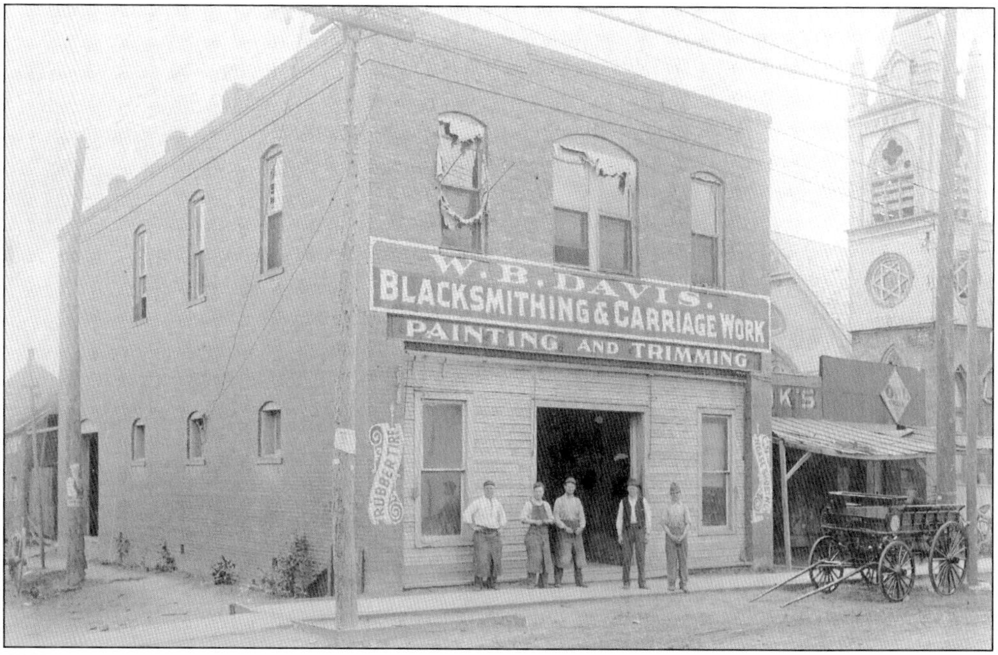

W.B. Davis Blacksmithing & Carriage Work, c. 1910. W.B. Davis Blacksmithing & Carriage Work was located at 301 South Travis Street. The diamond shaped sign on the building to the right says "Owl Cigars." The church to the far right is the Travis Street Methodist Episcopal Church. (Courtesy of the City of Sherman.)

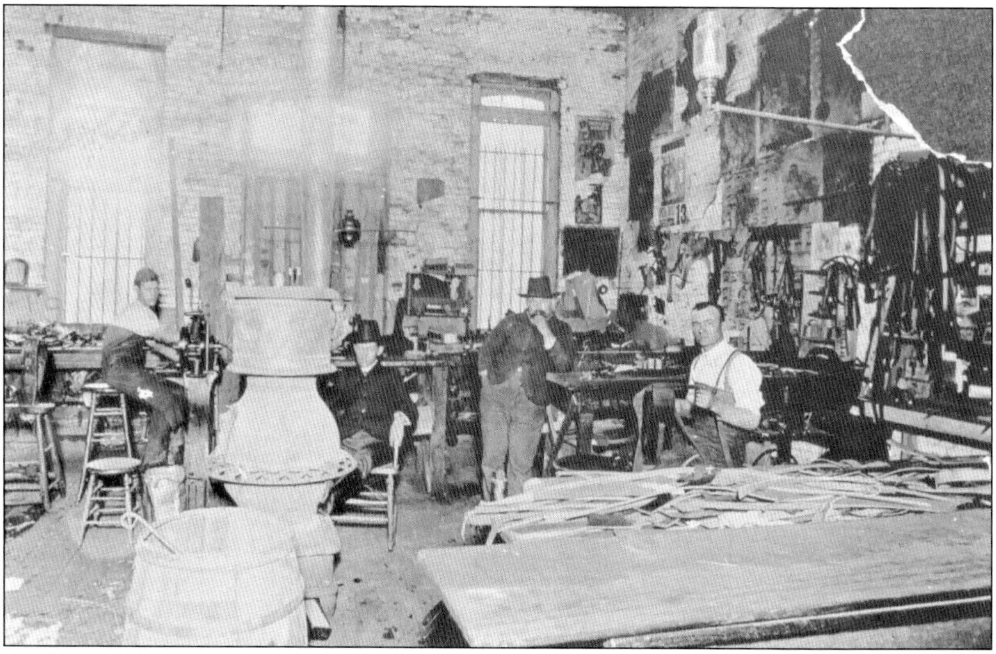

W.P. Gunn Harness Shop, 1905. William Parks Gunn was the owner of the harness shop, a leather and saddlery store where hand-tooled saddles were manufactured. The shop was located at 116 West Lamar Street. Gunn also had a large dairy outside of Sherman and owned a saloon at 119 South Travis Street. (Courtesy of the City of Sherman.)

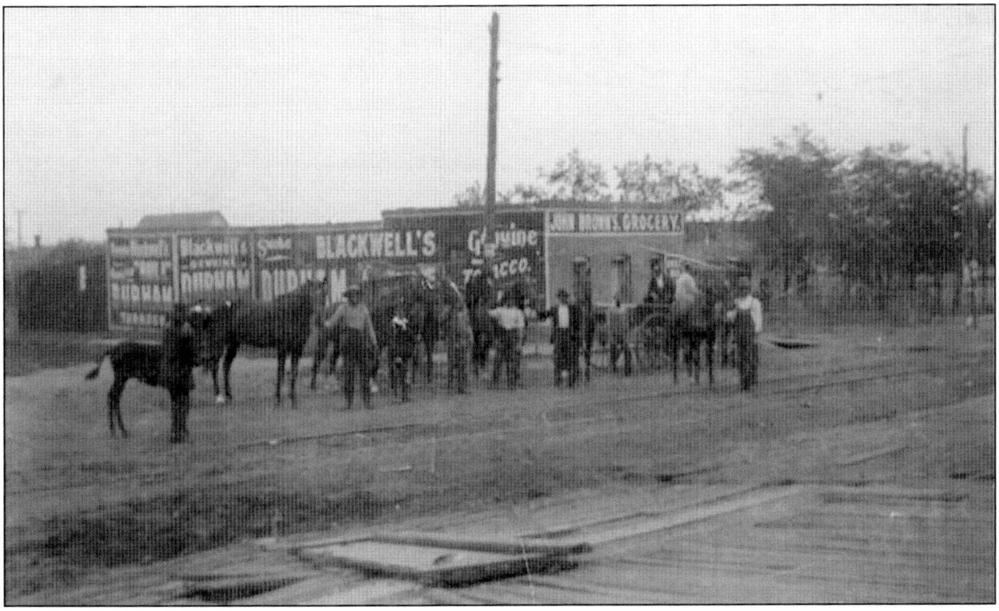

JOHN BROWN'S GROCERY. John Brown owned a grocery store in the late 1890s in the black community at 123 East Pecan Street. A group of black men with horses and wagons are standing in front of the store. There is also a sign for "Blackwell's Genuine Durham Tobacco." (Courtesy of the Sherman Museum.)

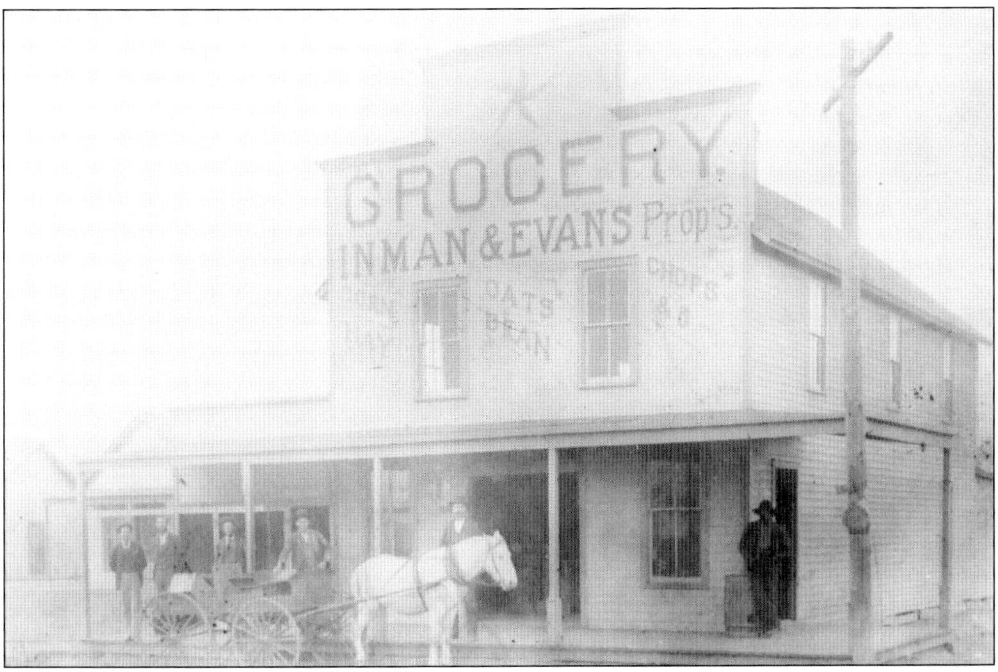

INMAN & EVANS GROCERY STORE. Inman's Grocery Store began in 1885 and was known as Inman & Sons, Thomas Inman & Sons, and Inman & Evans. In 1904, the store was moved to the corner of Willow and Pecan Streets and occupied a two-story building. Later, a brick store was constructed on the same site. The store finally closed in 1981. (Courtesy of the Sherman Museum.)

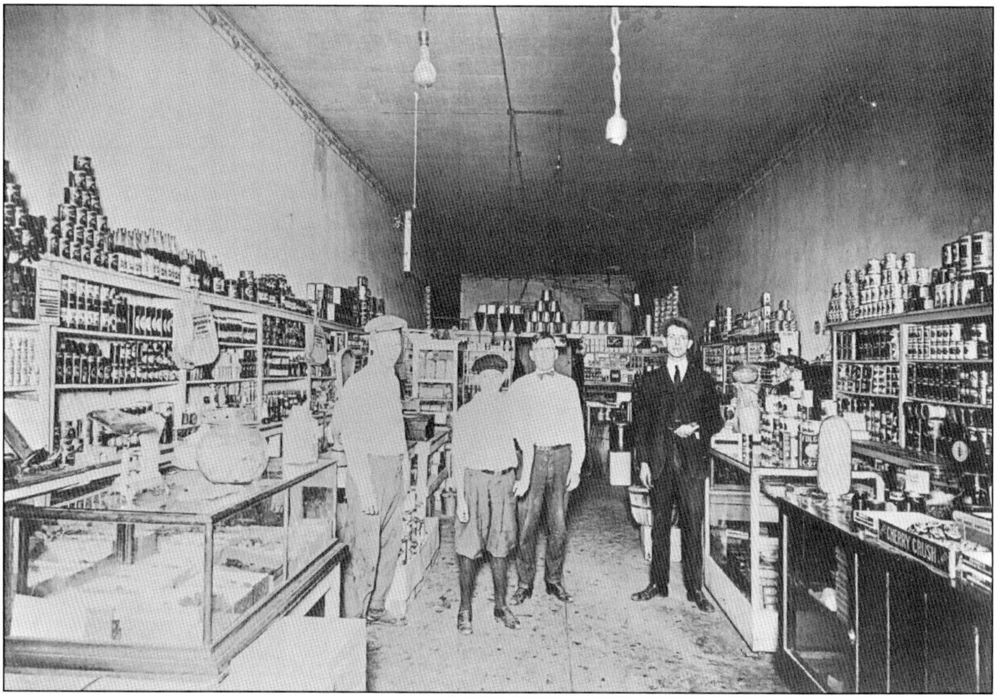

Neighborhood Grocery Stores. The top photograph shows Crutchfield Grocery about 1925. Ed Crutchfield (right) was the owner of the store, which was located at 203 South Travis Street. The bottom photograph is J.E. Cunningham and Company. Many times store employees would gather customer orders in the morning and return with the merchandise in the afternoon. Since few people had "ice boxes" it was sometimes necessary to make an early morning delivery of the breakfast meat. (Above, courtesy of the City of Sherman; below, courtesy of the Sherman Museum.)

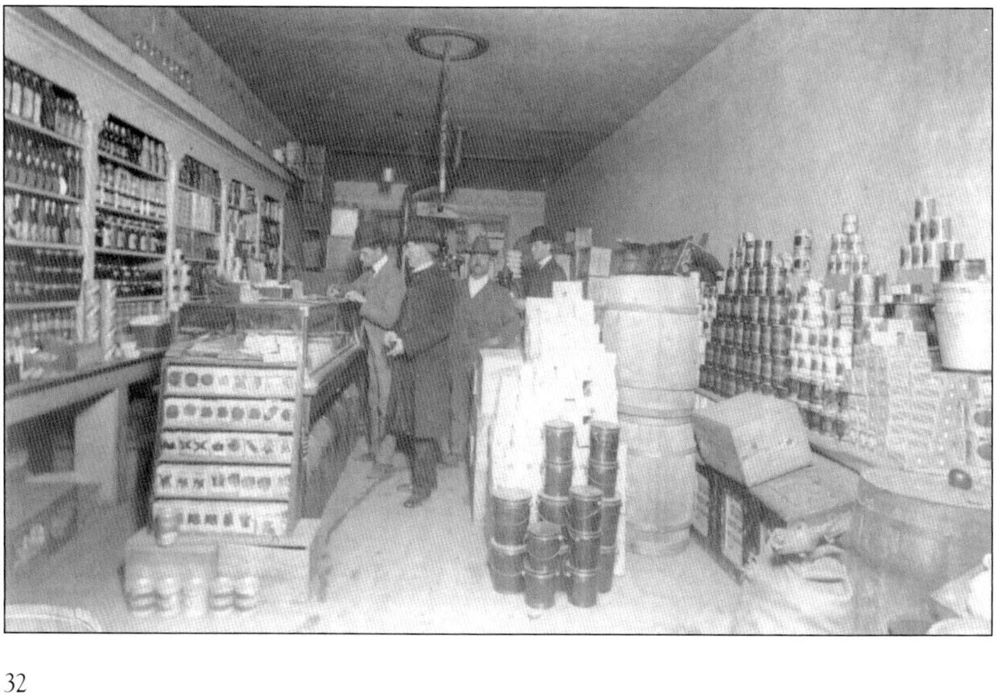

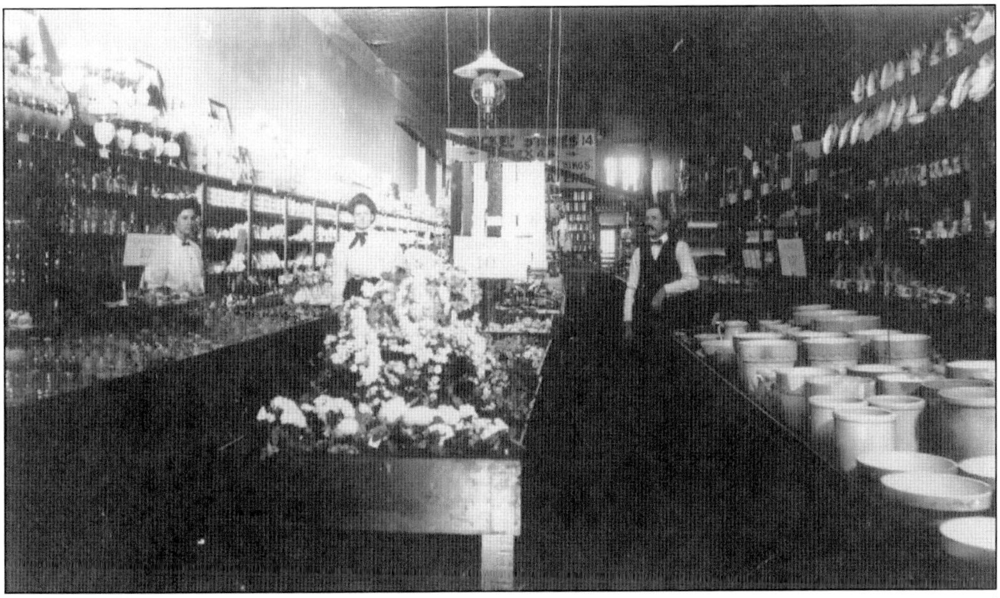

Duke and Ayers. Duke and Ayers was the first five-and-dime store in Sherman and was located at 111 North Travis. It was first known as the Nickel Store in 1901. S.H. Kress and Company sprang up about the same time and was followed by F.W. Woolworth and Company. (Courtesy of the Sherman Museum.)

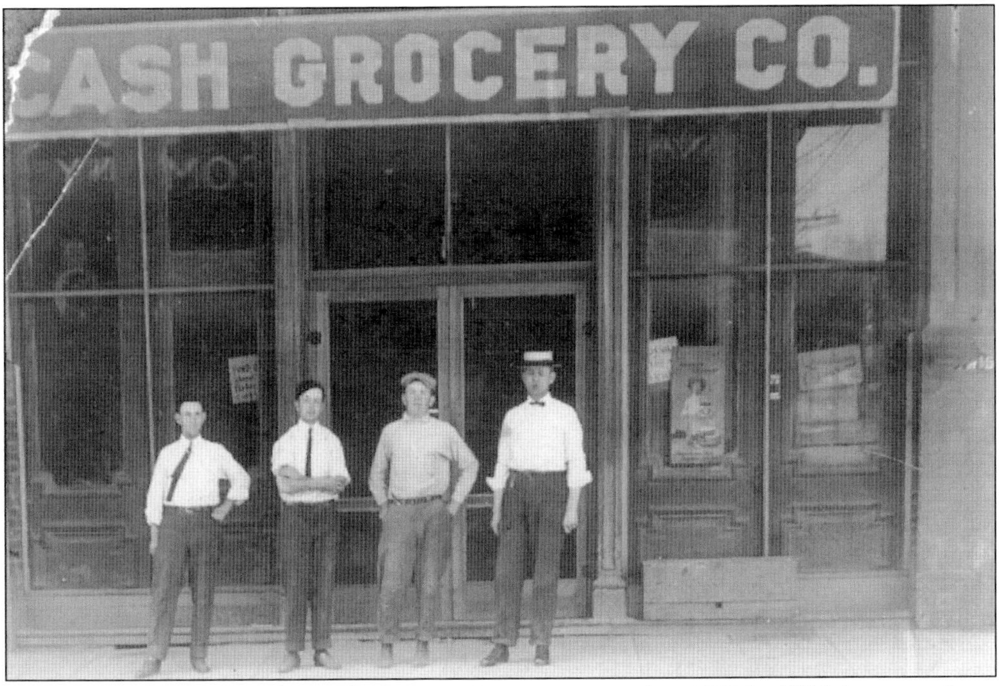

Cash Grocery Store. The Cash Grocery Store was started in 1909 by W.H. Lucas and was located on the north side of the square. Three years later it moved to the northwest corner of the square. In 1921, J.E. Marshall purchased an interest in the store and the name was changed to the L. and M. Store. Eventually Lucas would operate six neighborhood grocery stores in Sherman. (Courtesy of the Sherman Museum.)

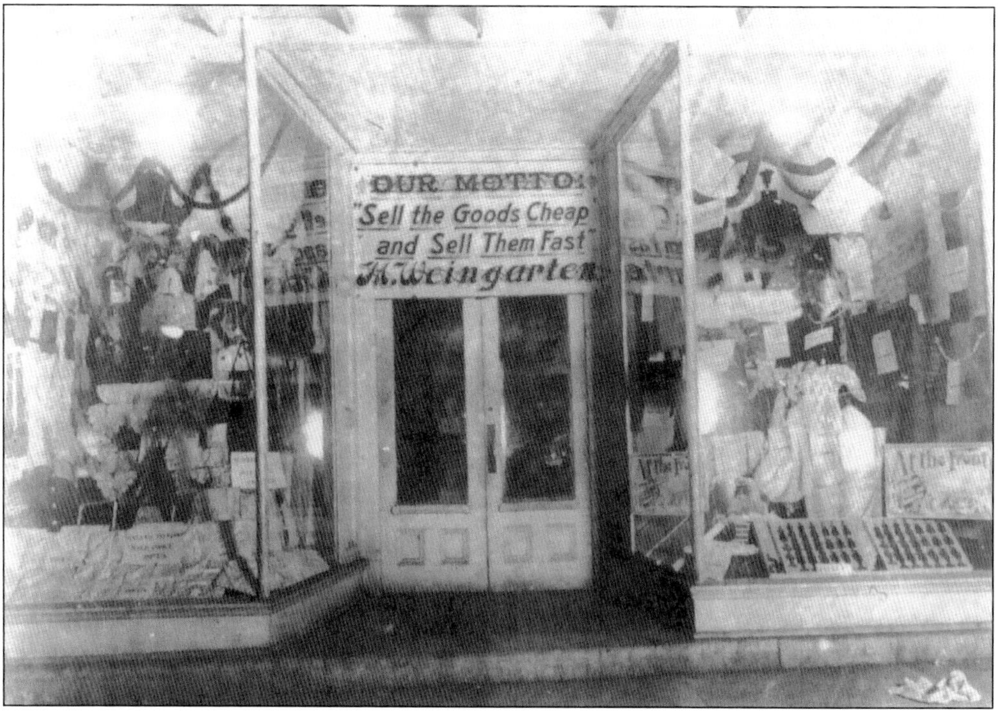

MANDEL WEINGARTEN STORE. The Mandel Weingarten Store was a dry goods store that was located on North Travis Street in the mid-1900s and moved to South Crockett Street by 1923. It was the first store in Sherman with glass display windows. Their motto was "Sell the Goods Cheap and Sell Them Fast." (Courtesy of the Sherman Museum.)

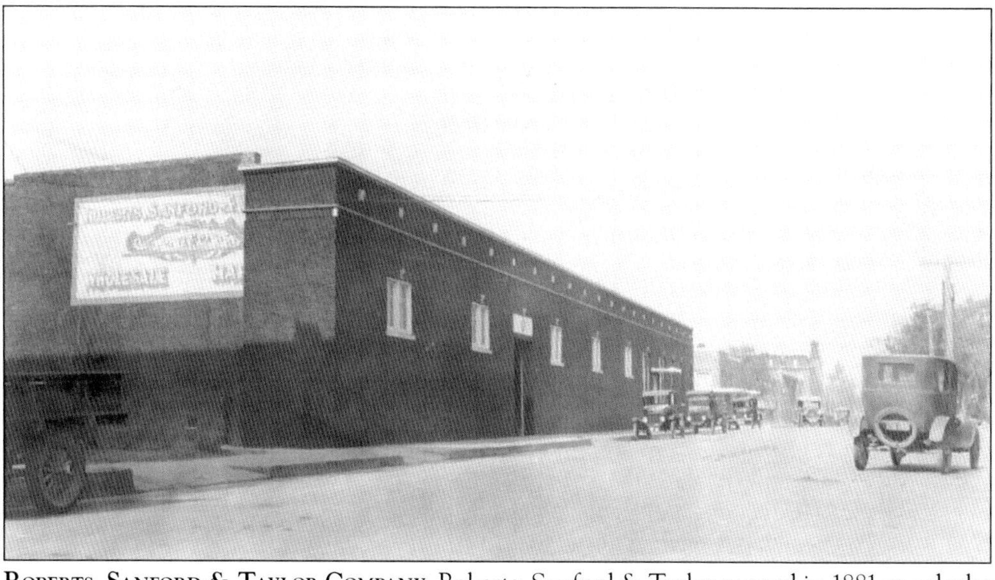

ROBERTS, SANFORD & TAYLOR COMPANY. Roberts, Sanford & Taylor opened in 1881 as a dealer in retail hardware. In 1904, the retail department closed and they began selling at wholesale prices. Then in 1964, they added sporting goods. The company was originally founded by C.N. Roberts, George E. Hardwicke, and W.W. Taylor. It became Roberts, Sanford & Taylor in 1898. (Courtesy of the Sherman Museum.)

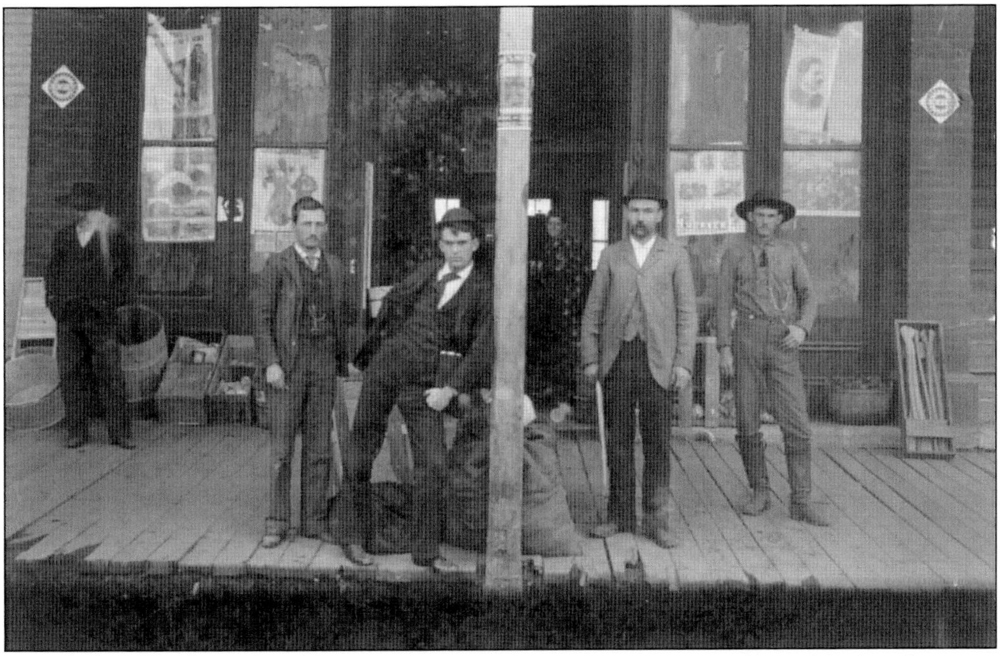

Neighborhood Grocery Stores. In Sherman's early history, the small neighborhood grocery stores served the citizens with both groceries and neighborhood news. Many customers would make arrangements at the store to carry their purchases on a monthly account. Sometimes a customer would even wait to pay until their cotton crop came in. Most stock was carried in bulk and produce was offered only in season, and was mostly locally grown. The top photograph shows Aker and Webb Grocery, which was located on the south side of the square, around 1898. The bottom photograph is unidentified but is a typical grocery store selling produce and canned goods. (Both courtesy of the Sherman Museum.)

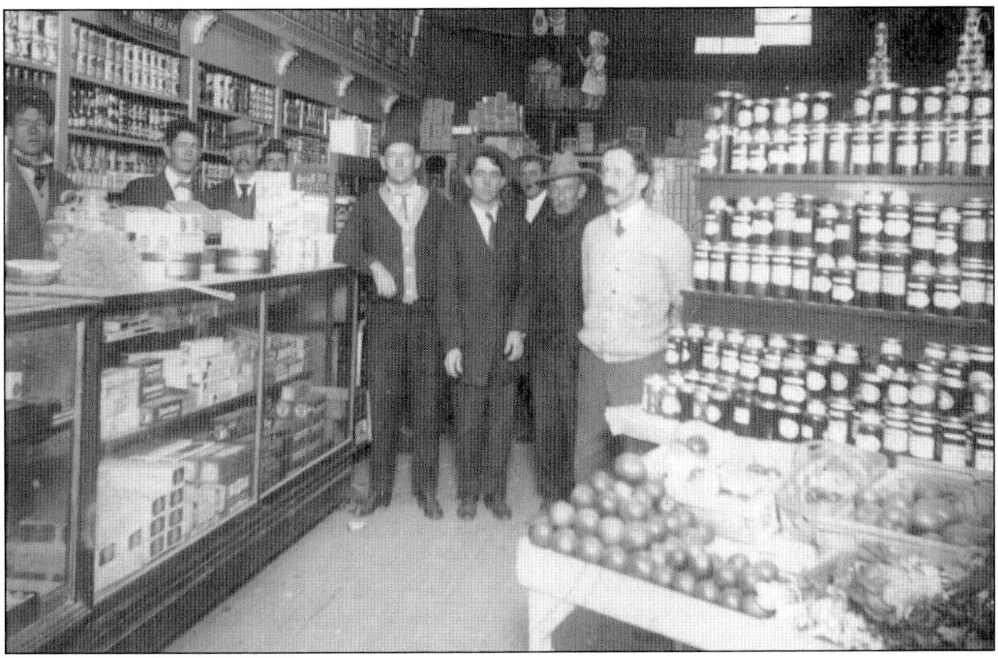

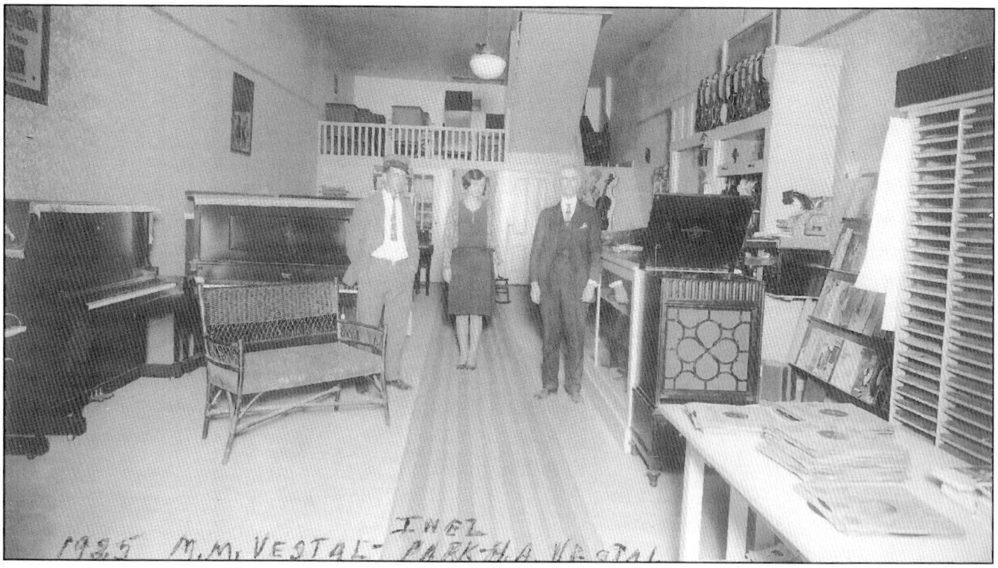

Vestal Music Company, 1925. H.A. Vestal established the Vestal Music Company in 1896 in his father's sewing machine store. He started with six organs and one piano, and the business grew to include other lines of musical instruments. In a 1929 advertisement, Vestal Music Company advertised "Baldwin pianos and new home sewing machines" for sale. Shown above, from left to right, are M.M. Vestal, Inez Park, and H.A. Vestal. (Courtesy of the Sherman Museum.)

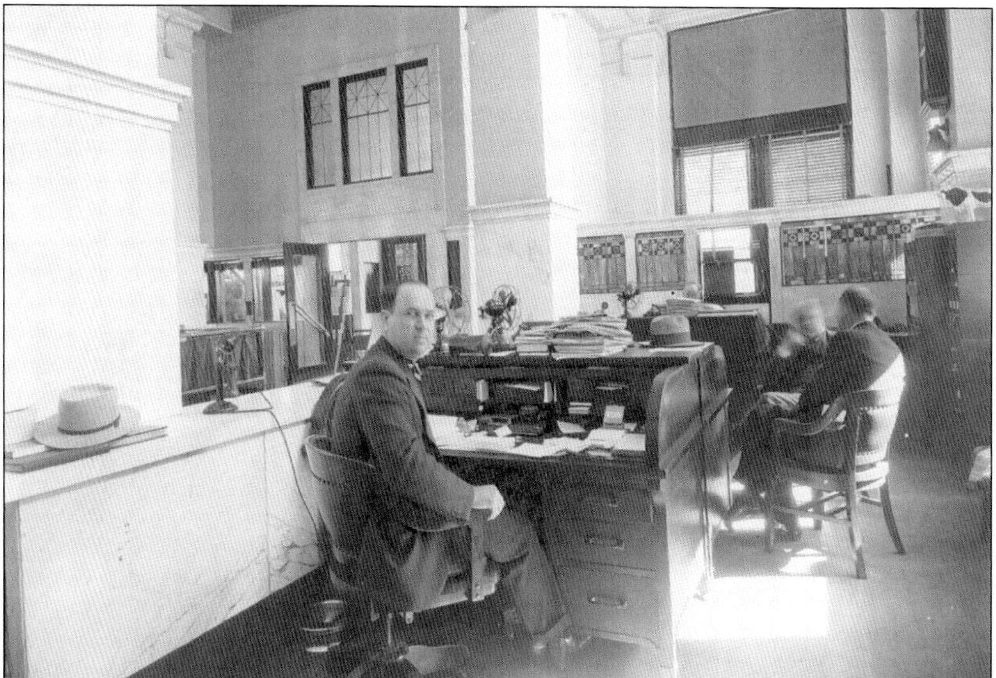

Replacing the Old Pecan Tree. The Merchants and Planters Bank opened to replace the old pecan tree bank that had been located on the courthouse square and served citizens for so long. L. Sale Omohundro is seen sitting at his desk in the bank. (Courtesy of the Sherman Museum.)

ORIGINAL MERCHANTS AND PLANTERS BANK. Constructed in 1873, this first Merchants and Planters Bank building was erected at a time when Sherman was growing. Schools were being established, railroads were coming to town, and settlers were flocking from the Old South to the New South. In 1885, Dunn and Bradstreet referred to Sherman as the "Texas financial center." (Courtesy of the Sherman Museum.)

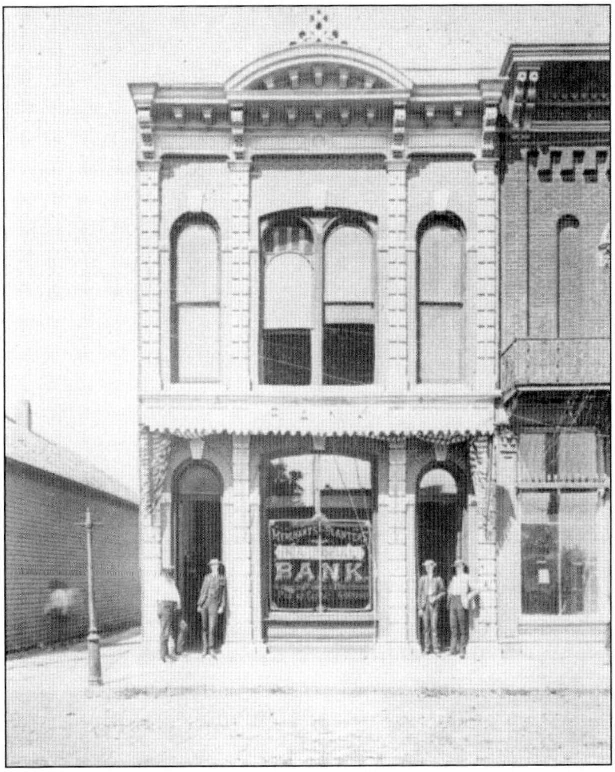

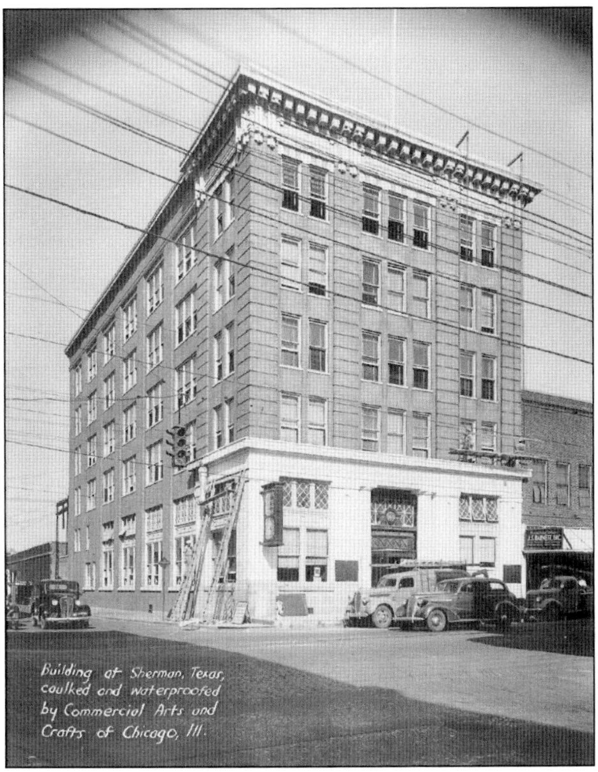

MERCHANTS AND PLANTERS BANK. Merchants and Planters National Bank was founded in 1872 with $150,000 capital. The original building was constructed at 200 North Travis Street in 1873 but was razed in 1912. The current building was completed that same year on the original site. Judge C.C. Binkley was the first president of the bank. (Courtesy of the Sherman Museum.)

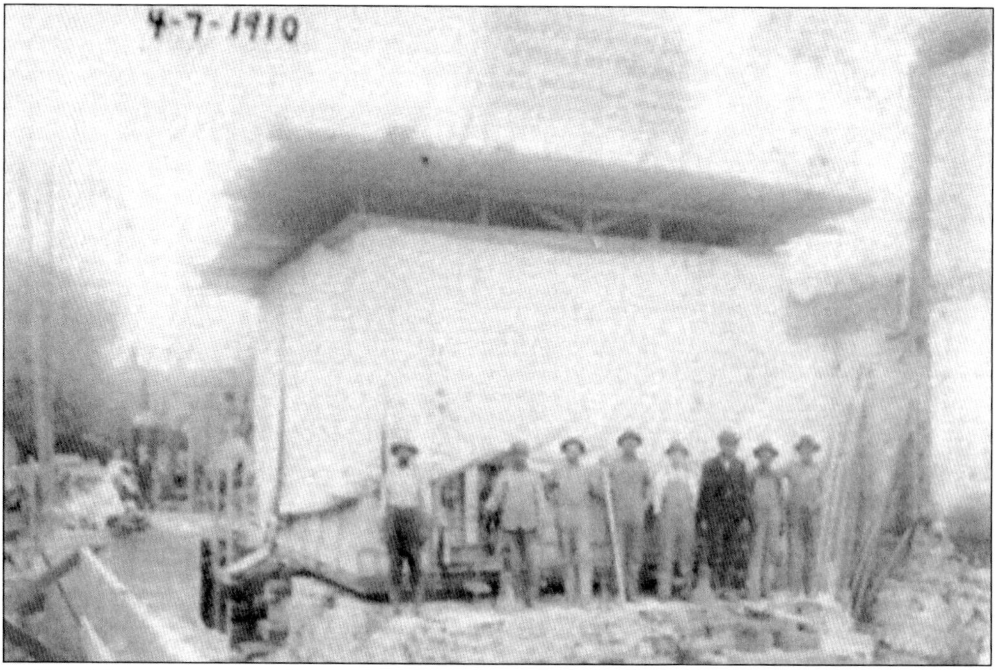

A New Merchants and Planters Bank. It was a big job to move the vault into the new Merchants and Planters National Bank in 1912. In the top photograph, C.A. Thomas and his crew are seen moving the bank vault after the razing of the original building. The sign on top of the vault says "Selden-Breck Constr. Co. General Contractors Malcolm S. Martin, architect." In the bottom photograph, the new, modern lobby is displayed after remodeling. In 1953, Merchants and Planters National Bank was still the largest bank between Dallas and Oklahoma City. (Both courtesy of the Sherman Museum.)

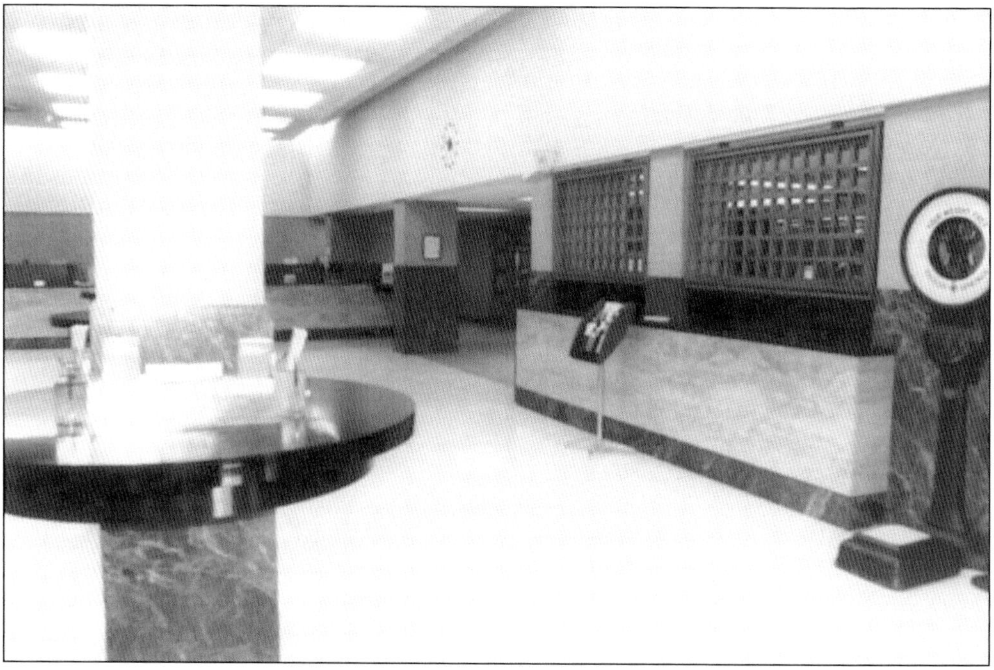

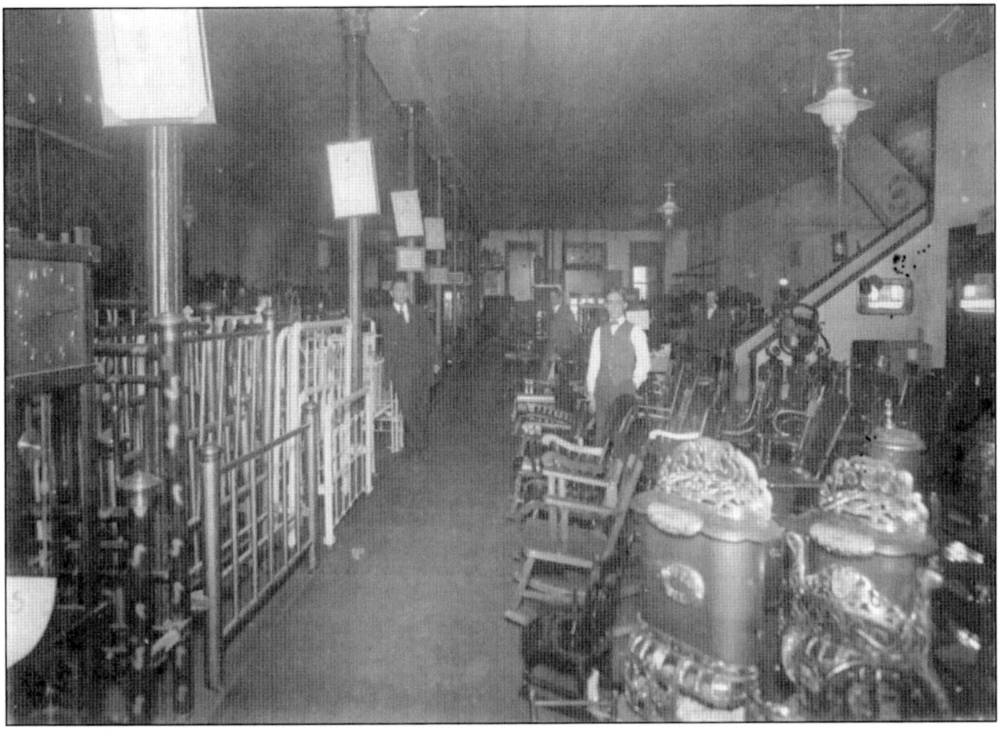

Taliaferro Furniture Store, c. 1908. J.C. Taliaferro operated the Taliaferro Furniture Store on East Houston Street for over 30 years. Taliaferro married Susiebel Carr in 1915, and they moved into the Carr home at 516 North Grand Avenue. Many items from the Taliaferro's collection of local antiques were donated to the Sherman Historical Museum. Both photographs show the interior of the furniture store. (Both courtesy of the Sherman Museum.)

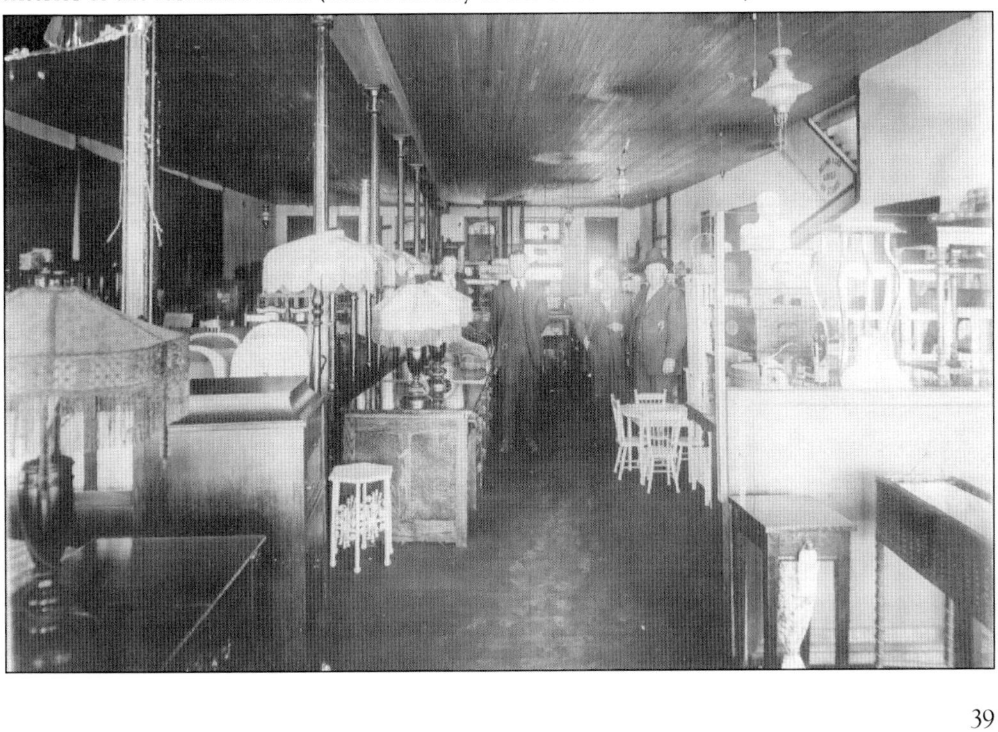

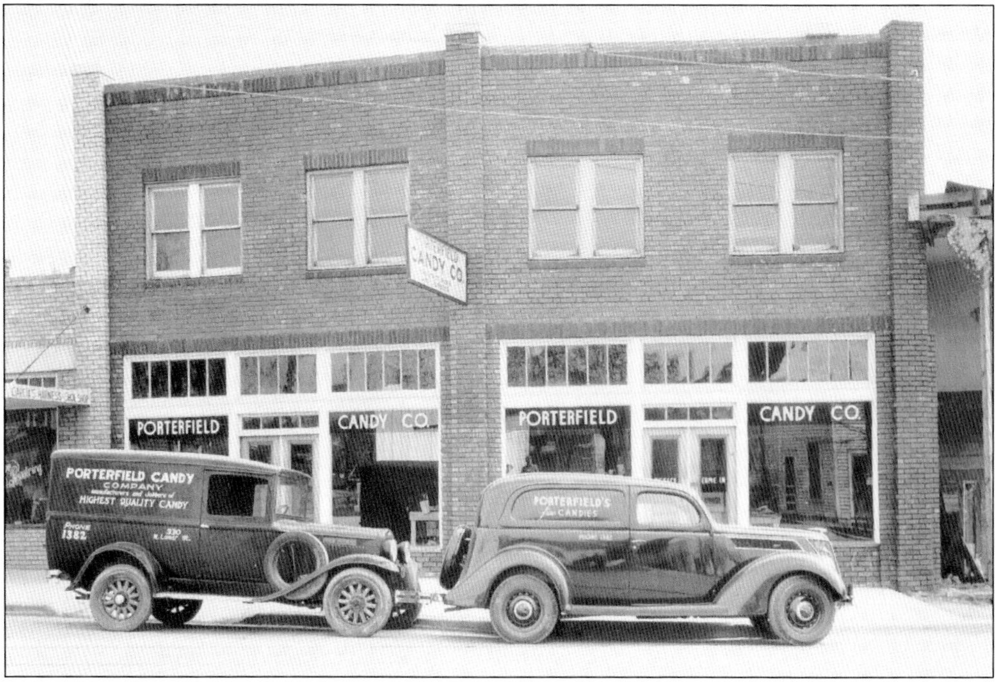

PORTERFIELD CANDY COMPANY, C. 1935. Porterfield Candy Company was located at the southeast corner of Rusk and Lamar Streets, across the street from the old Steam Laundry Building. J.D. Porterfield was the president and Addie Porterfield was the secretary-treasurer. The ABC Candy Company and the Hartt Candy Company were also located in Sherman during the mid-1930s. (Courtesy of the City of Sherman.)

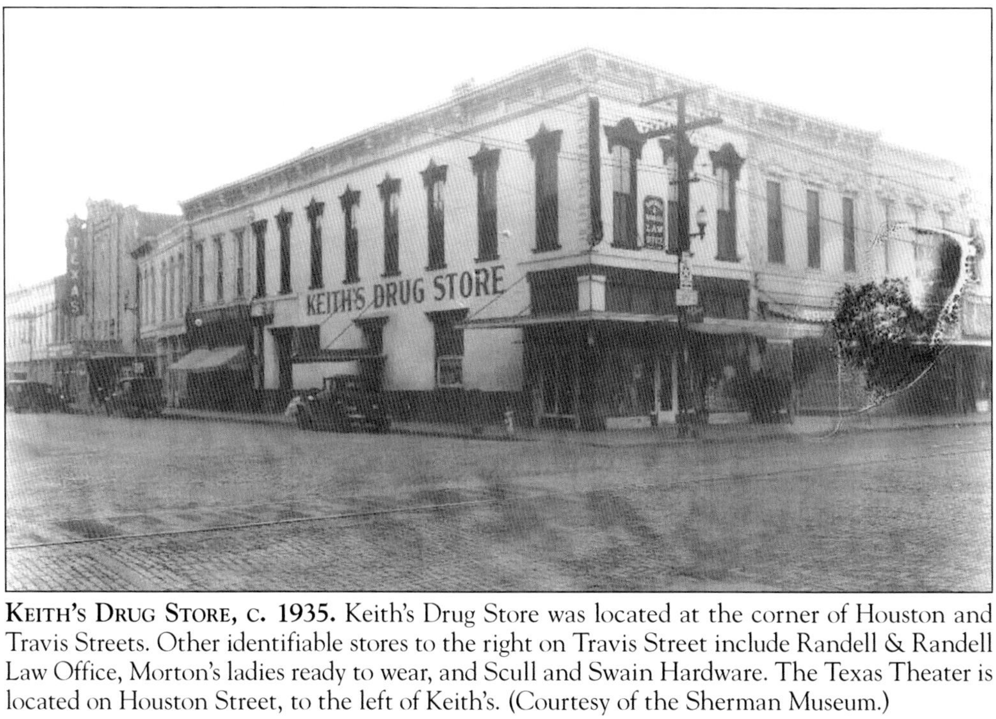

KEITH'S DRUG STORE, C. 1935. Keith's Drug Store was located at the corner of Houston and Travis Streets. Other identifiable stores to the right on Travis Street include Randell & Randell Law Office, Morton's ladies ready to wear, and Scull and Swain Hardware. The Texas Theater is located on Houston Street, to the left of Keith's. (Courtesy of the Sherman Museum.)

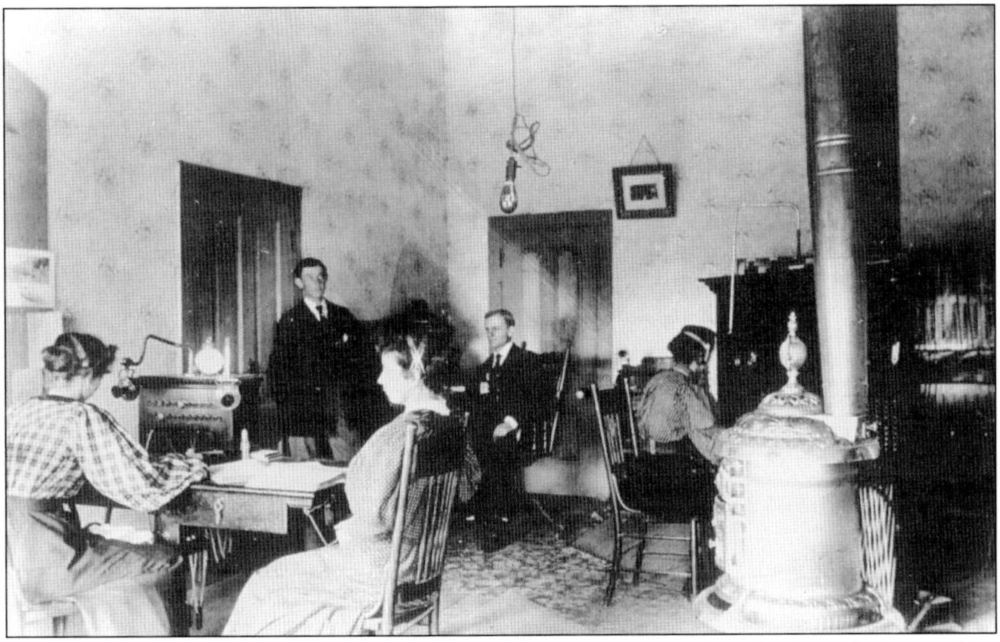

Southwestern Telegraph and Telephone, 1890s. Operators work at the first telephone office in Sherman, which was located in the Murphy Dry Goods Building at the northeast corner of Travis and Houston Streets. (Courtesy of the Sherman Museum.)

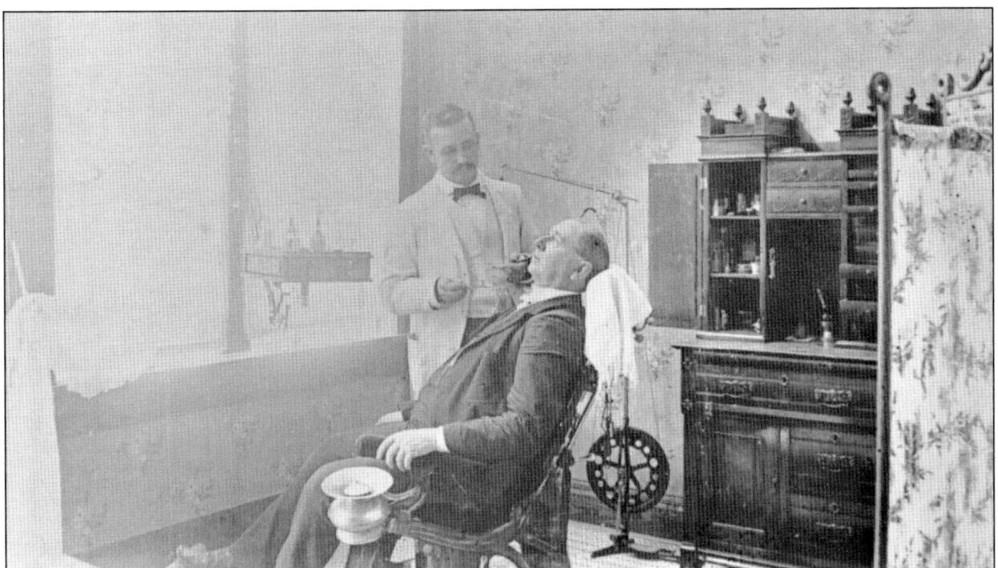

A Local Dentist. Judge John T. Cunningham is in the dentist's chair having a tooth pulled, probably by Dr. George Staples. His office was located in the Murphy's Dry Goods building at the northeast corner of Travis and Houston Streets. (Courtesy of the City of Sherman.)

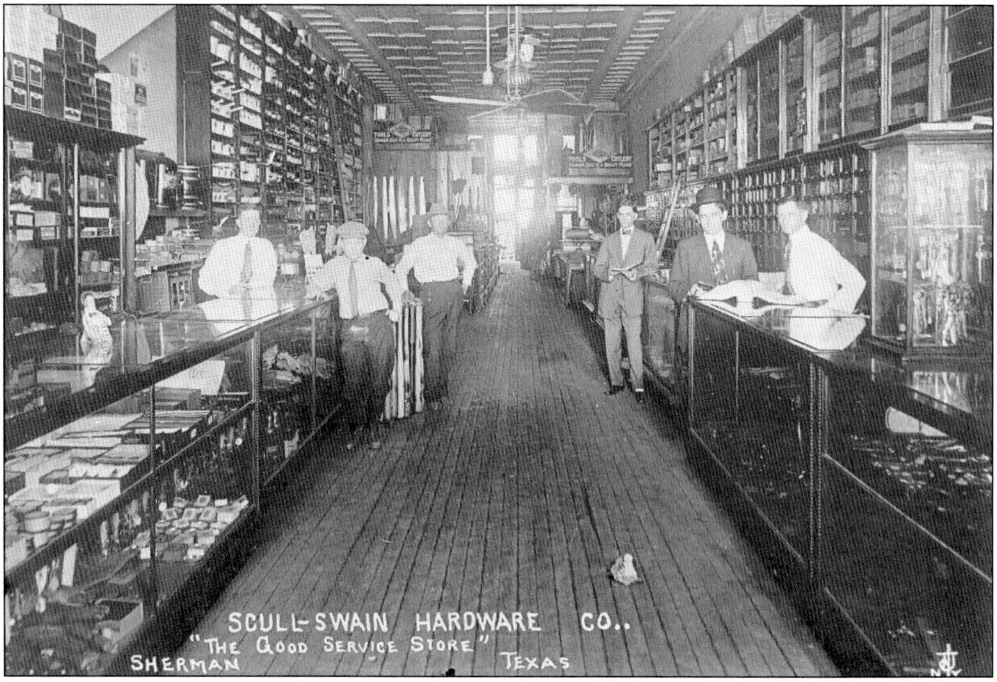

SCULL-SWAIN HARDWARE COMPANY, 1900S. Scull-Swain Hardware Company was the first hardware store on the square. It was located at 105 North Travis Street and was known as the "Good Service Store." It was the predecessor of Scull, Swain, and Wallace. (Courtesy of the City of Sherman.)

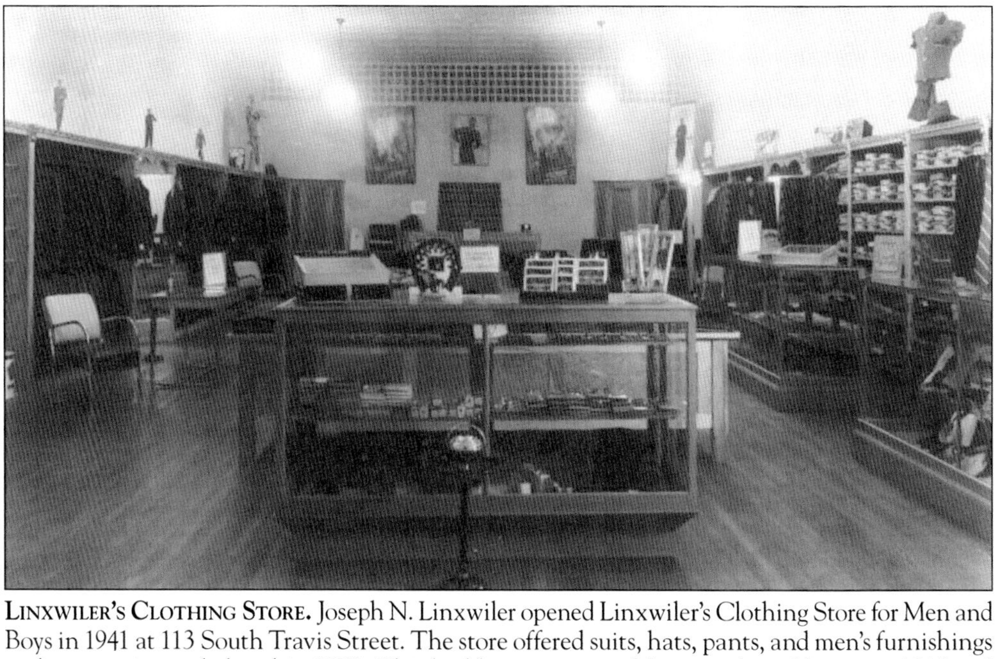

LINXWILER'S CLOTHING STORE. Joseph N. Linxwiler opened Linxwiler's Clothing Store for Men and Boys in 1941 at 113 South Travis Street. The store offered suits, hats, pants, and men's furnishings and accessories and closed in 1972. This building was one of four purchased between 1916 and 1918 by Leo Kelly, a trunk salesman. He placed a common brick facade on all the buildings, and they became known as the Kelly Building. (Courtesy of the Sherman Museum.)

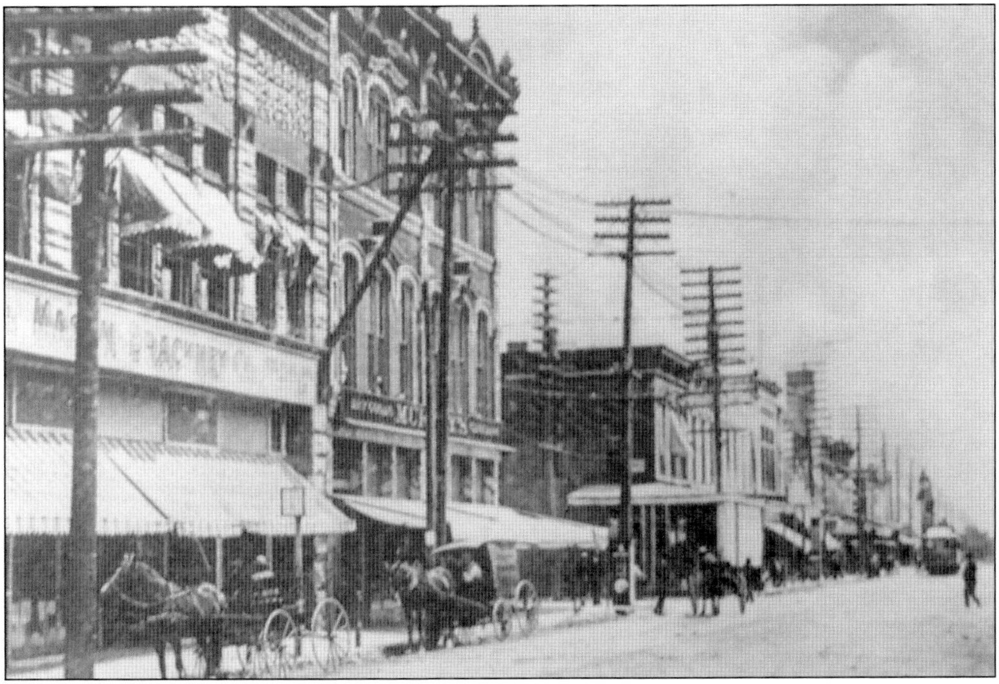

MURPHY'S DRY GOODS. Murphy's Dry Goods (center), was located at the northeast corner of Travis and Houston Streets. Over the years, the building housed Schneider Brothers and Company, Murphy's Dry Goods, Marks Brothers, Bass Parrish and Taylor, Taylor and Vaughan, Vaughan's, and finally Price's. (Courtesy of the Sherman Museum.)

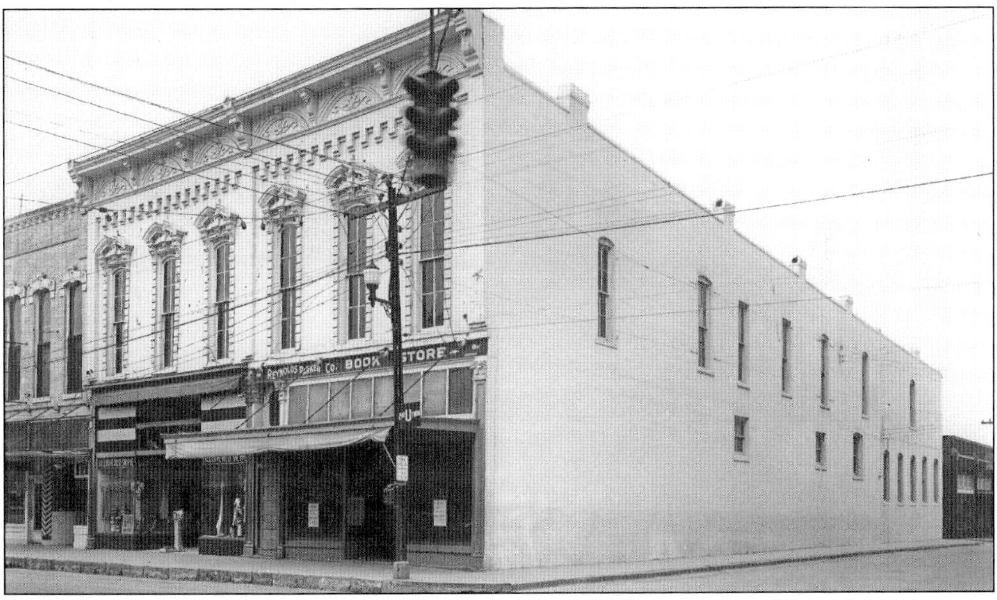

REYNOLDS PARKER BOOK STORE. The Reynolds Parker Book Store originally began in the early 1900s as a printing company established by Lewis J. Reynolds and Charles W. Parker. They advertised that they published *The Daily Register*, but also published books and commercial jobs. The store was located at the corner of Travis and Wall Streets, but closed in the mid-to-late 1930s. (Courtesy of A Touch of Class Antique Mall.)

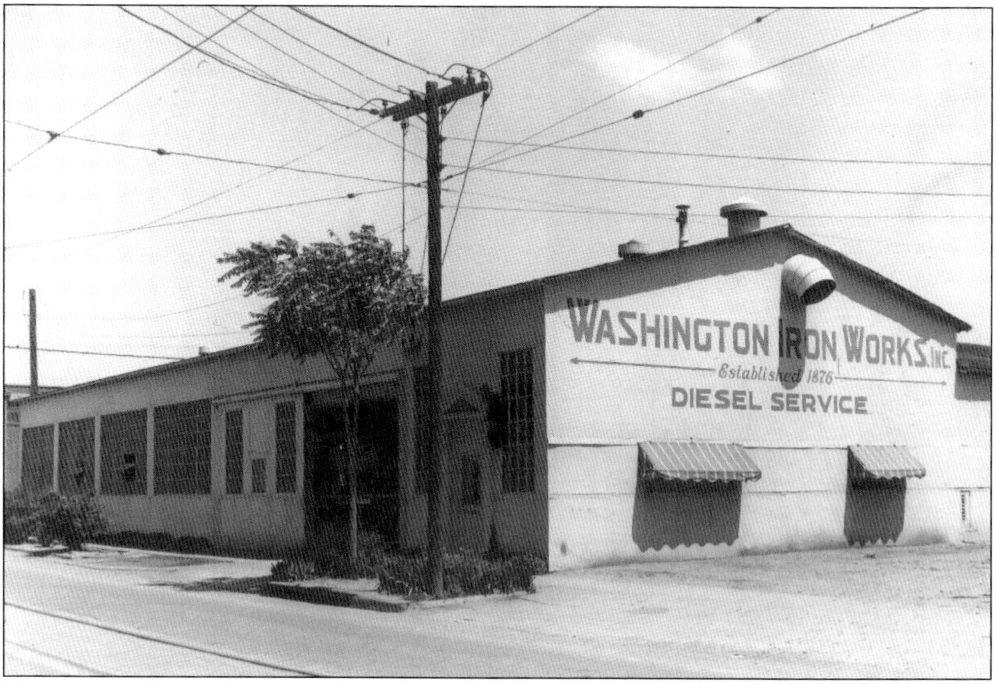

Washington Iron Works. Washington Iron Works was established in 1876 as Totten Brothers blacksmith shop and was located on Cherry Street. The Totten boys originally moved to Sherman because it was on the Butterfield and Overland Stage route. The company originally produced wagon wheels, then specialized in the repair and maintenance of steam engines. The company was incorporated in 1881 as Washington Iron Works. (Courtesy of the Sherman Museum.)

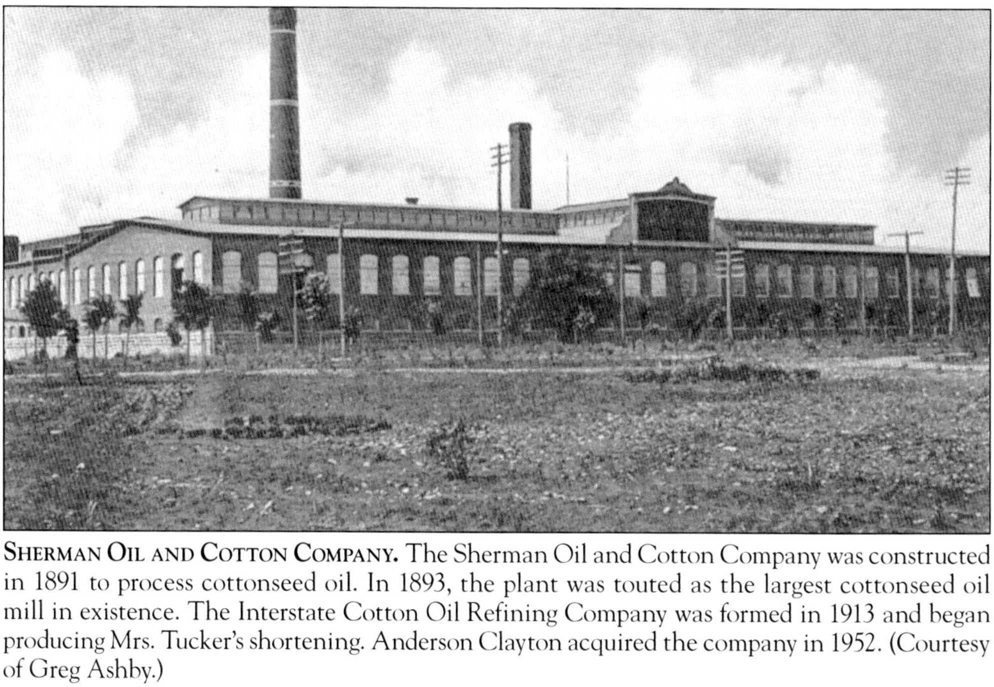

Sherman Oil and Cotton Company. The Sherman Oil and Cotton Company was constructed in 1891 to process cottonseed oil. In 1893, the plant was touted as the largest cottonseed oil mill in existence. The Interstate Cotton Oil Refining Company was formed in 1913 and began producing Mrs. Tucker's shortening. Anderson Clayton acquired the company in 1952. (Courtesy of Greg Ashby.)

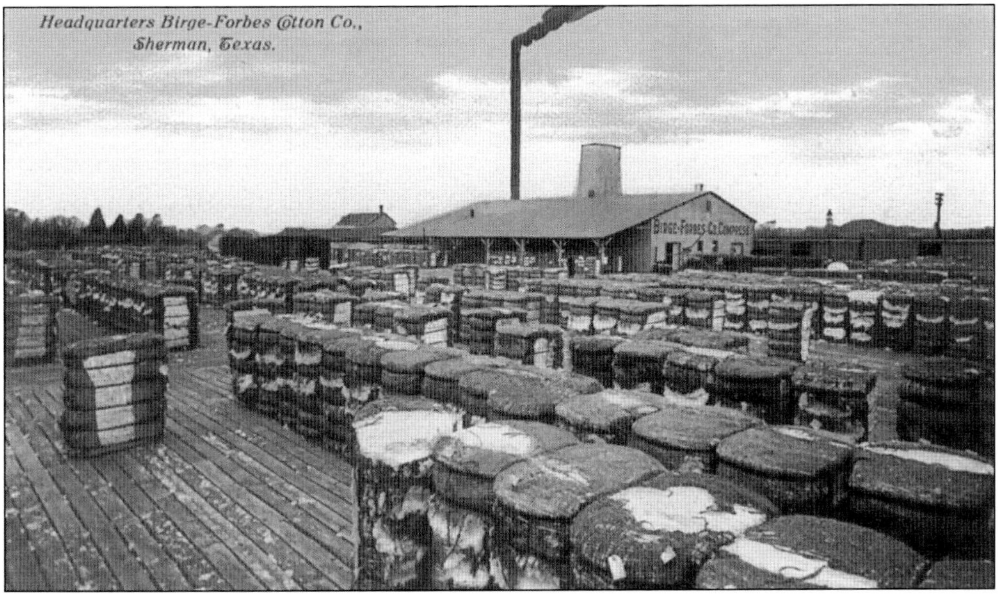

Birge-Forbes Cotton Company. This 1895 postcard shows cotton bales ready for shipment to the cotton mill. In 1894, Noble A. Birge and Tom Forbes created the Birge-Forbes Cotton Brokers. Expansions of the company were made to include other related cotton, cottonseed, and land businesses. In 1902, Birge died and his son Nat Birge continued to operate the Cotton and Land Company. In 1911, he purchased interest in what became the Interstate Cotton Oil Company. (Courtesy of Greg Ashby.)

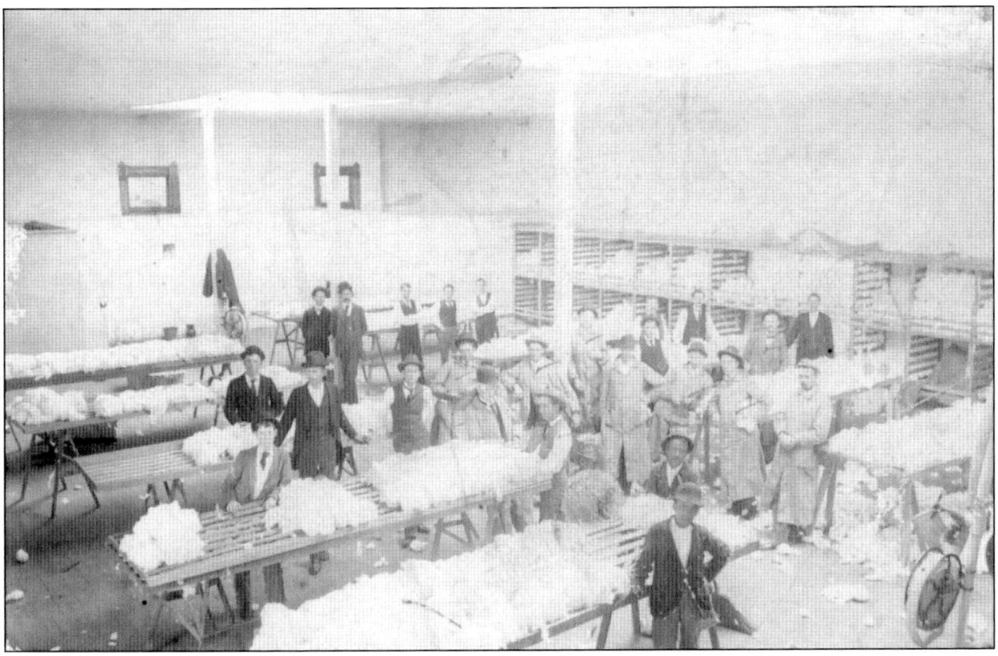

Classing Cotton, c. 1900. In 1898, more than 11,000 bales of cotton were shipped to Sherman for processing at the Birge-Forbes Cotton Company. Workers would pull and sample cotton for its quality and sort it accordingly. Birge-Forbes Cotton and Land Company ceased operation in the late 1930s. (Courtesy of the Sherman Museum.)

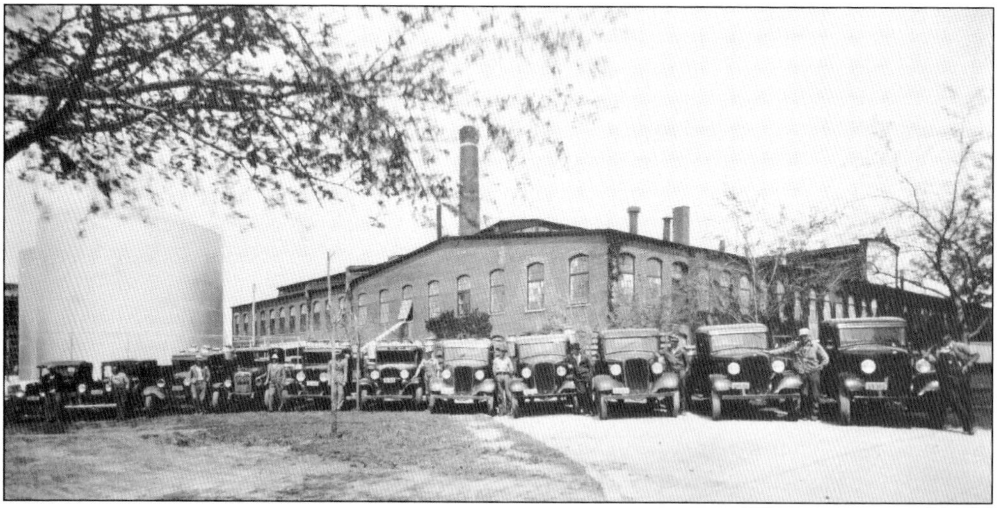

ANDERSON CLAYTON FOODS, C. 1928–1929. Built in 1891, the plant was originally known as the Sherman Oil and Cotton Company. The plant's name changed to Mrs. Tucker's Foods in 1947. The company merged with Anderson Clayton and Company in 1952 and became Mrs. Tucker's Food Product Division. Kraft Food Ingredients purchased the plant in 1987, and it was again sold in 1992 to Ag Processing, Inc. (Courtesy of the City of Sherman.)

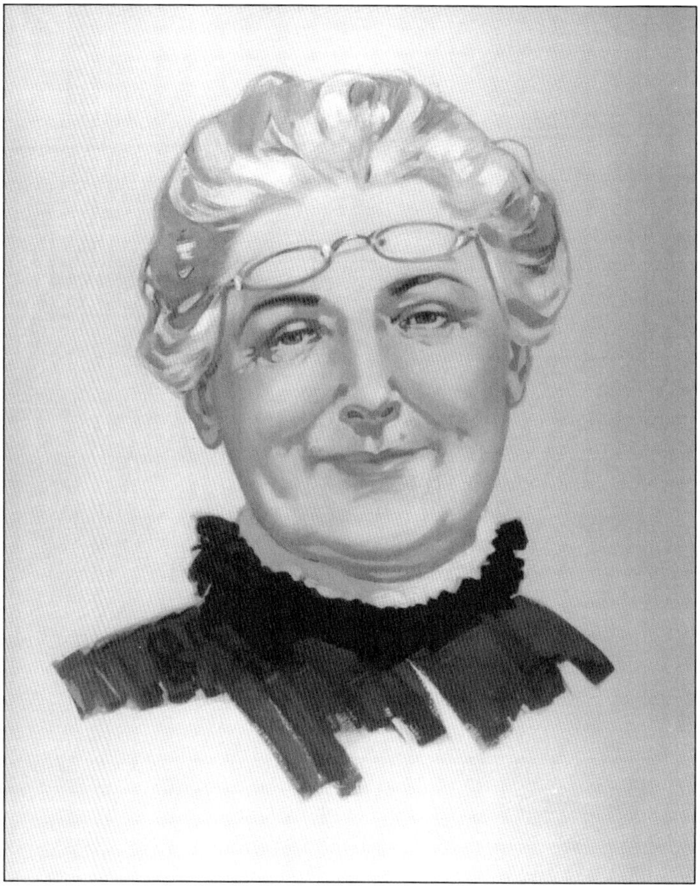

MRS. TUCKER'S FOODS. Mrs. Tucker's shortening was originally produced at the Interstate Cotton Oil Refining Company and was followed by lines of cooking oil and margarine. In 1962, Anderson Clayton introduced Chiffon margarine, the first soft tub margarine sold in a table service plastic container. In the 1970s, their slogan was "It's Not Nice to Fool Mother Nature." (Courtesy of the Sherman Museum.)

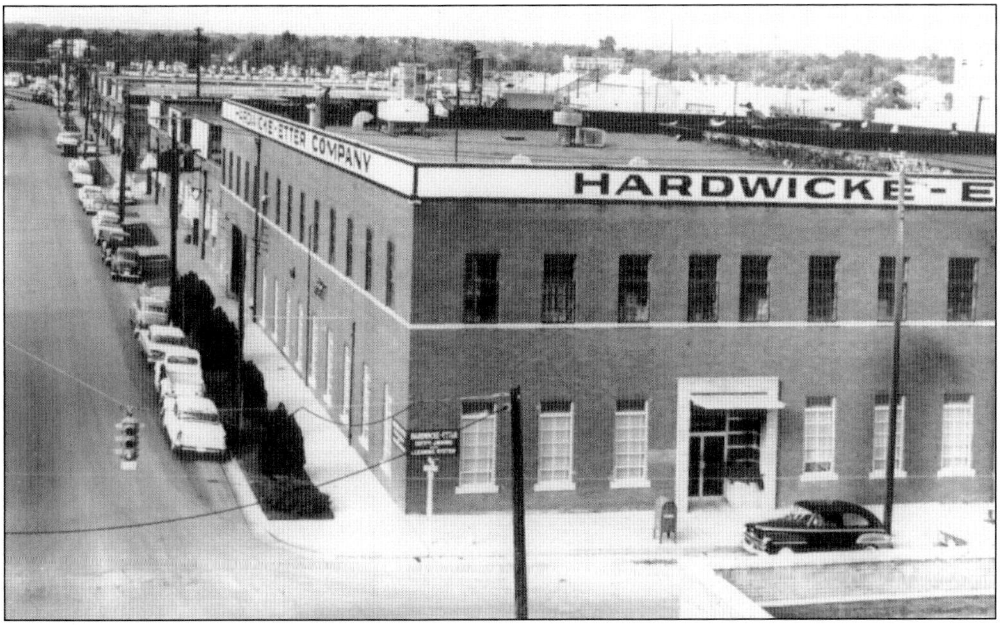

HARDWICKE-ETTER COMPANY. George E. Hardwicke and Joe F. Etter established Hardwicke-Etter in 1902, and it became one of the most respected cotton equipment manufacturers in the country. Located at Houston and Montgomery Streets, they eventually added cotton-cleaning and cotton gin equipment. During World War II more than three million 4.2-millimeter chemical mortar shells were produced at the plant. (Courtesy of the Sherman Economic Development Corporation.)

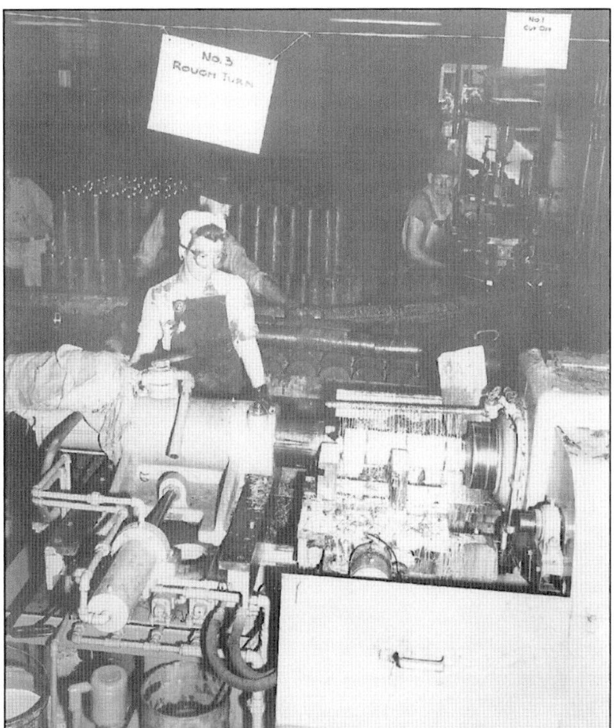

COTTON GIN EQUIPMENT. Hardwicke-Etter Company was one of the most respected cotton equipment manufacturers in the United States. They manufactured cotton-cleaning equipment and, by the 1940s, produced a complete line of cotton gin equipment. In 1948, Hardwicke-Etter had 450 employees and a $1-million payroll. Hardwicke-Etter closed in 1992 after 106 years of continuous operation. (Courtesy of the Sherman Museum.)

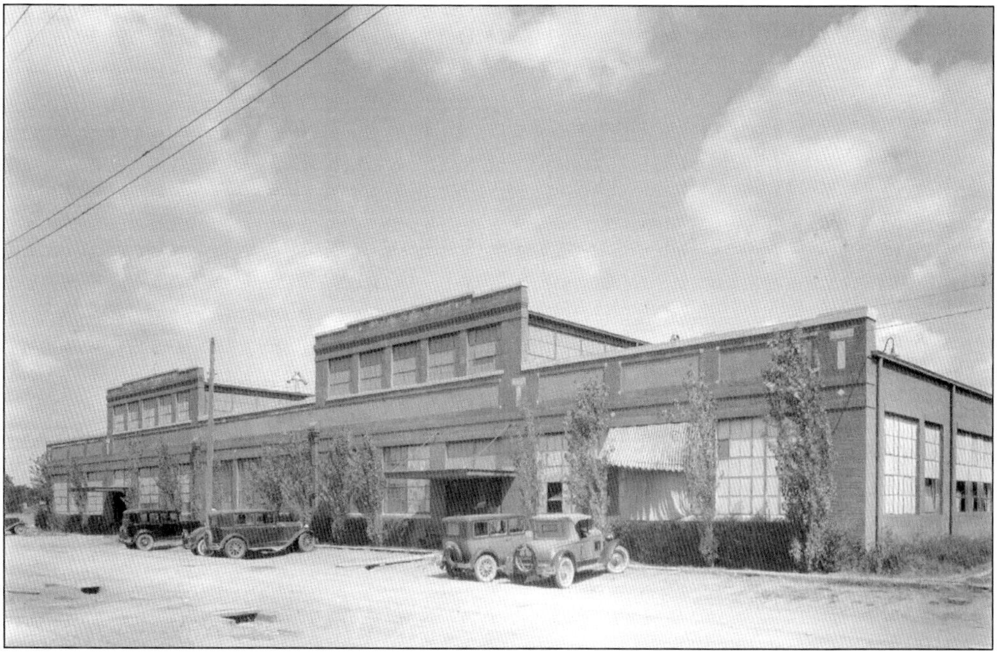

Pool Manufacturing Company. Sherman Overall Manufacturing was originally chartered in 1909 and sold to R.F. Pool Sr. in 1911. The name was changed to Pool Manufacturing Company in 1925, and they opened their new facility on South Montgomery Street in 1928. At that time, the company boasted 650 employees and 525 sewing machines. (Courtesy of the Sherman Museum.)

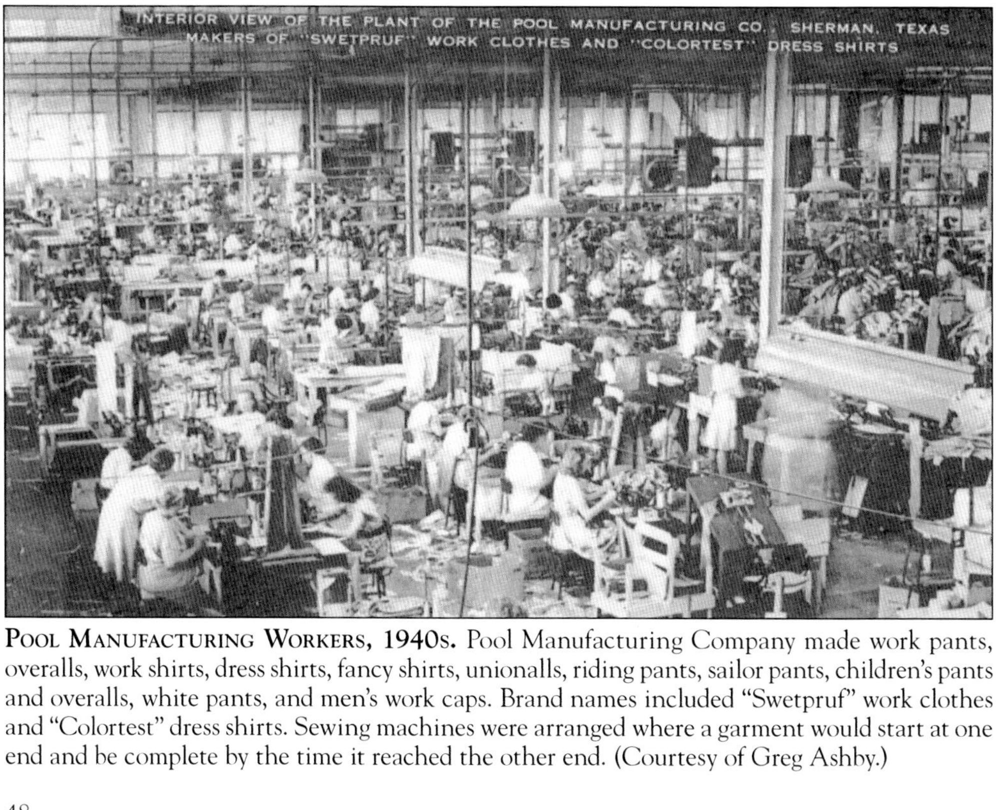

Pool Manufacturing Workers, 1940s. Pool Manufacturing Company made work pants, overalls, work shirts, dress shirts, fancy shirts, unionalls, riding pants, sailor pants, children's pants and overalls, white pants, and men's work caps. Brand names included "Swetpruf" work clothes and "Colortest" dress shirts. Sewing machines were arranged where a garment would start at one end and be complete by the time it reached the other end. (Courtesy of Greg Ashby.)

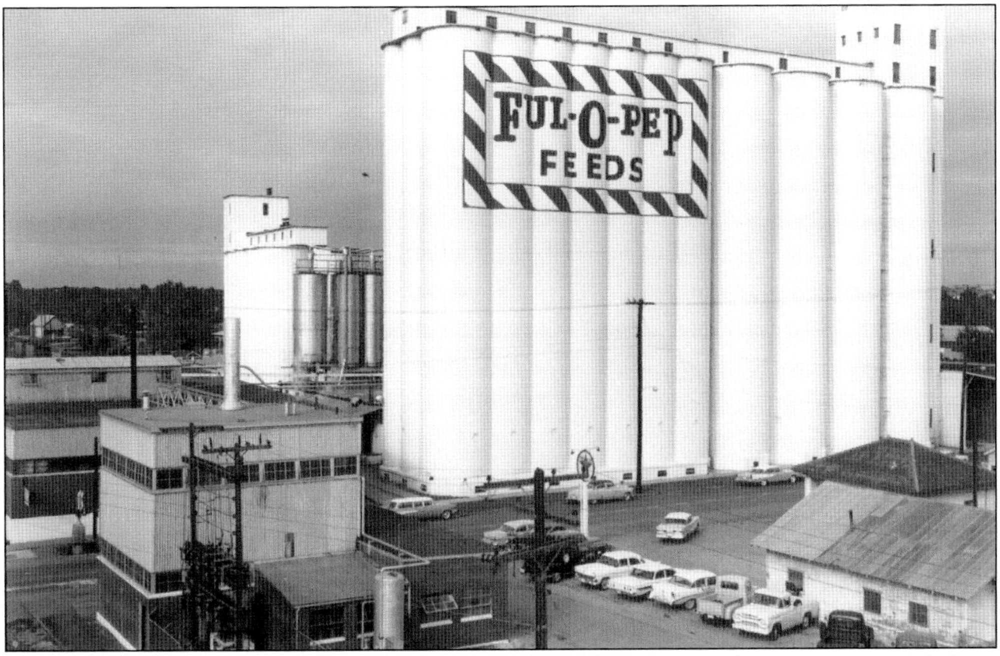

Ful-O-Pep Feeds. The Fant Milling Company produced flour, prepared mixes, cornmeal, baking powder, cereals, and dry stock feed. Trade names used by the company were Aunt Jemima, Quaker Oats, and Ful-O-Pep. Fant Milling Company was the first exclusive corn mill built in Texas. (Courtesy of the Sherman Museum.)

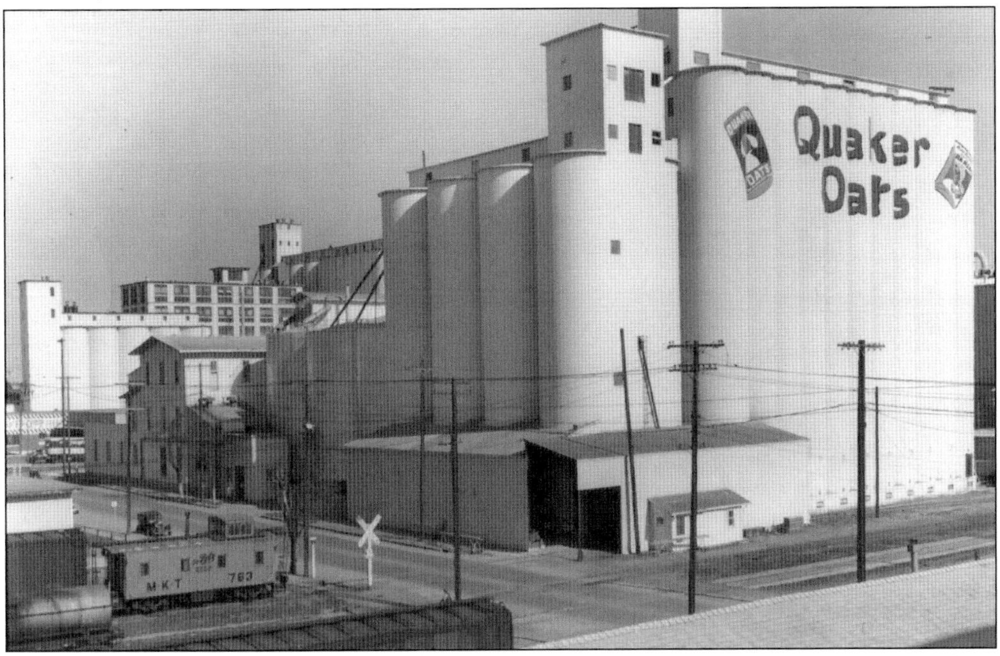

Quaker Oats. Quaker Oats opened their Sherman plant in 1941, acquiring the Kimbell Milling Company and later the G.B.R. Smith Milling Company. Quaker Oats manufactured rolled oats, cornmeal, flour, hominy grits, and livestock feed. In 1948, the company had a payroll of more than $1 million a year for approximately 475 employees. (Courtesy of the Sherman Museum.)

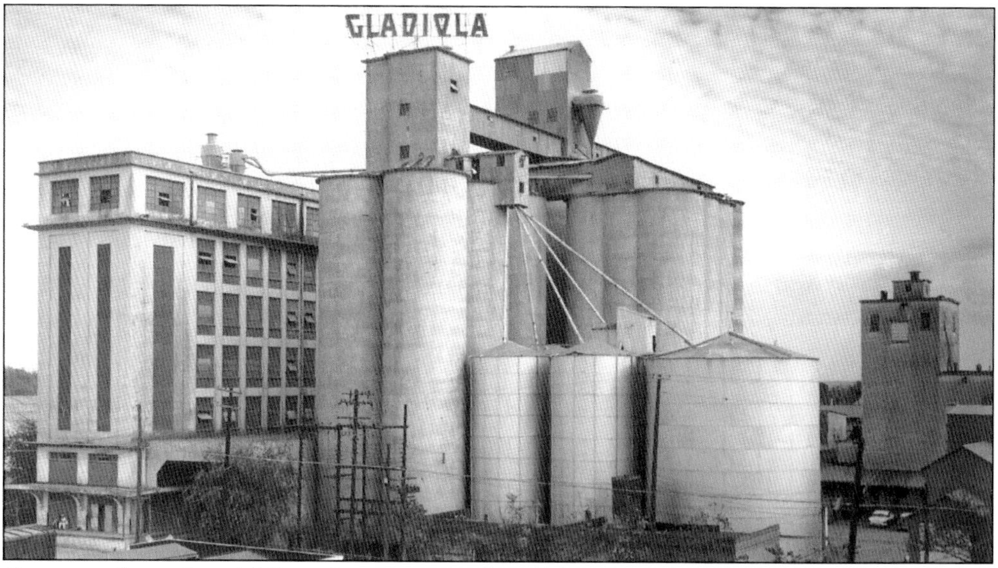

GLADIOLA SIGN. Fant Milling Company was founded in 1898 as a grain brokerage. In 1921, a stock company headed by E.T. Fant purchased Gladney Milling Company from Sam Gladney, and began its operation as Fant Milling Company. Flour was packed under the Gladiola label and sold extensively throughout the nation. In 1941, Fant acquired two other milling companies. The name changed to ConAgra in 1971. (Courtesy of the Sherman Museum.)

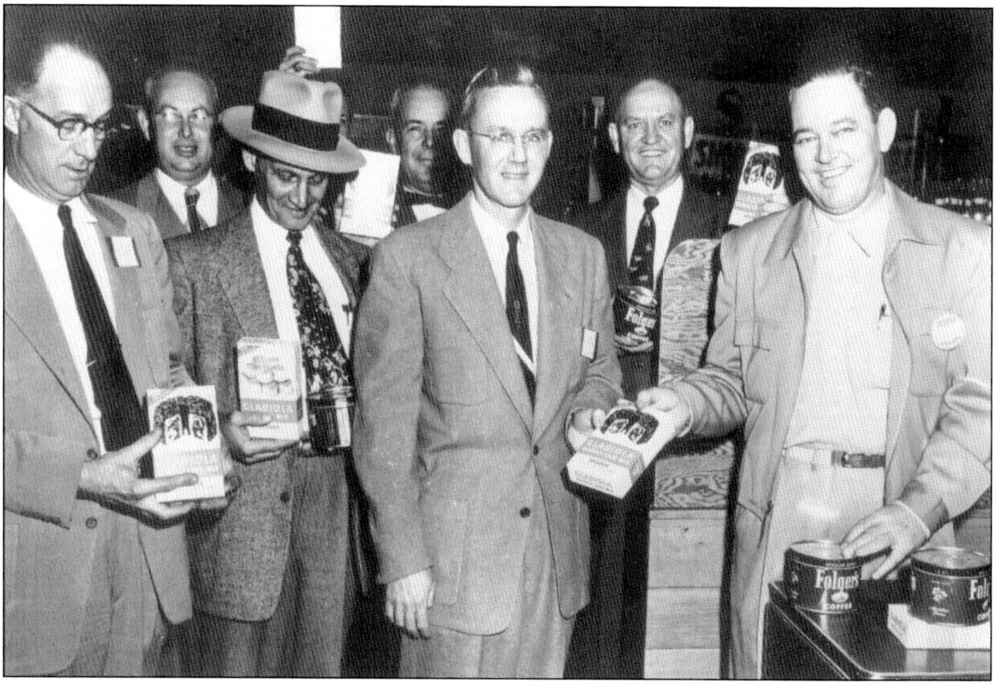

GLADIOLA FLOUR MILL TOUR. Local dignitaries toured Fant Milling Company, the maker of Gladiola flour. From left to right are (first row) Chris S. Schluree, Schluree Hardware Store; Ed Barcus, pastor, First Methodist Church; E.T. "Euclid" Fant Jr., Fant Milling Company; and unidentified; (second row) Jack Hannah, Hannah and Son Florists; Howard Hestand Sr., Hestand Pharmacy; and E.B. Chapman, Texas Oil Company. (Courtesy of the Sherman Museum.)

Three

A Town Becomes a City

As Sherman grew, so did the city services. In 1868, the *Sherman Courier* was established, while the *Patriot*, the second newspaper, began publication in 1870. Also in 1870, the city's first water system was set up and consisted of four cisterns on the public square. The cisterns caught rainwater from the courthouse roof.

The first city hall was constructed at Travis and Cherry Streets in 1873, and Capt. L.F. Ely started a new courthouse in 1875. The *Sherman Democrat* began publication in 1879 and became a daily newspaper three years later. By 1879, Sherman's first telephone system had secured the required number of 50 subscribers that would ensure the success of the telephone exchange.

By 1886, the city's first water mains were laid, and the city switched to a deep-water well system, digging a well at the south plant. The first Trinity well was added to the system in 1891.

The Sisters of St. Vincent de Paul established the first hospital, St. Vincent's, in 1902, and Sherman Hospital was built in 1913. Its name was later changed to Wilson N. Jones Hospital.

The first pavement was laid in Sherman in 1905, the same year that Pres. Theodore Roosevelt visited the community. The free city library opened in 1912, and the Carnegie Public Library opened in 1915, a gift from the Andrew Carnegie Foundation. A new city hall was built in 1913 at a cost of $13,000, and in 1915, the city adopted the city charter, setting up the city manager-commissioner form of government. The city fathers adopted a plan for orderly development in 1918, designed by George Kessler, which also resulted in the beginning of the park system.

By 1930, Sherman's population reached 15,713. A year later, the city purchased 160 acres at a cost of $10,000, for a municipal airport. City planning continued with the adoption of a zoning ordinance in 1936. The following year, the city purchased the old Kidd-Key Conservatory property and razed most of the buildings. The only remaining building, which was unfinished, was completed as the municipal building in 1938, to house the city offices. The same year, the school stadium was built and the municipal swimming pool opened.

St. Vincent's Hospital closed in 1954 and reopened the following year as Sherman Community Hospital. The Municipal Airport building was completed in 1955, and a city bond issue passed to begin construction on the new route for US Highway 75.

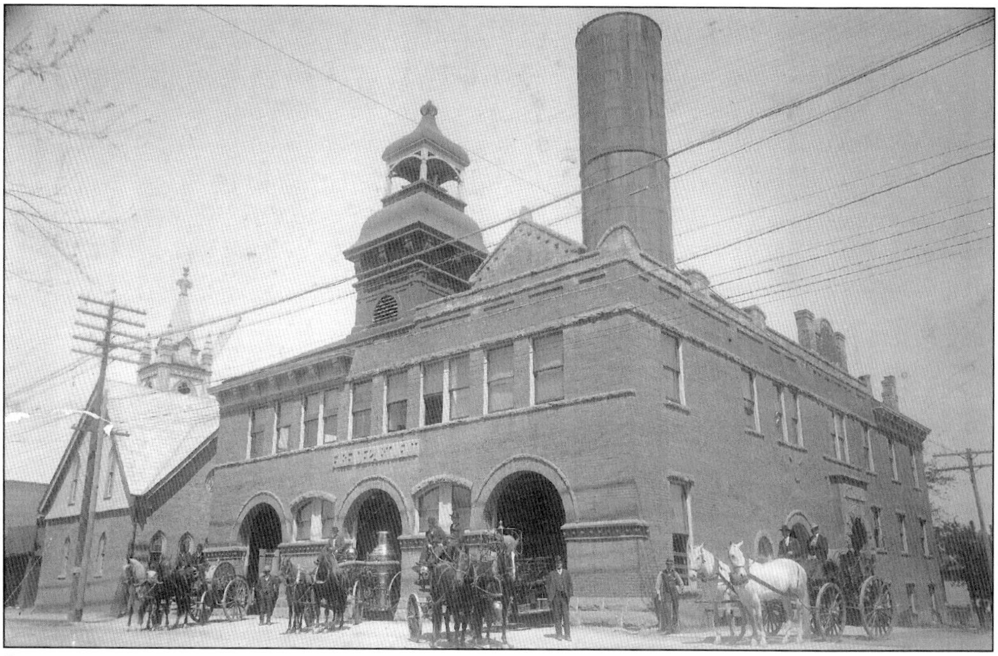

Sherman Fire Department. The fire department was organized in 1873, and the new facility was built in 1893 at a cost of $13,000. The building housed the fire department and city hall and was located at the corner of Travis and Cherry Streets. The building was torn down in 1965, and the fire department moved across the street. (Courtesy of the Sherman Museum.)

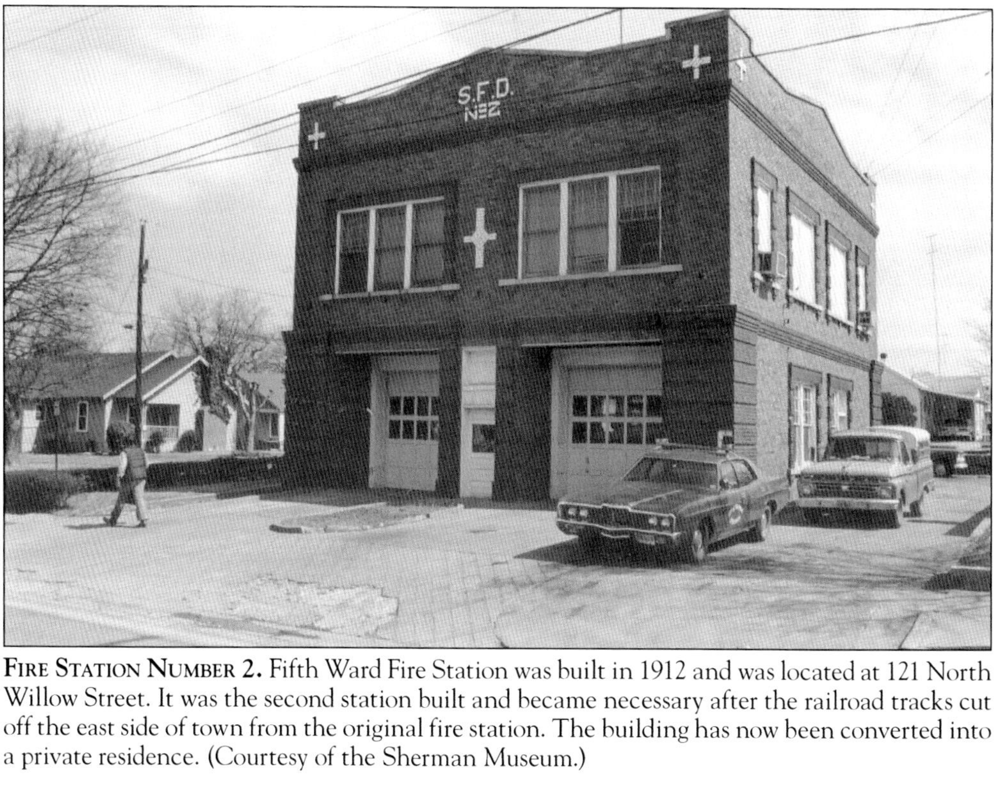

Fire Station Number 2. Fifth Ward Fire Station was built in 1912 and was located at 121 North Willow Street. It was the second station built and became necessary after the railroad tracks cut off the east side of town from the original fire station. The building has now been converted into a private residence. (Courtesy of the Sherman Museum.)

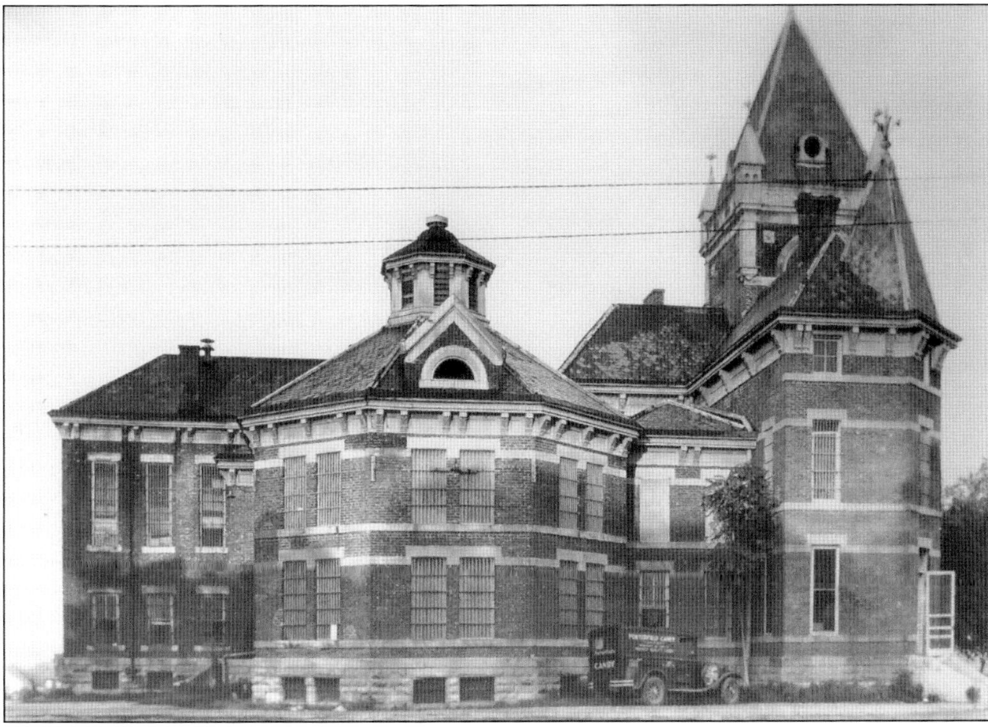

Grayson County Jail. The Grayson County Jail was erected in 1887 at a cost of $100,000 and had space for 100 prisoners. It also featured a rotary cellblock, which was found to be impractical, and was replaced by stationary cells in 1912. The rail for the rotary cell is now used as an archway over the entrance to Loy Lake Park. (Courtesy of the Sherman Museum.)

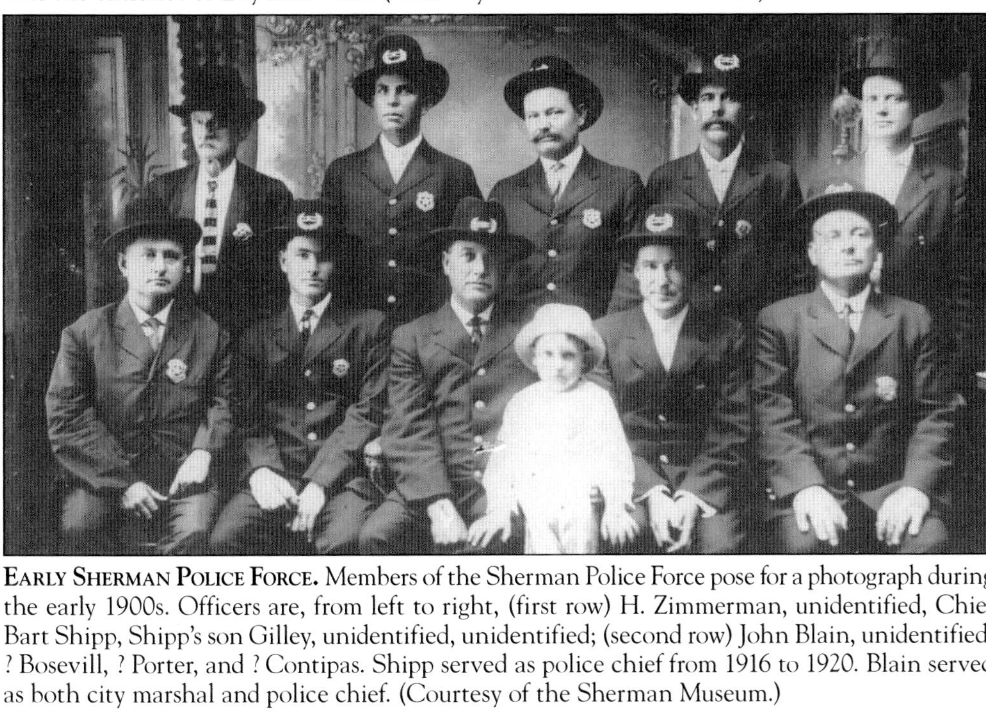

Early Sherman Police Force. Members of the Sherman Police Force pose for a photograph during the early 1900s. Officers are, from left to right, (first row) H. Zimmerman, unidentified, Chief Bart Shipp, Shipp's son Gilley, unidentified, unidentified; (second row) John Blain, unidentified, ? Bosevill, ? Porter, and ? Contipas. Shipp served as police chief from 1916 to 1920. Blain served as both city marshal and police chief. (Courtesy of the Sherman Museum.)

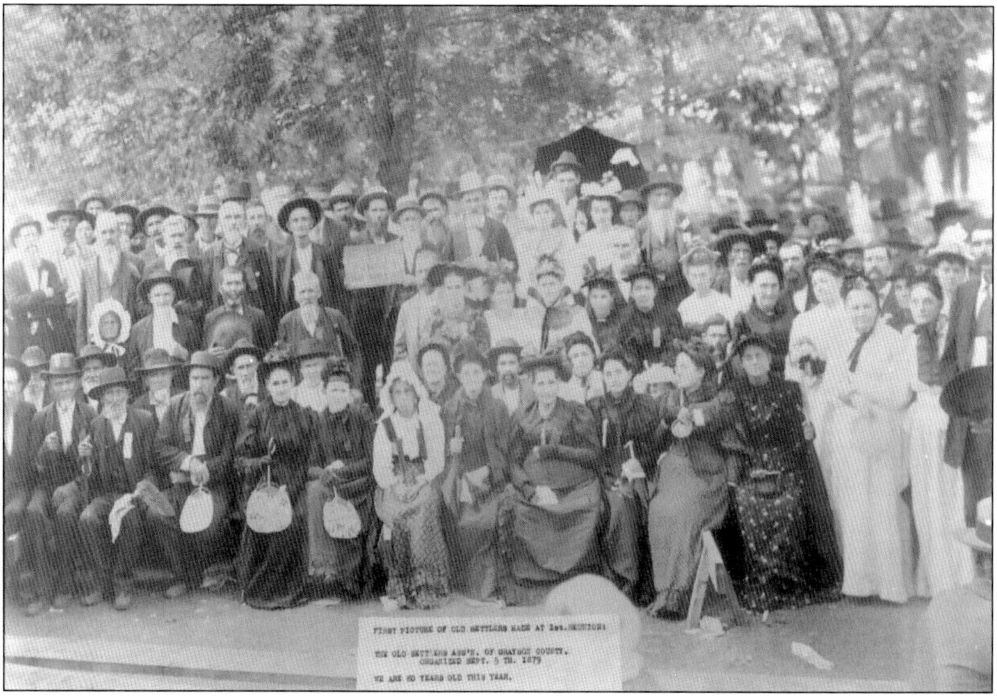

OLD SETTLERS ASSOCIATION. The Old Settlers Association was founded in 1879 and originally met at McKinstry's Grove, south of Sherman, to reminisce about the days of the Republic of Texas, the frontier, and the southern Confederacy. This photograph was made at the first reunion, even though the sign says, "We are 30 years old this year." (Courtesy of the Sherman Museum.)

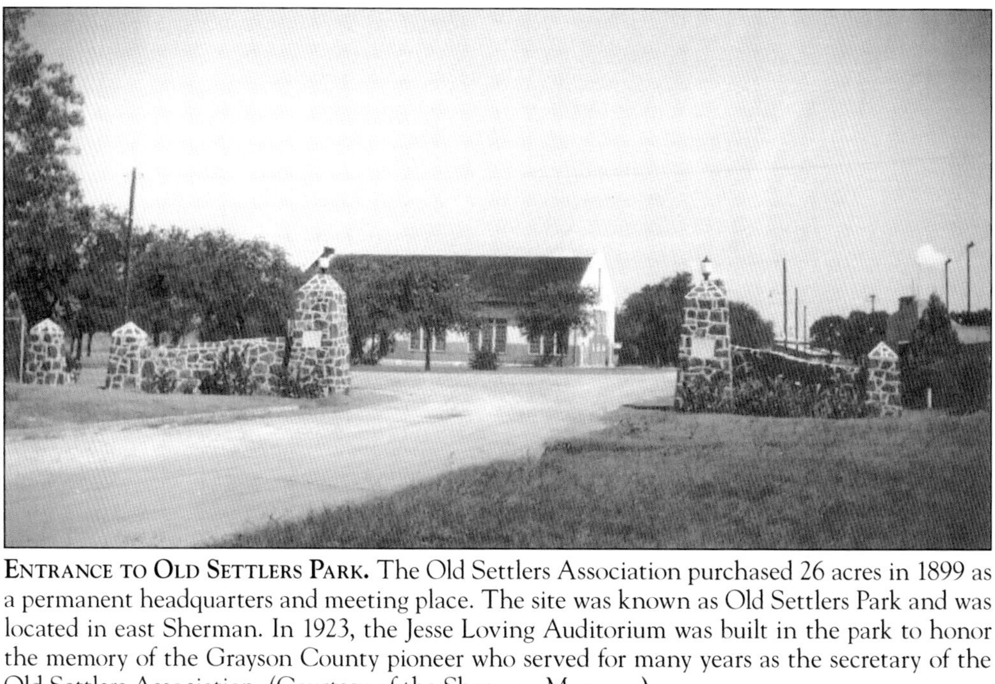

ENTRANCE TO OLD SETTLERS PARK. The Old Settlers Association purchased 26 acres in 1899 as a permanent headquarters and meeting place. The site was known as Old Settlers Park and was located in east Sherman. In 1923, the Jesse Loving Auditorium was built in the park to honor the memory of the Grayson County pioneer who served for many years as the secretary of the Old Settlers Association. (Courtesy of the Sherman Museum.)

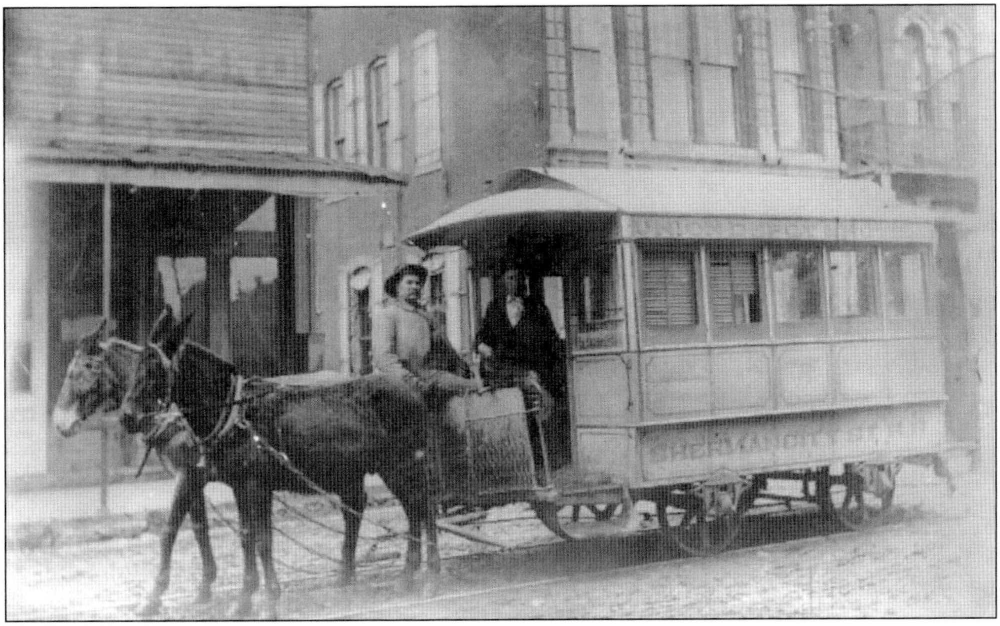

City Street Railway Company, 1877. The City Street Railway Company began operating mule-drawn streetcars out of Union Station in 1877. M.P. "Dad" Hill was one of the first drivers of the streetcars. They operated from the east end of Mulberry Street, west to Travis Street, and then south to Lake Street. The first electric cars began operating in 1889. (Courtesy of the Sherman Museum.)

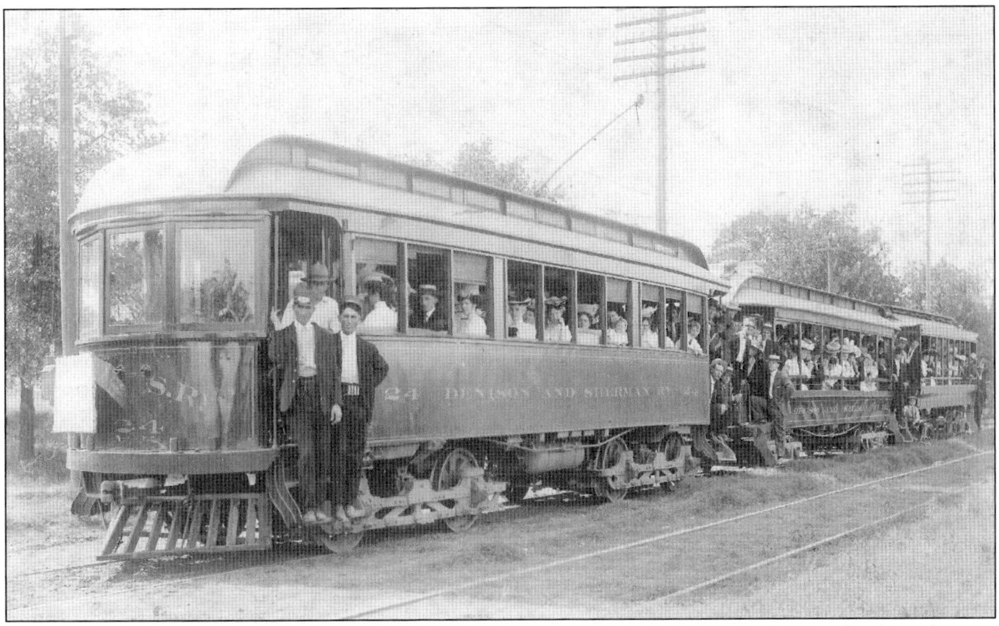

Interurban. In 1901, the Sherman-Denison Railway Company began operating the first electric railway line in Texas, going from Sherman to Denison. There were no local ticket offices, and tickets were purchased from drugstores and hotels. The line became part of the Texas Traction Company in 1907, and was incorporated into the Texas Electric Railway 10 years later. The company was dissolved in 1948. (Courtesy of the Sherman Museum.)

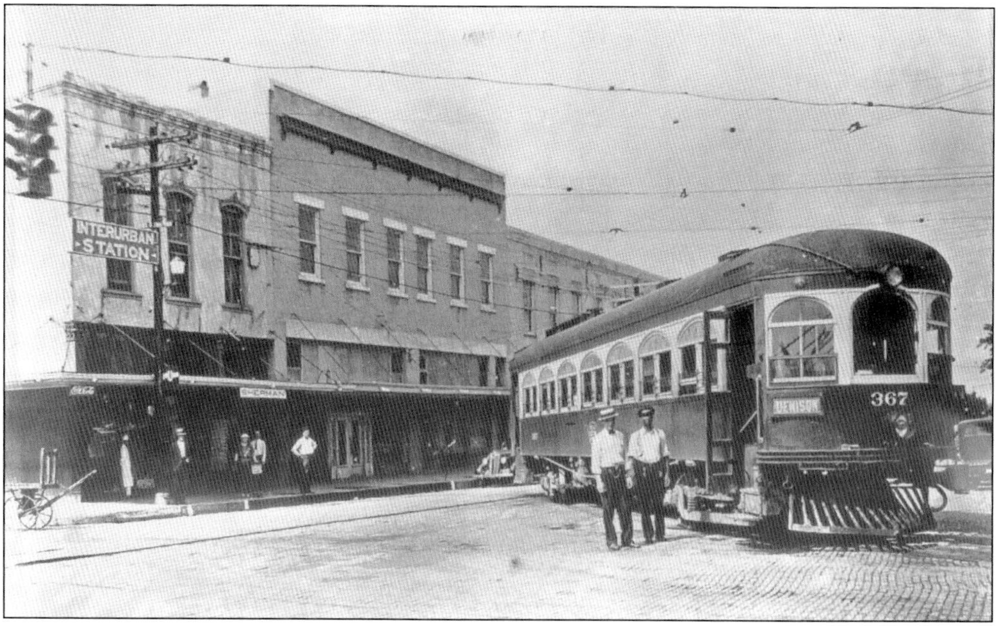

SHERMAN INTERURBAN STATION, c. 1940. The Interurban station was located at the corner of Lamar and Travis Streets. The "Limited" left for Dallas every hour, stopping at the Baker Hotel, then continuing on different routes to Waco, Fort Worth, Corsicana, or Cleburne. The "Local" left every half-hour and stopped wherever passengers wanted. The last Interurban ran in 1948. (Courtesy of the City of Sherman.)

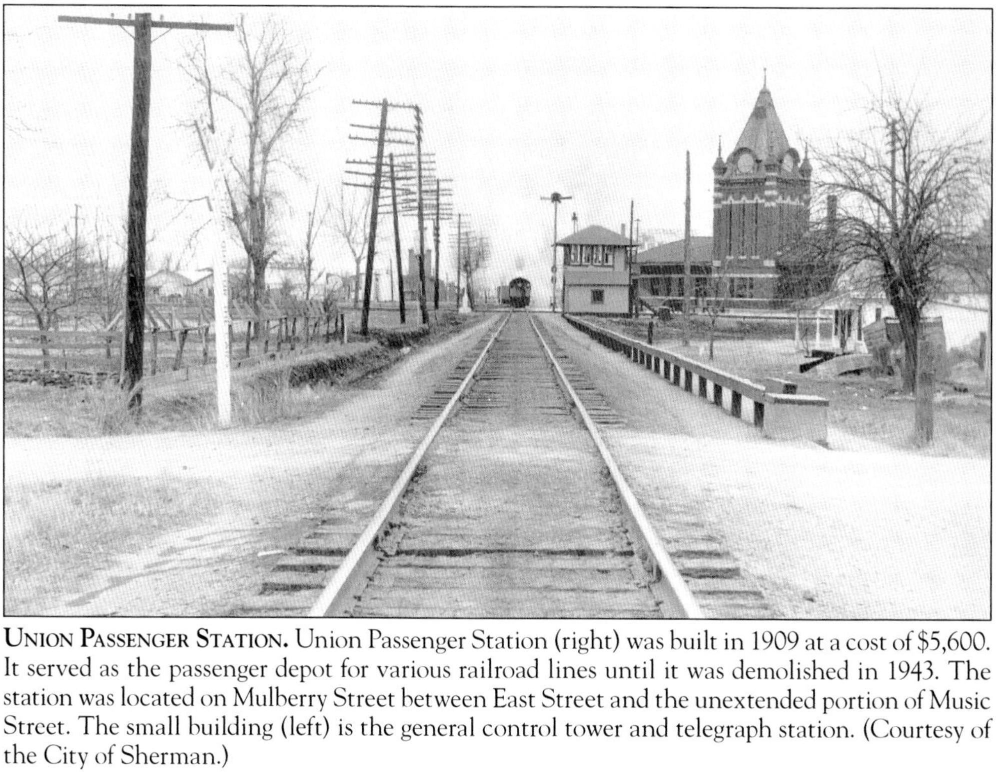

UNION PASSENGER STATION. Union Passenger Station (right) was built in 1909 at a cost of $5,600. It served as the passenger depot for various railroad lines until it was demolished in 1943. The station was located on Mulberry Street between East Street and the unextended portion of Music Street. The small building (left) is the general control tower and telegraph station. (Courtesy of the City of Sherman.)

FEDERAL BUILDING AND POST OFFICE. In 1906, the excavation for the federal building and post office was underway at the corner of Travis and Pecan Streets. The post office was later moved but the federal building remains at this location. In the background is the Franklin School, the first building built specifically as a school. It was located at Walnut and Mulberry Streets. (Courtesy of the City of Sherman.)

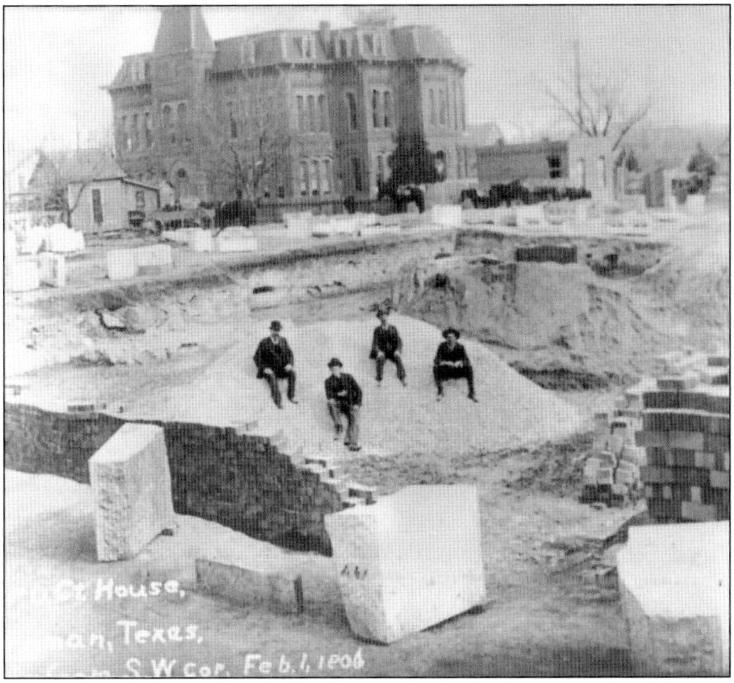

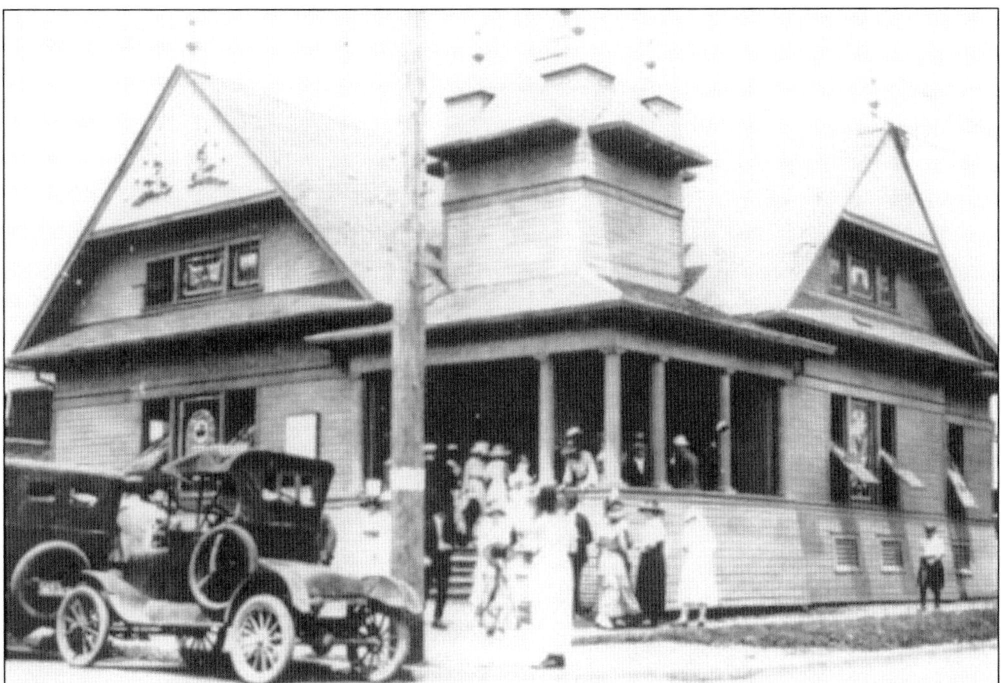

HOUSTON STREET CHURCH OF CHRIST. The Houston Street Church of Christ was located at 225 East Houston Street in the 1920s. Two Model T cars are parked in front of the church. The building later housed Locke the Tinner and eventually burned. (Courtesy of the Sherman Museum.)

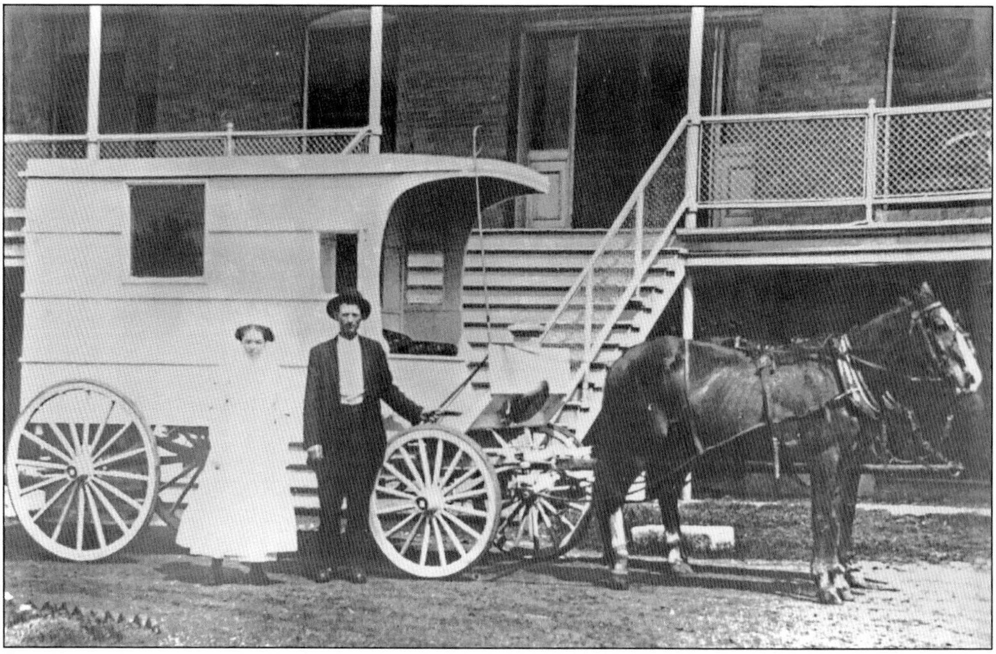

St. Vincent's Ambulance. The horse-drawn ambulance is shown on the south side of St. Vincent's Sanitarium facing Odneal Street. St. Vincent's brought the latest medical innovations to Sherman including the first use of oxygen in 1930 and the first EKG machine in the early 1930s. (Courtesy of the City of Sherman.)

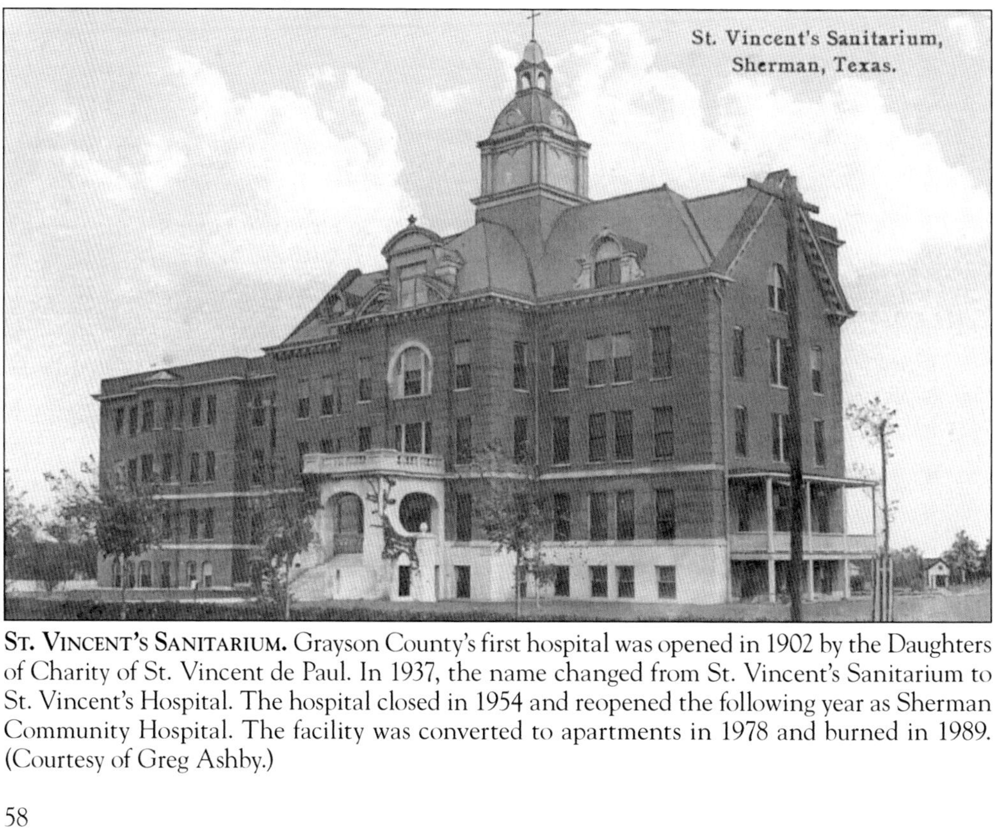

St. Vincent's Sanitarium. Grayson County's first hospital was opened in 1902 by the Daughters of Charity of St. Vincent de Paul. In 1937, the name changed from St. Vincent's Sanitarium to St. Vincent's Hospital. The hospital closed in 1954 and reopened the following year as Sherman Community Hospital. The facility was converted to apartments in 1978 and burned in 1989. (Courtesy of Greg Ashby.)

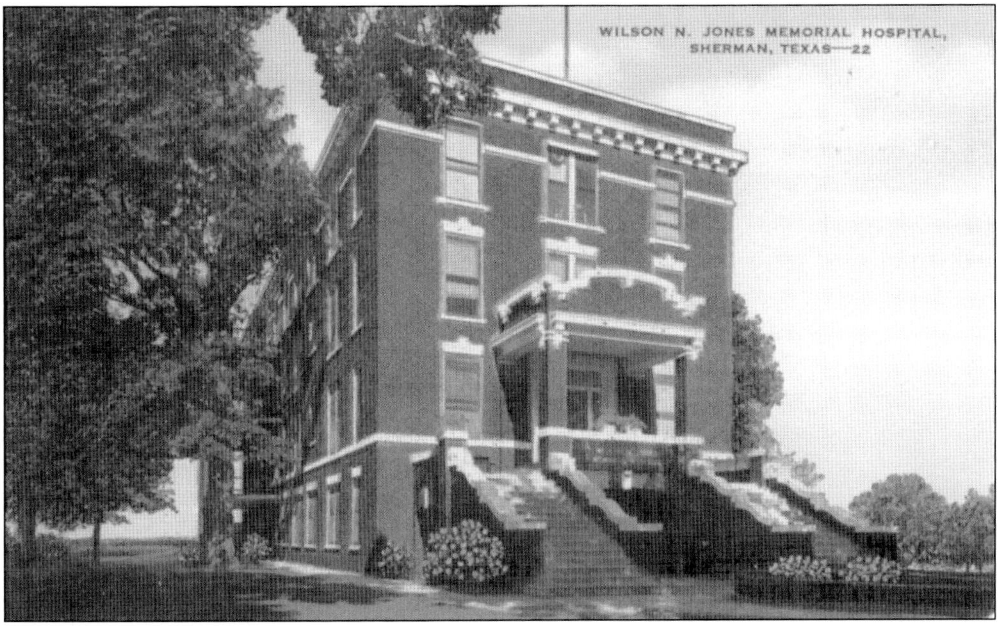

WILSON N. JONES HOSPITAL. Sherman Hospital Company was erected in 1914 by Dr. E.J. Neathery. Wilson Nathaniel Jones, governor of the Choctaw Nation, left a portion of his estate for the establishment of a hospital in Sherman. He died in 1901, but by the time his estate was finally settled in 1928, the other hospital was in operation. Trustees of the estate purchased Sherman Hospital and renamed it Wilson N. Jones Hospital. (Courtesy of the Sherman Museum.)

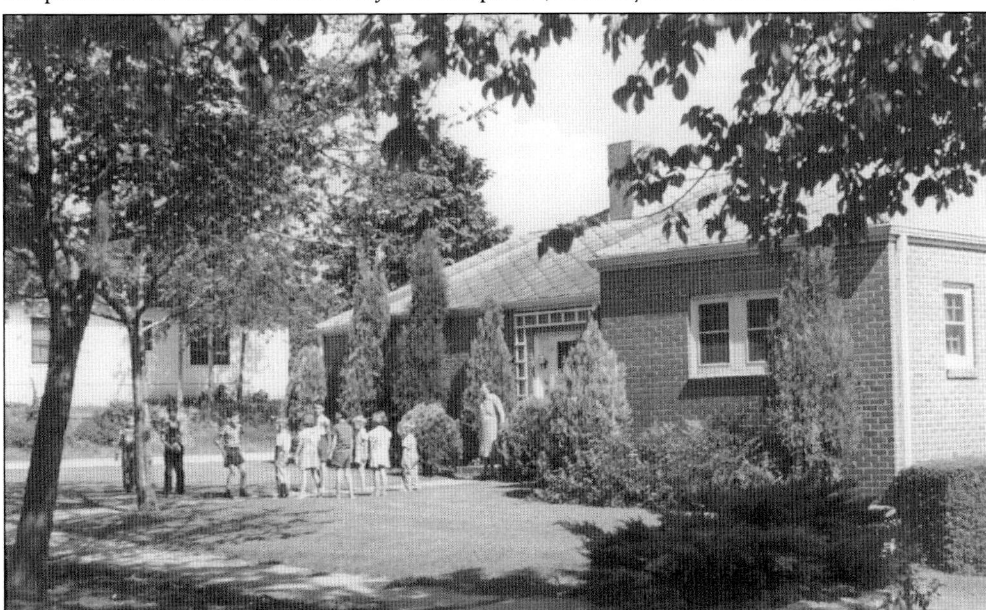

SHERMAN DAY NURSERY. Edna Gladney founded Sherman Day Nursery in 1918 as a daily home for preschool children of working mothers. It was originally located on the corner of Cherry and Branch Streets. Gladney moved to Fort Worth, and various sponsors assumed responsibility for the nursery. In 1927, the City of Sherman took over administration of the nursery, and it finally closed in 2008. (Courtesy of the Sherman Museum.)

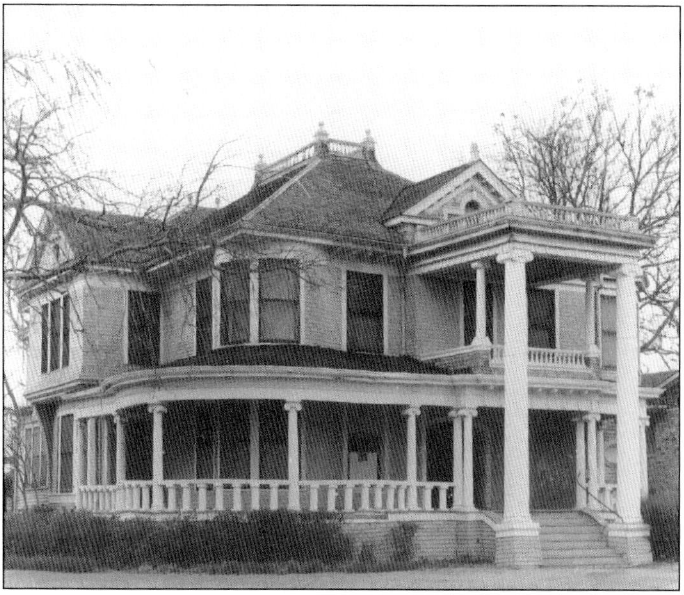

Keliehor House. The Keliehor house was located at 812 South Travis Street and was originally built by H. Stinnets, president of the Diamond Milling Company and the first automobile dealer in Sherman. C.L. Keliehor, a cattleman, dentist, contractor, and bank director, purchased the house in 1912. The house had 14 rooms and featured marble baths, fireplaces with massive mantles, and a Tiffany leaded window on the stairway landing. (Courtesy of the Sherman Museum.)

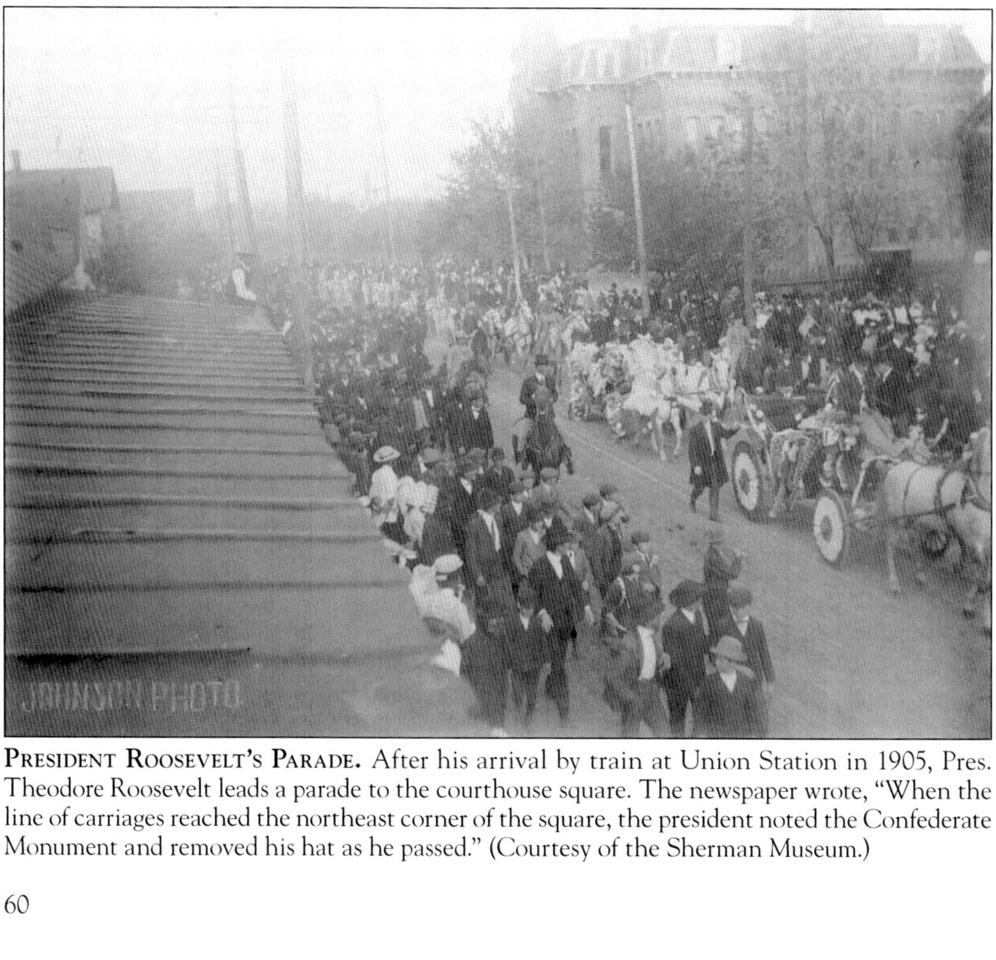

President Roosevelt's Parade. After his arrival by train at Union Station in 1905, Pres. Theodore Roosevelt leads a parade to the courthouse square. The newspaper wrote, "When the line of carriages reached the northeast corner of the square, the president noted the Confederate Monument and removed his hat as he passed." (Courtesy of the Sherman Museum.)

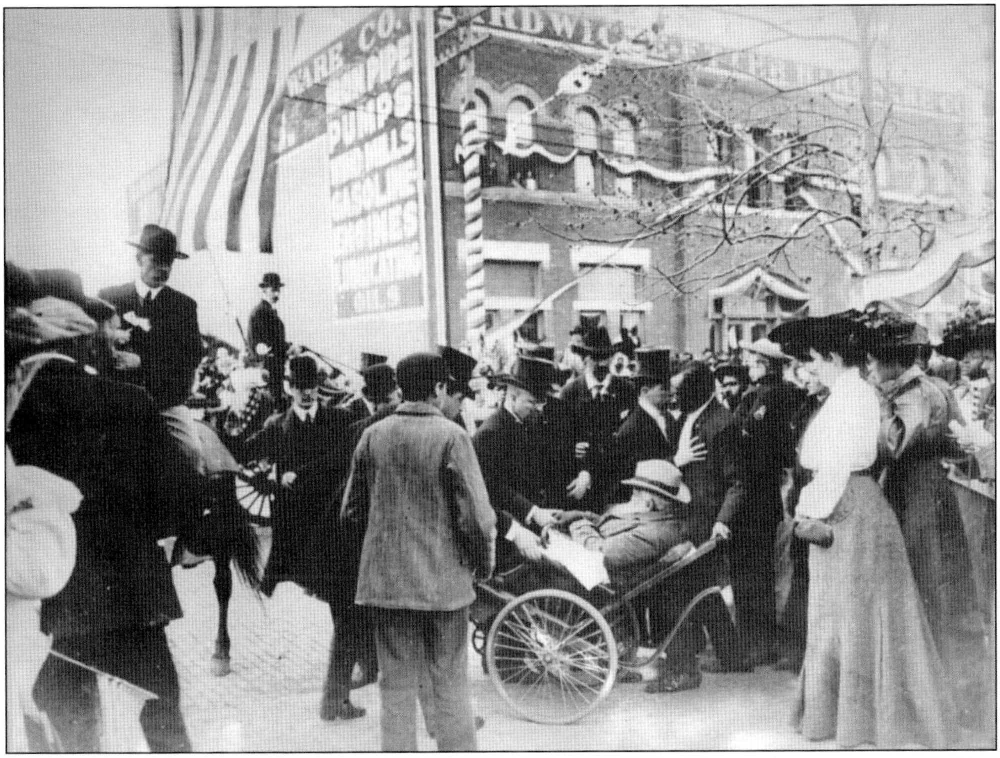

PRESIDENT ROOSEVELT GREETS CAPT. O.T. LYON. Pres. Theodore Roosevelt was en route to San Antonio to attend a reunion of his Rough Riders. His main Texas host was Republican national committeeman Col. Cecil Lyon of Sherman. The president is pictured shaking hands with Colonel Lyon's father, Capt. O.T. Lyon, seated in the wheelchair. (Courtesy of the City of Sherman.)

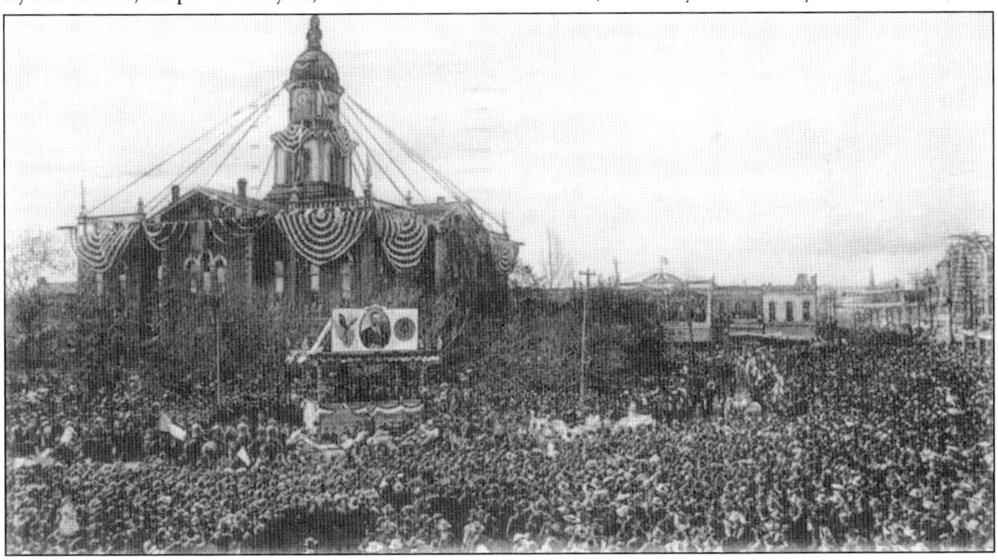

PRESIDENT ROOSEVELT ADDRESSES THE CROWDS. On April 5, 1905, Pres. Theodore Roosevelt spoke to an estimated crowd of 30,000 to 60,000 visitors in Sherman. He arrived at the square in the decorated carriages in front of the speakers stand. Mounted Rough Riders are also seen on the left side of the stand. (Courtesy of the Sherman Museum.)

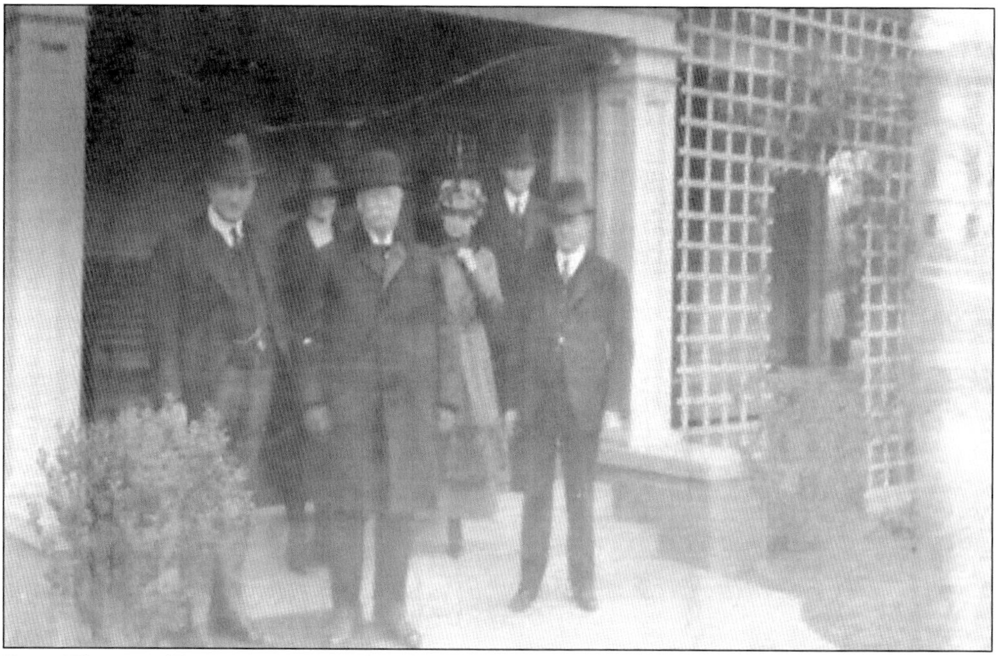

Pres. Howard Taft. Pres. Howard Taft visited Sherman twice after he left office, as a guest of Austin College president Dr. T.S. Clyce and May Clyce. His first visit was in April 1919, when he spoke to 1,200 people at Austin College's Sherman Hall. He visited again in April 1920 and spoke to college students at chapel in Sherman Hall. (Courtesy of the Sherman Museum.)

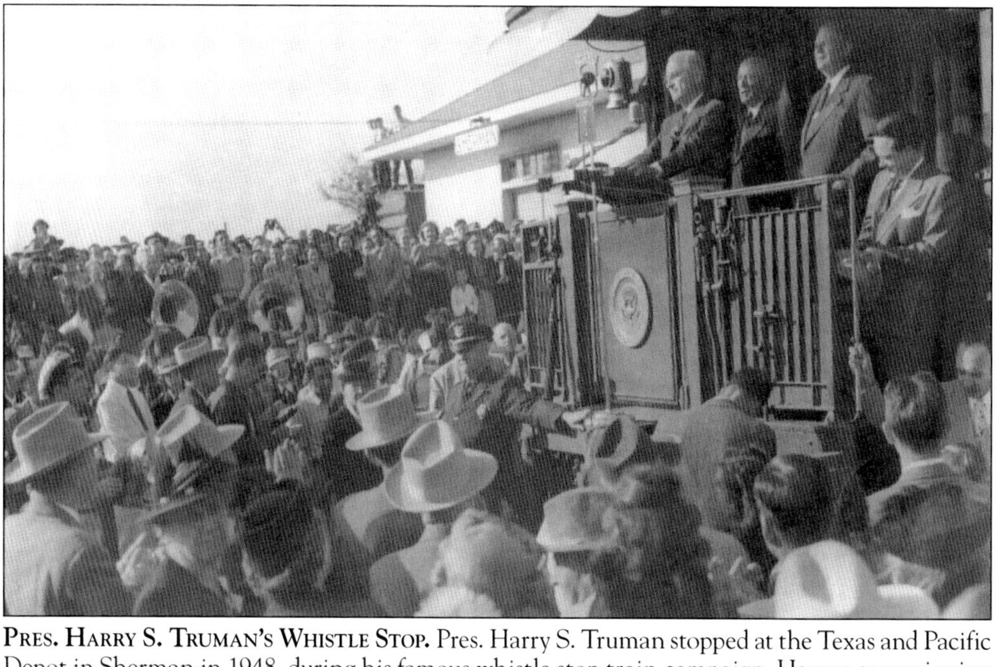

Pres. Harry S. Truman's Whistle Stop. Pres. Harry S. Truman stopped at the Texas and Pacific Depot in Sherman in 1948, during his famous whistle stop train campaign. He was campaigning for his first full term as president of the United States, even though he had been serving since Franklin D. Roosevelt's death in 1945. Texas congressman Sam Rayburn is shown standing behind Truman on the train's platform. (Courtesy of the Sherman Museum.)

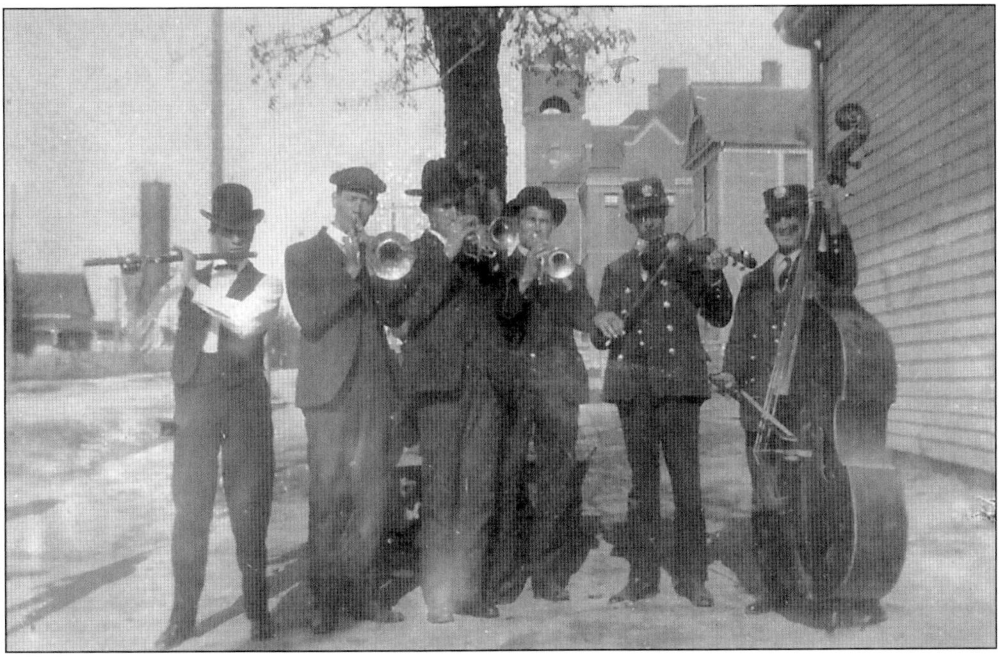

Fifth Ward Fire Department Band. Around 1910, musicians formed the Fifth Ward Orchestra. The band members are, from left to right, Aubrey Smith, Cecil Able, Eli Boatman, Harold Burk, Ed Holmes, and Fred Duer. The Fifth Ward Fire Station bell tower is seen in the background. (Courtesy of the Sherman Museum.)

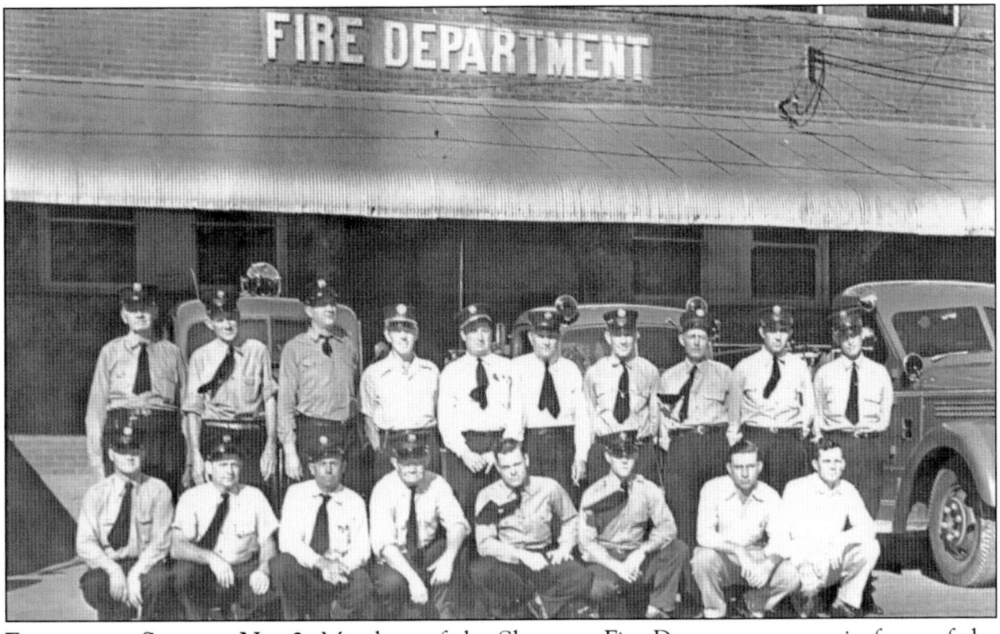

Firemen at Station No. 2. Members of the Sherman Fire Department pose in front of the Fifth Ward Fire Station. Firemen are, from left to right, (first row) D.O. Bledsoe, D. Francis, L. Belknap, Bob Long, T. Rasor, D. McGill, ? Carender, and Roy Clayton; (second row) C. Calhoun, C. Moore, J. Romain, C. Burris, Chief Jones, A.L. McQuire, Ed Tate, G. Miller, W.T. Dollins, and H. Willaby. (Courtesy of the Sherman Fire Department.)

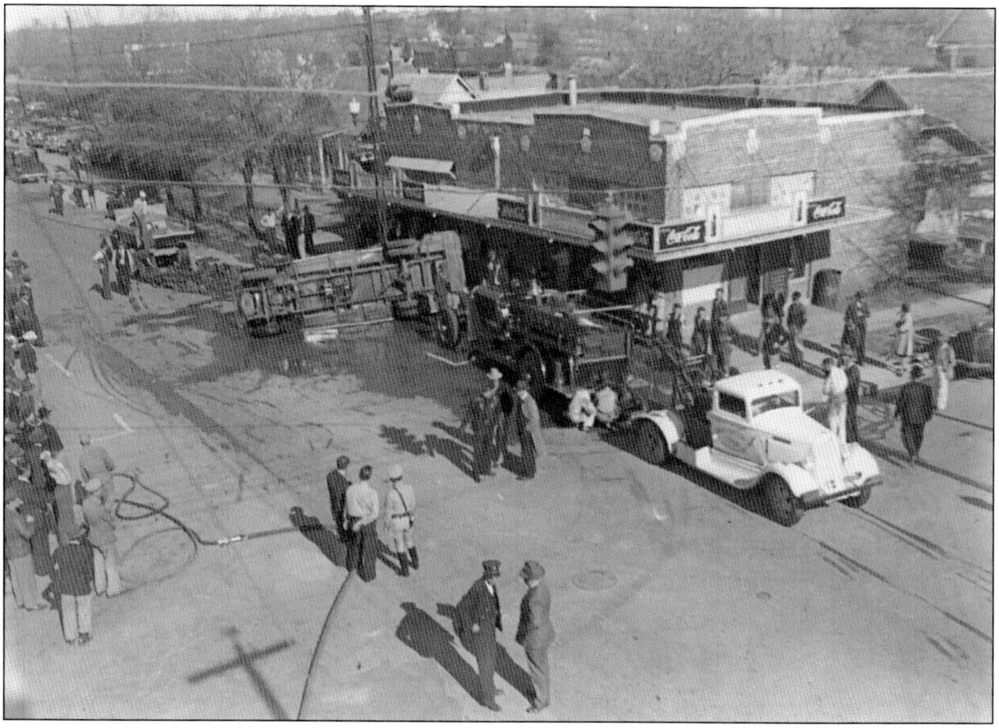

Fire Department Accident. On December 15, 1941, fireman E.G. "Big Hoss" Miller was killed and fireman Harvey Head was injured when the 1941 Ford fire engine and the Stutz pumper collided in front of E.T. Gwaltney Grocery at the corner of Walnut and Pecan Streets. The two men in the center of the photograph are mayor R.L. Hall and fire chief J.M. Andrews. (Courtesy of the Sherman Fire Department)

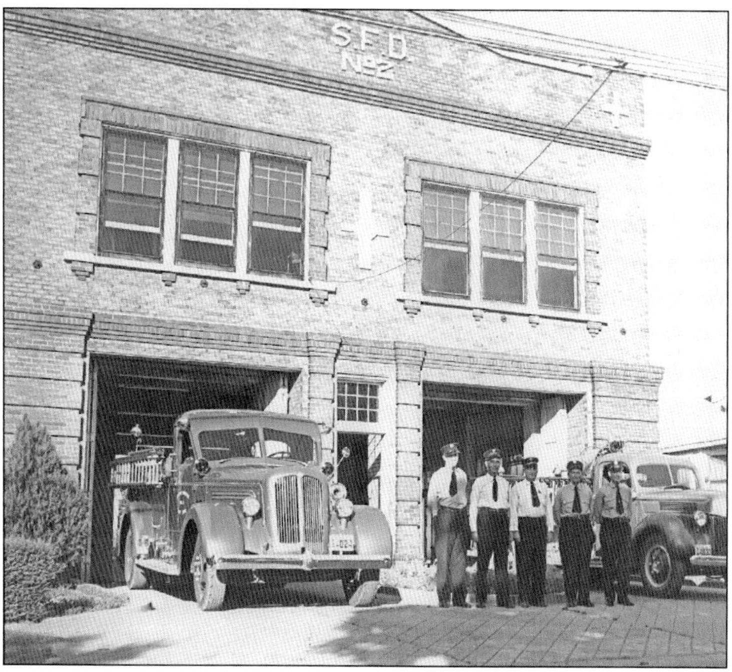

Fifth Ward Fire Station, 1953. Firemen, left to right, J. Romain, J. Jacks, chief A.C. Jones, G. Miller, and Ed Tate show off their equipment at the Fifth Ward Fire Station. Sherman's fire department formed in 1873 but consisted of volunteers. In 1885, two or three firemen were put on salary of room, board, and $15 per month, but the rest of the firemen were still volunteers. (Courtesy of the Sherman Fire Department.)

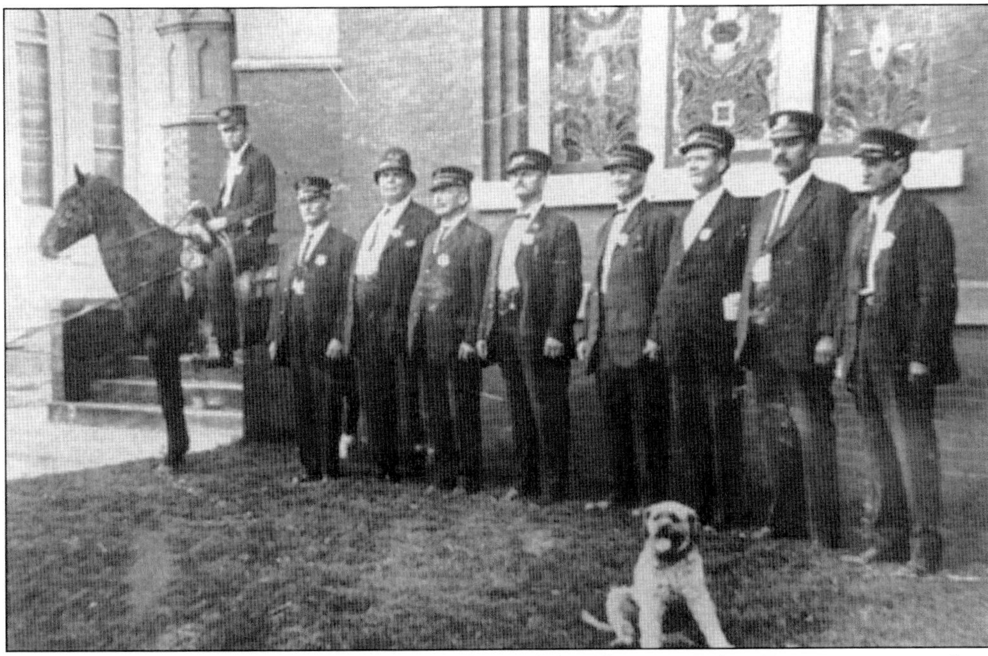

Sherman Police Department, 1910. Members of the Sherman Police Department pose for a photograph. The officers are, from left to right, Charles Stamps, Sam McAfee, Dad Hill, Henry Despain, Andy Burrus, Jap Phillips, Joe Doty, John Ramsey, and Jimmy Gee. (Courtesy of the Sherman Museum.)

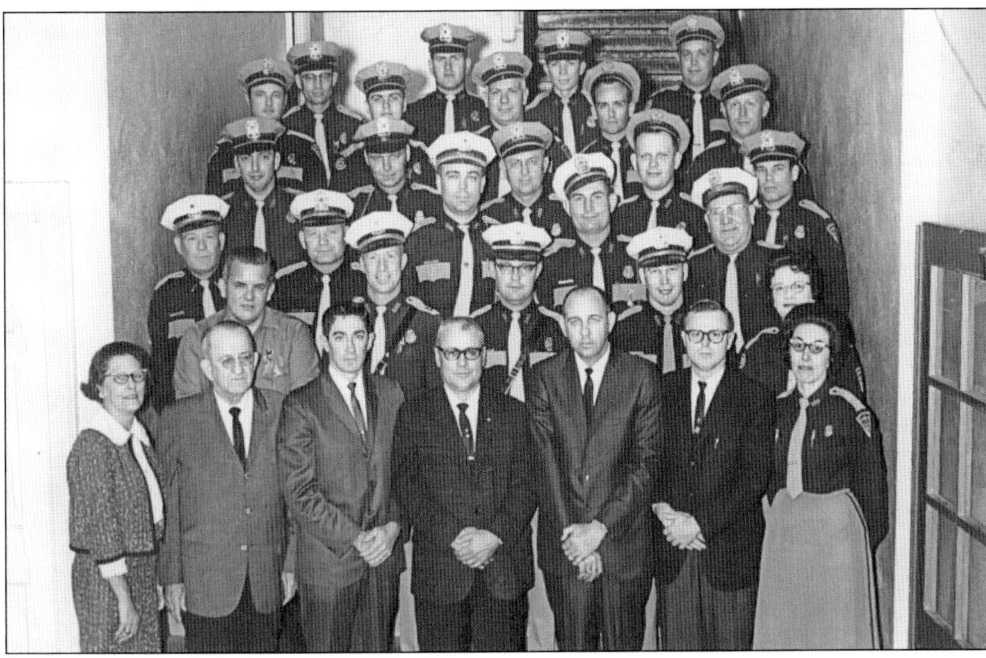

Sherman Police Department, 1965. Members of the Sherman Police Department pose for a photograph in December 1965. Johnny Burleson (first row, center) was the police chief. At that time, the city's population was about 30,660, and the town covered an area a little over eight-and-a-half square miles and had a total of 126 miles of streets. (Courtesy of Margaret Williams.)

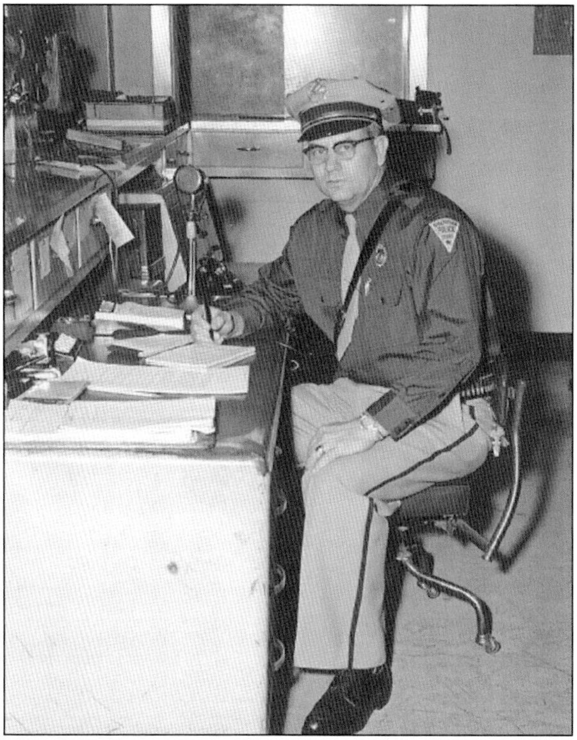

Police Chief Les Tribble. G.L. "Les" Tribble served as police chief from 1940 to 1947 and again from 1953 to 1961. He also served as Grayson County judge from 1963 to 1978. During the 1940s, the police department had 13 officers and three cars. Day shift officers walked their beat and captains rode in the cars. (Courtesy of the Sherman Police Department.)

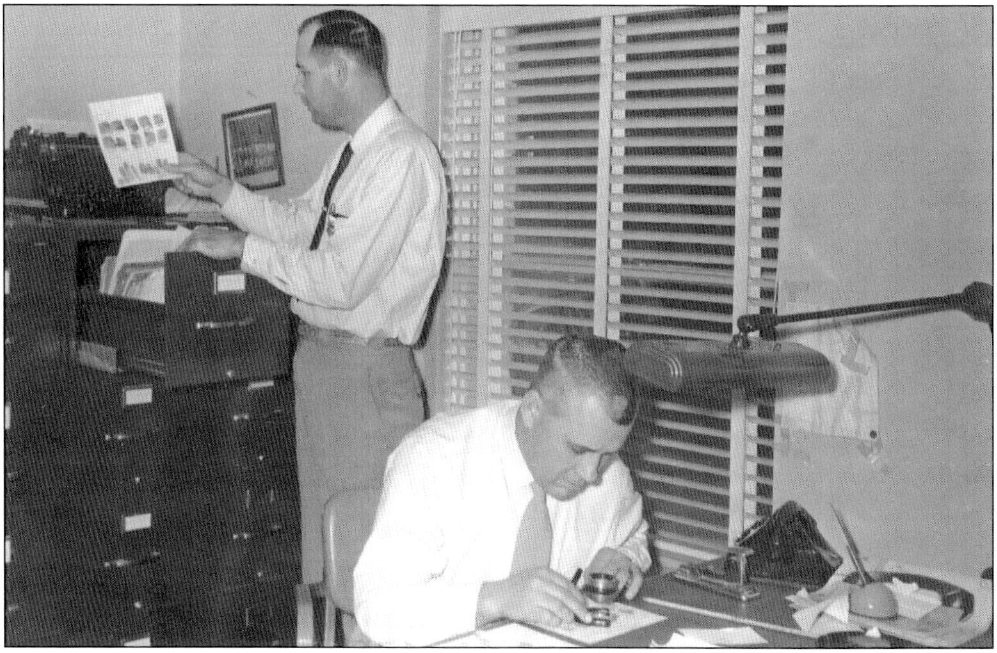

Two Police Chiefs. J.D. Pickens (left) and Johnny Burleson review fingerprints. Both later served as police chief for the Sherman Police Department. Burleson was hired in 1946 and served as police chief from 1961 until his retirement in 1979. Pickens was hired in 1953 and served as chief from 1981 until his retirement in 1988. As of 2011, there have been 16 police chiefs in Sherman's history. (Courtesy of Margaret Williams.)

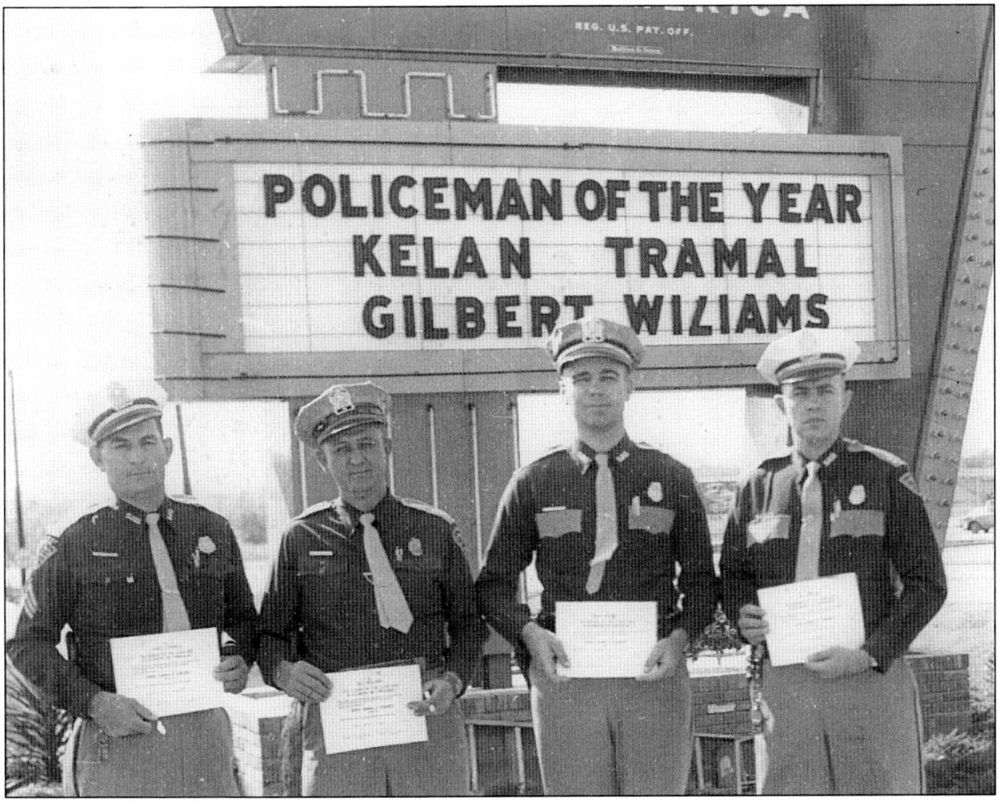

POLICEMEN OF THE YEAR. Sherman police officers, from left to right, James Tramell, W.A. "Bill" Williams, T.O. Gilbert, and W.P. Keelan, were named Policemen of the Year in 1963 or 1964. (Courtesy of Margaret Williams.)

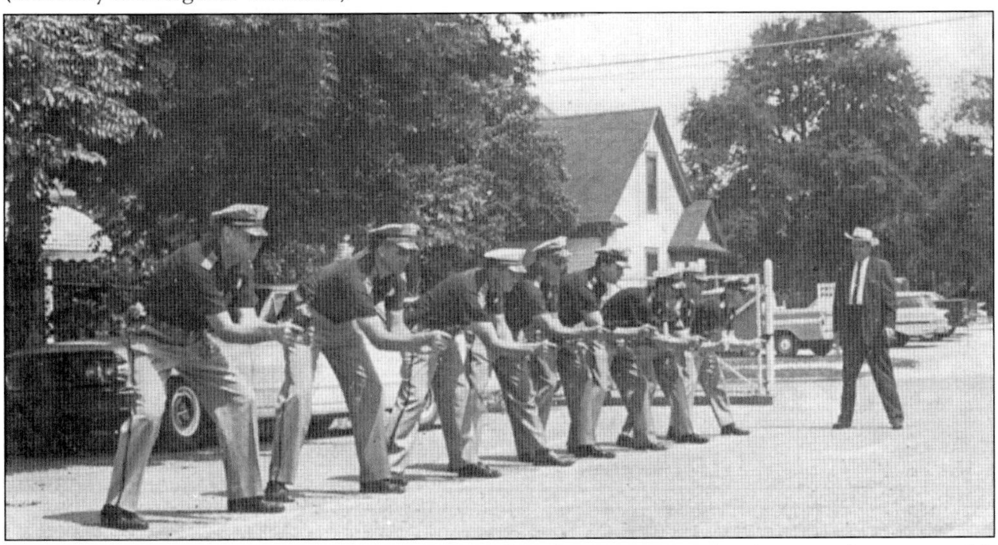

POLICE FIREARMS TRAINING. Police officers are "hip shooting" in 1964 after completing a week's training in firearms, which was taught by FBI agent Roby Robertson (right). Officers are, from left to right, Tom Flowers, T.O. Gilbert, Capt. L.W. Jackson, W.A. "Bill" Williams, J.F. McClure, Sgt. L.D. Gudgel, Jack Driscoll, and unidentified. (Courtesy of Margaret Williams.)

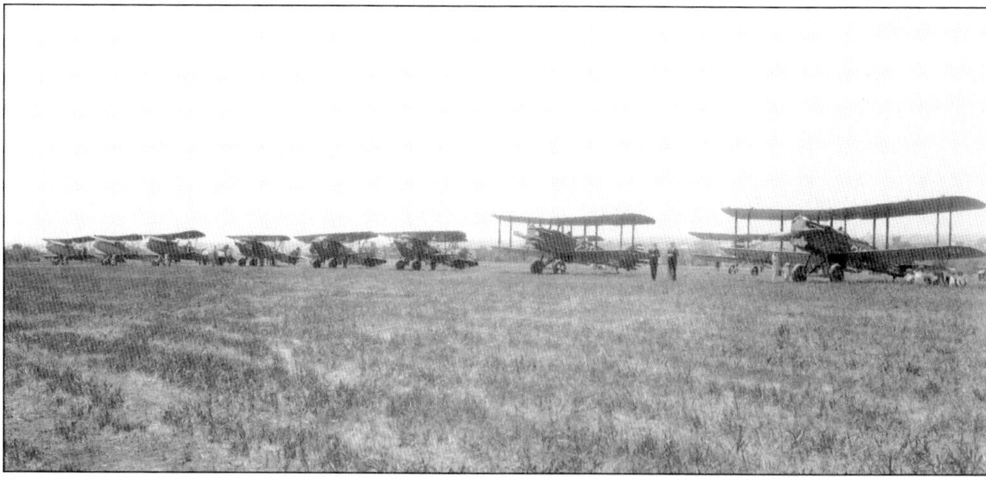

Opening of the Sherman Municipal Airport. In May 1929, the Sherman Municipal Airport opened on a 160-acre tract of land that was leased by the city. The land was purchased in 1931. Prior to this, pilots used a wheat field located near Woodlawn Country Club as their landing field. (Courtesy of the Sherman Museum.)

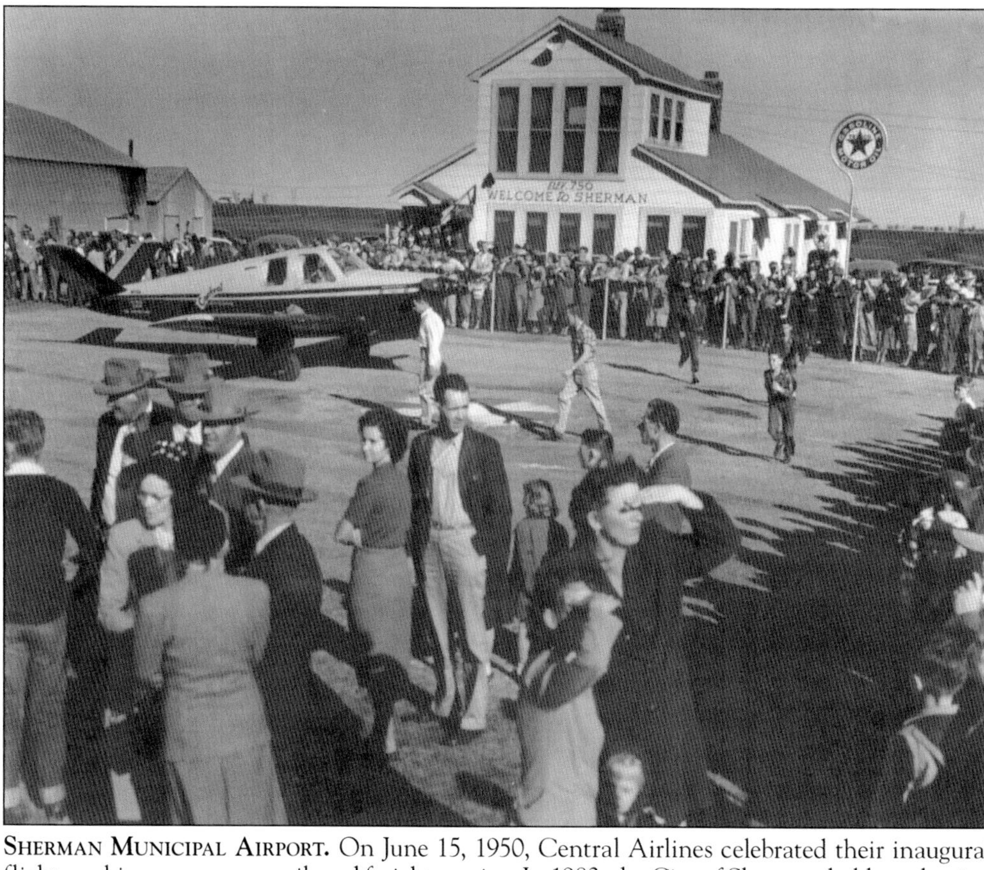

Sherman Municipal Airport. On June 15, 1950, Central Airlines celebrated their inaugural flight marking passenger, mail, and freight service. In 1983, the City of Sherman held an election to close the airport, however it failed by 199 votes, and the airport remained open. (Courtesy of the Sherman Museum.)

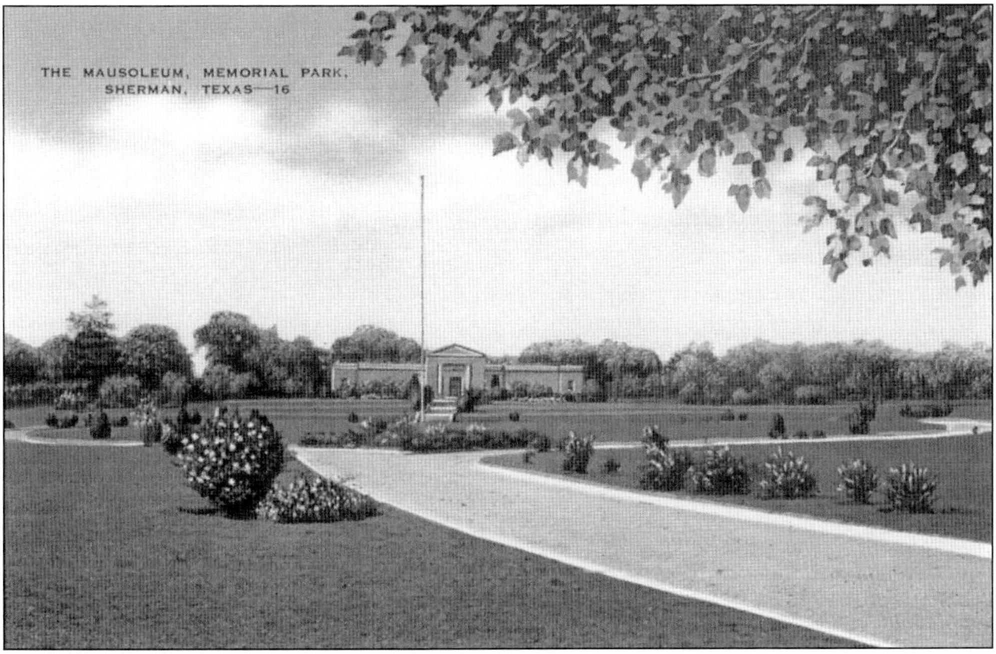

WEST HILL CEMETERY AND MAUSOLEUM. West Hill Cemetery began around 1860 and is located on 125 acres. Construction on the mausoleum began in 1920 and was completed in 1923. It was the first community mausoleum erected in Texas. West Hill graves mark the burial of Thomas Jefferson Shannon, the "father of Sherman;" Olive Ann Oatman Fairchild, who was kidnapped by Indians; and many of the dead from the 1896 cyclone. (Courtesy of Greg Ashby.)

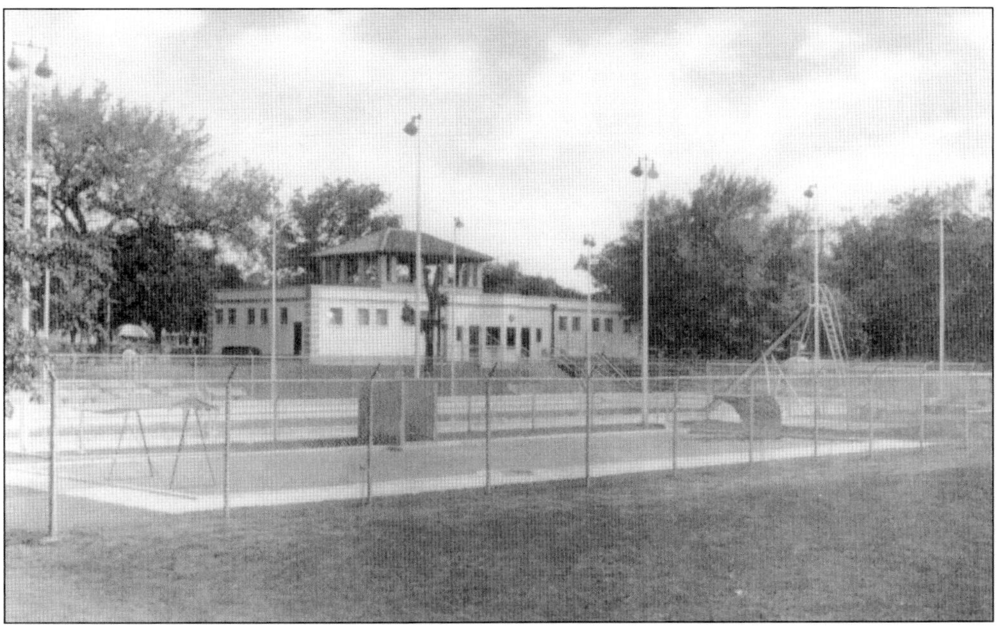

MUNICIPAL SWIMMING POOL. The Municipal Bathhouse was built in 1938 at a cost of $76,116. The bathhouse faced Houston Street, and the swimming pool was located on the north side of the building. Band concerts were held in the pavilion on top of the bathhouse. The swimming pool closed in 1961, and Fairview Swimming Pool opened in 1962. (Courtesy of the City of Sherman.)

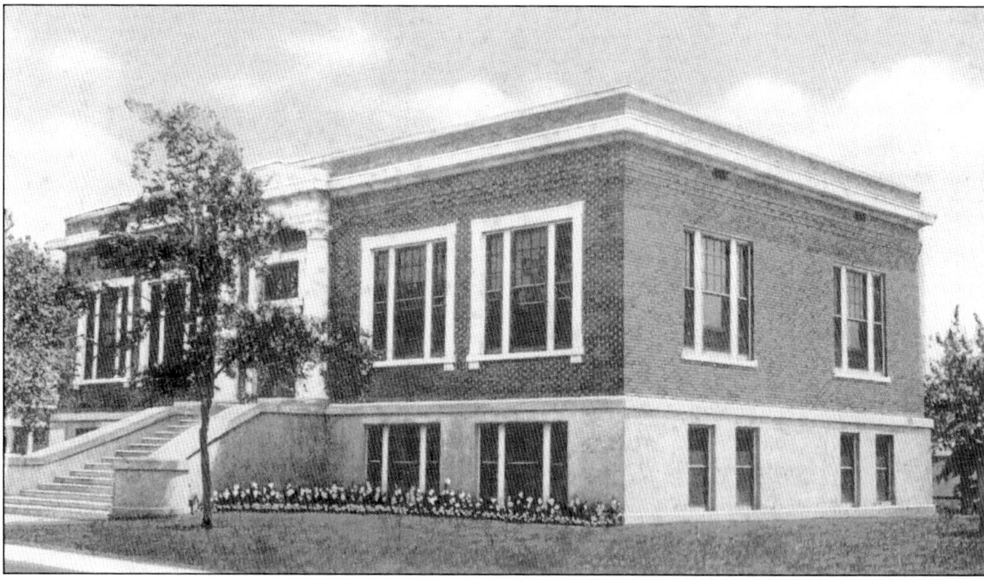

Carnegie Library. On April 3, 1912, Sherman was awarded a $20,000 grant from the Andrew Carnegie Foundation to build a library. The grant required matching contributions from the community. The city purchased the lot in 1912 for $2,500, and the building served as a library from 1915 to 1973. The building now houses the Sherman Museum. (Courtesy of the Sherman Museum.)

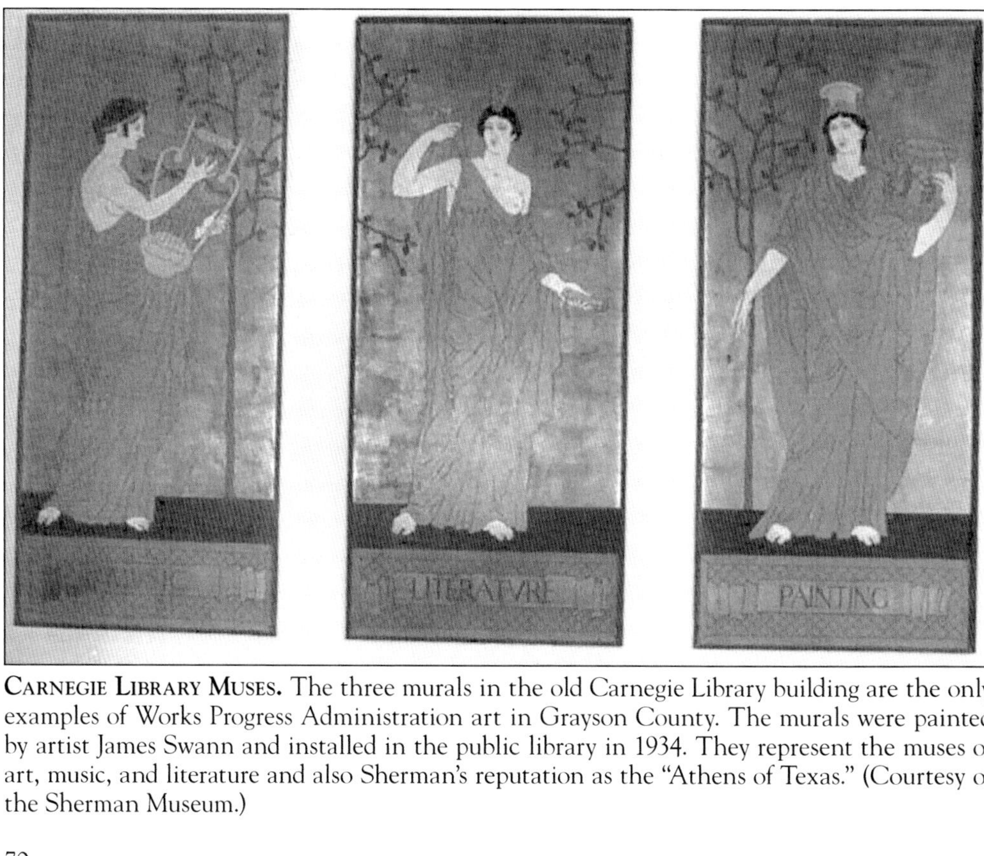

Carnegie Library Muses. The three murals in the old Carnegie Library building are the only examples of Works Progress Administration art in Grayson County. The murals were painted by artist James Swann and installed in the public library in 1934. They represent the muses of art, music, and literature and also Sherman's reputation as the "Athens of Texas." (Courtesy of the Sherman Museum.)

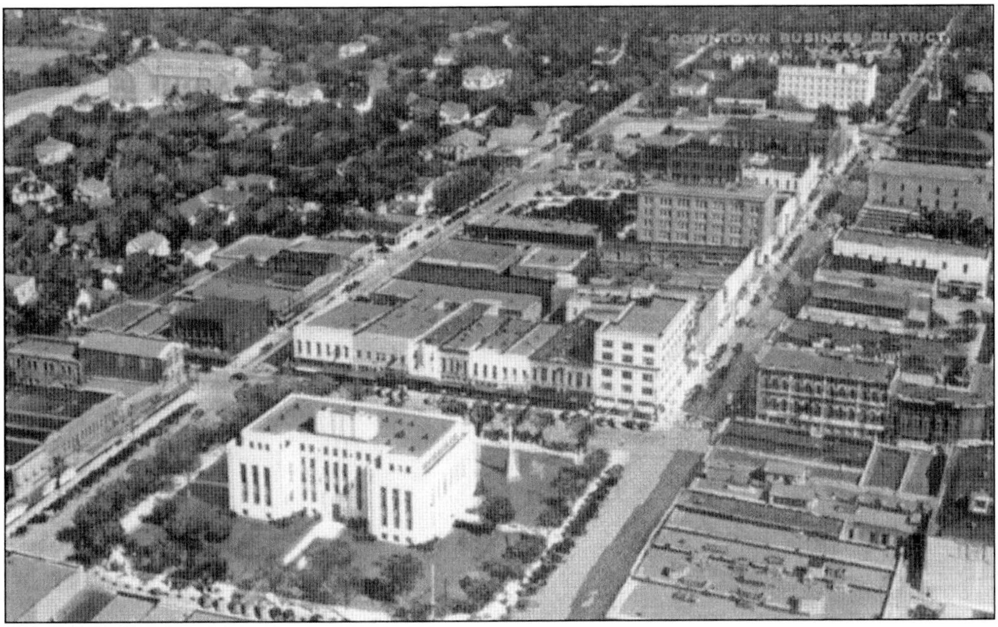

Aerial View of Downtown Sherman, c. 1948. This aerial photograph captures downtown Sherman after 100 years of existence. The population was about 26,000, and the community was hailed as the "industrial center of North Texas" by the *Sherman Democrat*. Sherman advertised that diversification was the key to their success. The Grayson County Courthouse is shown in the lower center of the photograph. (Courtesy of the Sherman Museum.)

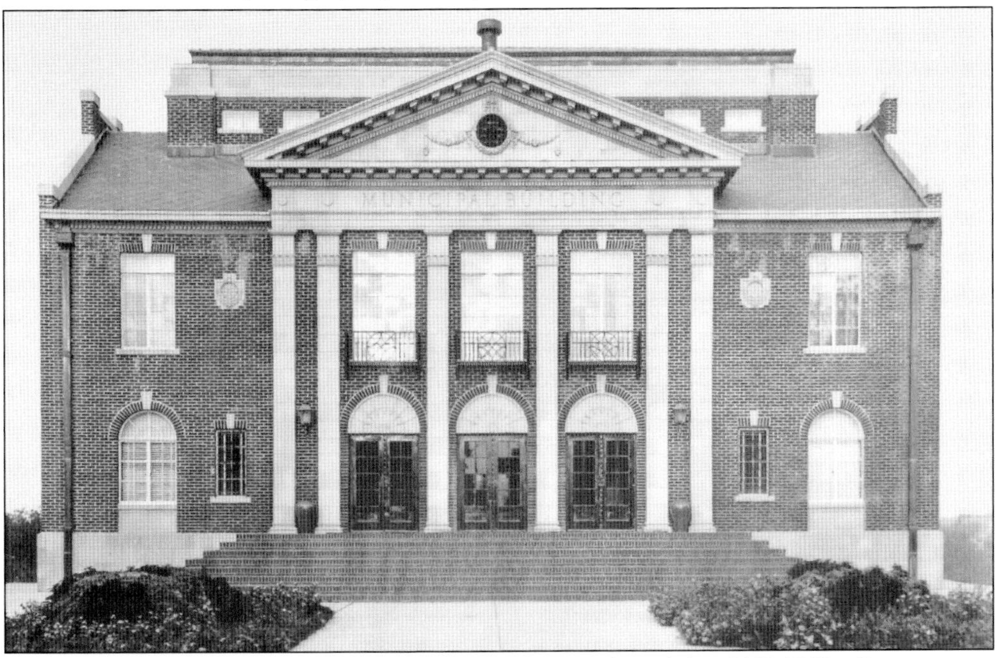

Kidd-Key Auditorium. In 1937, the City of Sherman purchased the old Kidd-Key Conservatory property for $40,000 and several of the buildings were razed. The college had closed in 1935 and the auditorium had remained unfinished. The municipal building was remodeled, and the auditorium was completed and opened in 1938 to house city offices. (Courtesy of the City of Sherman.)

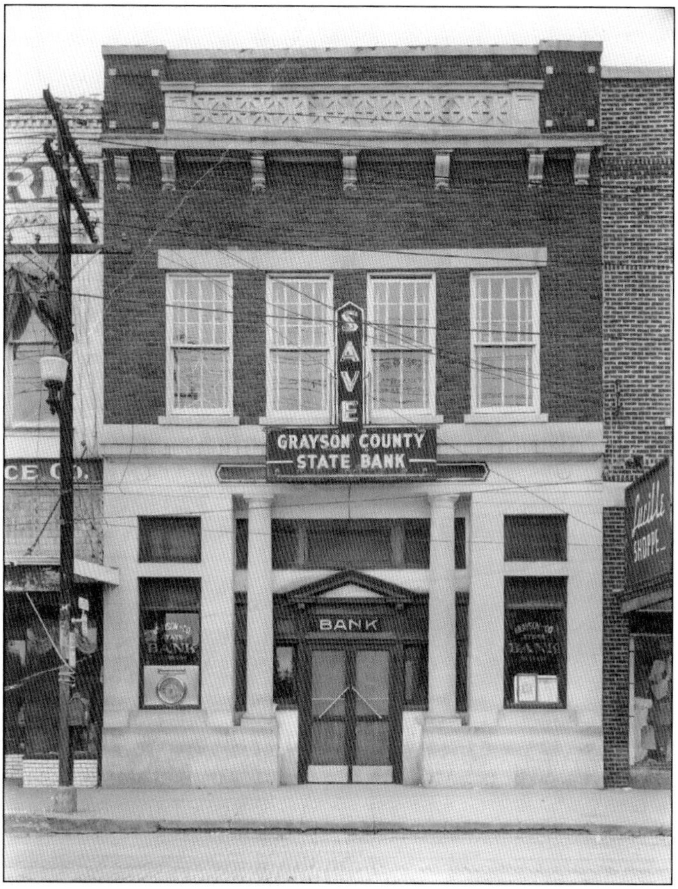

GRAYSON COUNTY STATE BANK, 1930S OR 1940S. Grayson County State Bank opened in 1936 at 109 South Travis Street. It was founded by John H. Perry with the backing of a group of local men and was called "the little man's" bank in a 1948 article in the *Sherman Democrat*. The building was previously the site of the Central State Bank. (Courtesy of the City of Sherman.)

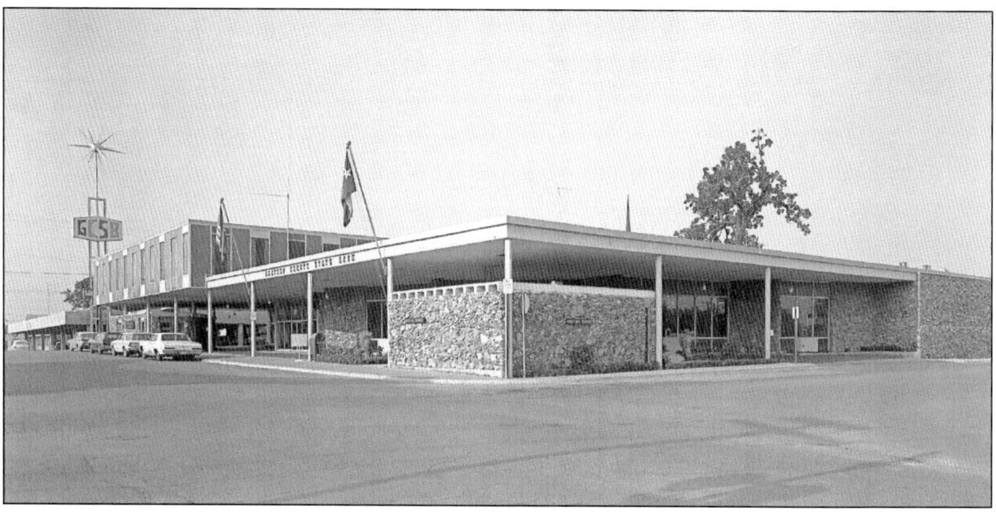

GRAYSON COUNTY STATE BANK'S NEW FACILITY. In September 1959, Grayson County State Bank moved to its new $500,000 facility at 400 North Crockett Street. The iconic symbol above the sign was known as "Sputnik." The new building featured the Oak Room, an informal coffee lounge. Charles A. Spears was chairman and major stockholder of the bank from 1954 until his death in 1987. (Courtesy of John Spears.)

Four

THE PASSAGE OF TIME

As the community grew, citizens expanded their horizon. In the mid-1930s, Sherman was advertised as "a well-balanced city" because of the many successful industrial plants and the rich, diversified agriculture. There were six steam and electric railways and a daily motor bus connection to all important towns within a radius of 100 miles.

Clubs such as the civic league, the Tuesday Literary Club, the chamber of commerce, the merchants association, and the Sherman Garden Club were formed. In 1936, the first broadcasts from radio station KRRV were heard across the airwaves.

Sherman had the Grayson Hotel with 100 "fireproof rooms and a bath in every room," the Binkley Hotel with 85 rooms, the Williams Hotel with 28 rooms, and the Oriental Hotel with 15 rooms.

The Texas Theater was billed as North Texas's largest and finest theater, with a seating capacity of 1,000. It was not the first building in Sherman to show motion pictures, but it was the first building constructed as a movie theater and the acoustics were especially designed for talking films.

By 1946, automobile registration in Grayson County totaled 14,691. In 1948, Sherman held a Centennial Celebration. Roy Acuff and his "Grand Ole Opry Gang" performed multiple shows at the municipal building.

By 1954, plans were finally underway for construction of the Mulberry Street Underpass, which would connect east Sherman with the main business section of town and take traffic under the existing railroad tracks. Bonds were originally approved two years earlier, but the project was delayed mainly because of long negotiations with the railways concerning relocation of the track and participation in the project.

KXII-TV became the first television station in town and began broadcasting in 1960. Sherman was designated a Standard Metropolitan Area by the US Census Bureau in 1967, the same year that building permits reached $7.9 million. The voters also approved a one percent city sales tax.

The Sherman School Board approved the total integration for all schools in 1965, saying, "no individual, regardless of race, color or creed, who is eligible to attend classes" would be denied admission to the school attendance area to which he is entitled to attend. The school system was previously in the second year of a grade-per-year program of integration, which started in the first grade.

By 1970, the population reached 30,000 and a new $8-million Sher-Den Mall opened on US Highway 75 between Sherman and Denison.

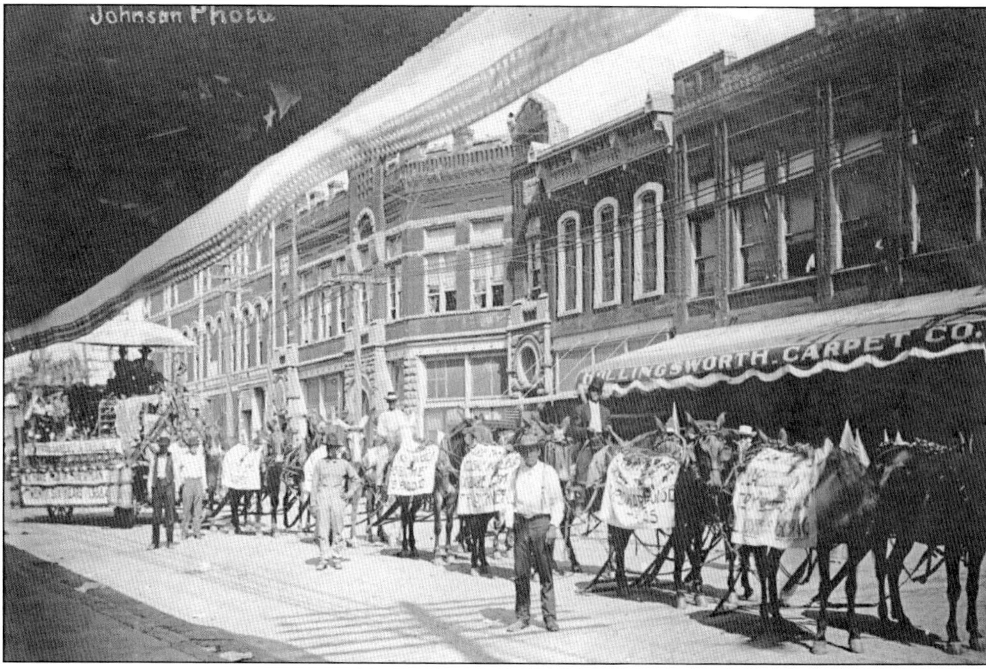

INDEPENDENCE DAY PARADE, 1909. The largest float in the 1909 Independence Day Parade was the 14-mule train from Roberts, Sanford & Taylor advertising that they had been in Sherman for 26 years. The wagon and load weighed 21,000 pounds and cost $400 to build. Each mule carried a cute saying such as "I'm just a mule but I'm stuck on my job." (Courtesy of A Touch of Class Antique Mall.)

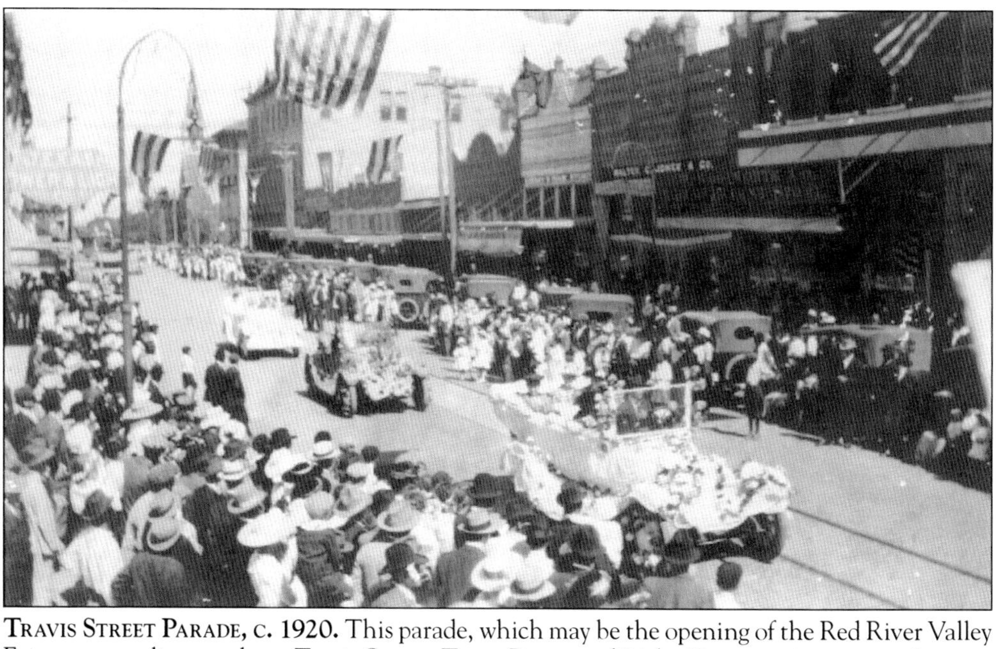

TRAVIS STREET PARADE, C. 1920. This parade, which may be the opening of the Red River Valley Fair, was traveling south on Travis Street. Texas Power and Light Company is seen on the west side of the street and the First Presbyterian Church is seen on the east side of the street in the rear. (Courtesy of the Sherman Museum.)

KU KLUX KLAN. These Klansmen are pictured about 1916, marching in Sherman in white robes with masks tied around their faces. In the background is J.D. Masters' Groceries, which was located on East Lamar Street. Prior to this time, John D. Masters was the owner of Staple and Fancy Groceries and was later a clerk at the W.E. Crutchfield Grocery. (Courtesy of the Sherman Museum.)

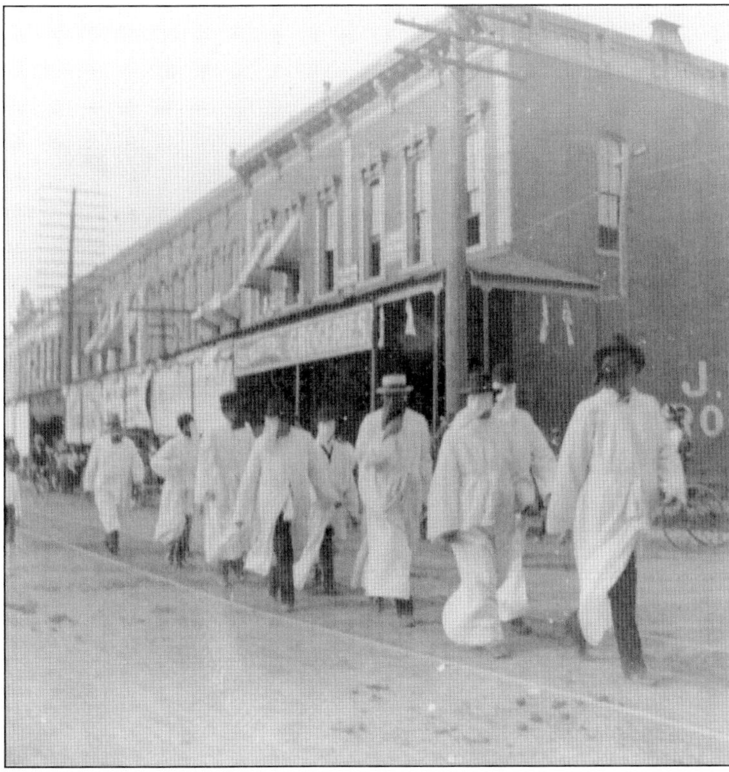

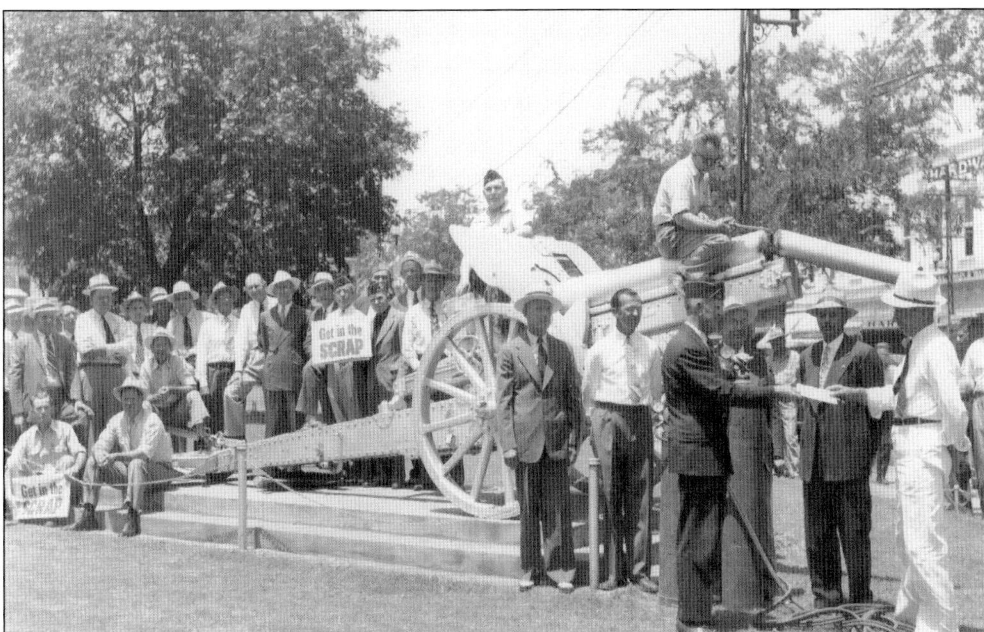

SCRAP DRIVE. During World War II, citizens held scrap drives promoting the collection of metal for use in the war production. In this photograph, they are cutting off the barrel of the cannon that is located on the courthouse lawn. The signs say "get in the scrap." (Courtesy of the Sherman Museum.)

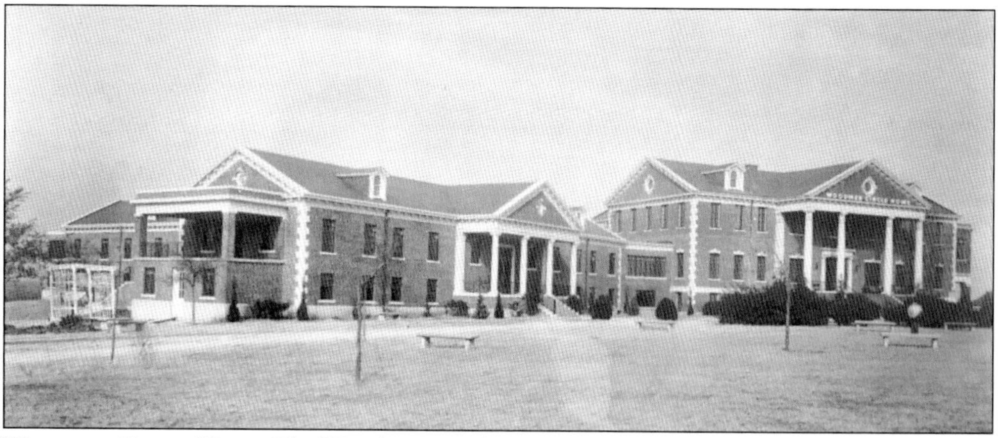

WOODMEN CIRCLE HOME. The Woodmen Circle Home was founded in 1930 by the Woodmen of the World and was located at the intersection of Highways 1417 and 56. The home was originally a rest home for the elderly and a foster home for children. The home closed in 1969 or 1970. (Courtesy of the City of Sherman.)

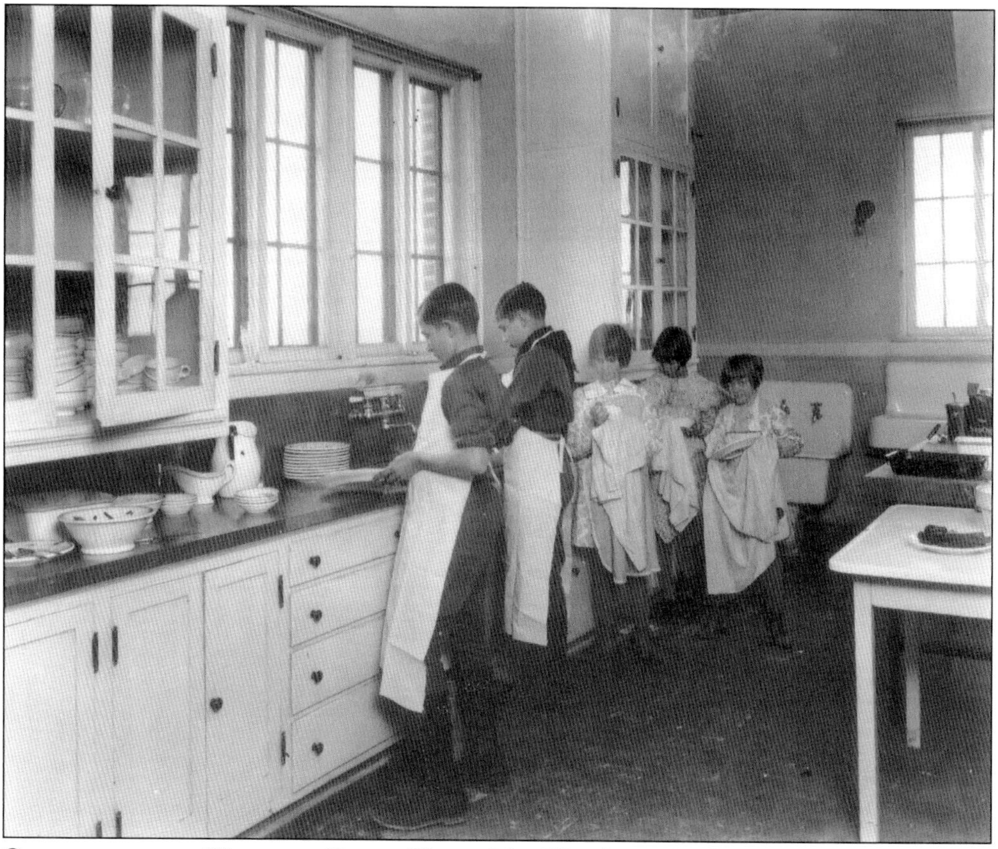

CHILDREN AT THE WOODMEN CIRCLE HOME. The Woodmen Circle Home was located on a 240-acre tract that included a little lake and enough land for the residents to raise much of their own food. In addition to an orchard, there were cows, chickens, vegetable gardens, and fields of alfalfa. Orphans at the home helped with the chores, including washing dishes. (Courtesy of the Sherman Museum.)

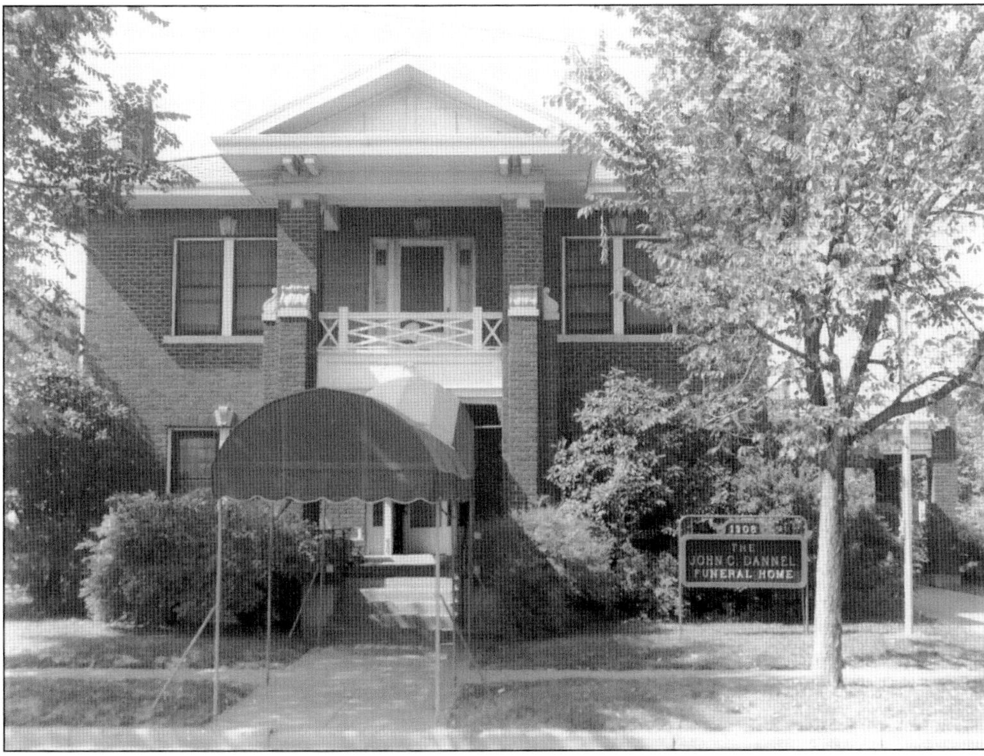

Dannel Funeral Home. In 1908, John C. Dannel bought the Sherman Undertaking Company and opened Dannel Funeral Home. In 1928, they consolidated with the Stewart M. Scott Company, and for a time the name was changed to Dannel-Scott Funeral Home. Their current building was built in 1923 and is located at the corner of Walnut and Jones Streets. In 2011, the fifth generation of Dannels operated the Dannel Funeral Home. (Courtesy of Pat Dannel.)

Waldo Funeral Home. R.R. Waldo (left) and Robert Waldo (right) stand with the salesman in front of a newly purchased hearse. The funeral home was founded in 1932 in Whitewright but was moved to Sherman in 1937 and was the first local funeral home to have a mortuary. Robert Waldo operated the business until 1980, when it was purchased by David Bedgood. (Courtesy of Waldo Funeral Home.)

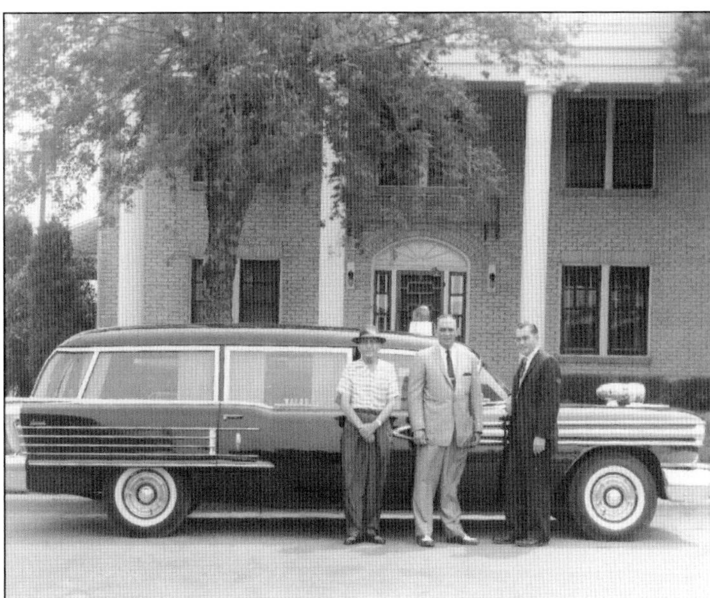

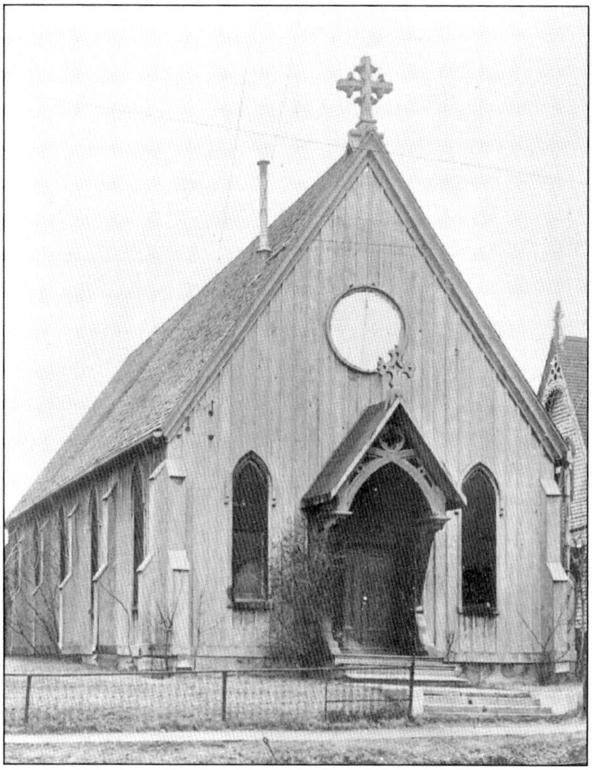

St. Stephen's Episcopal Church. The first building used as St. Stephen's Episcopal Church was erected between 1870 and 1880 and located near the railroad tracks on North Travis Street. In 1910, the building was sold to the Progressive Baptist Church and moved to East College Street, where it burned in 1916. In 1910, St. Stephen's built a new church on South Crockett Street, still used today. (Courtesy of the City of Sherman.)

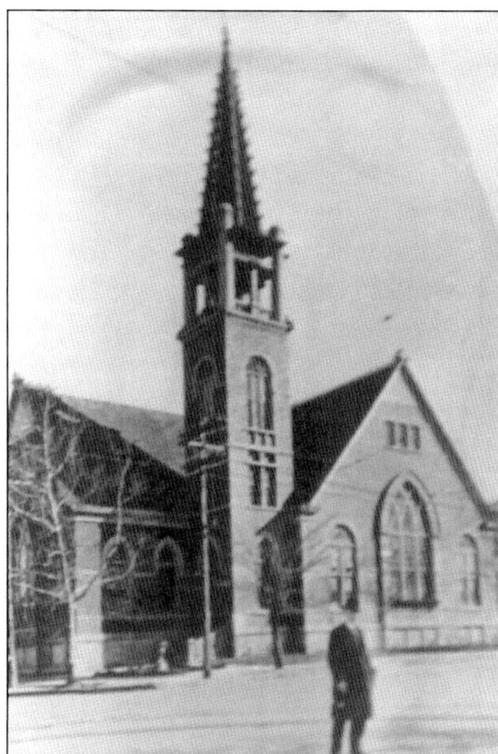

Red Brick Church. First Presbyterian Church, located on the southeast corner of Travis and Mulberry Streets, was called the "Red Brick Church." This building was erected in 1894 and replaced an 1874 frame structure. A new church building was completed at Rusk and Pecan Streets in 1955. Pictured in 1917 is Dr. T.A. Wharton, an early pastor of the church. (Courtesy of the Sherman Museum.)

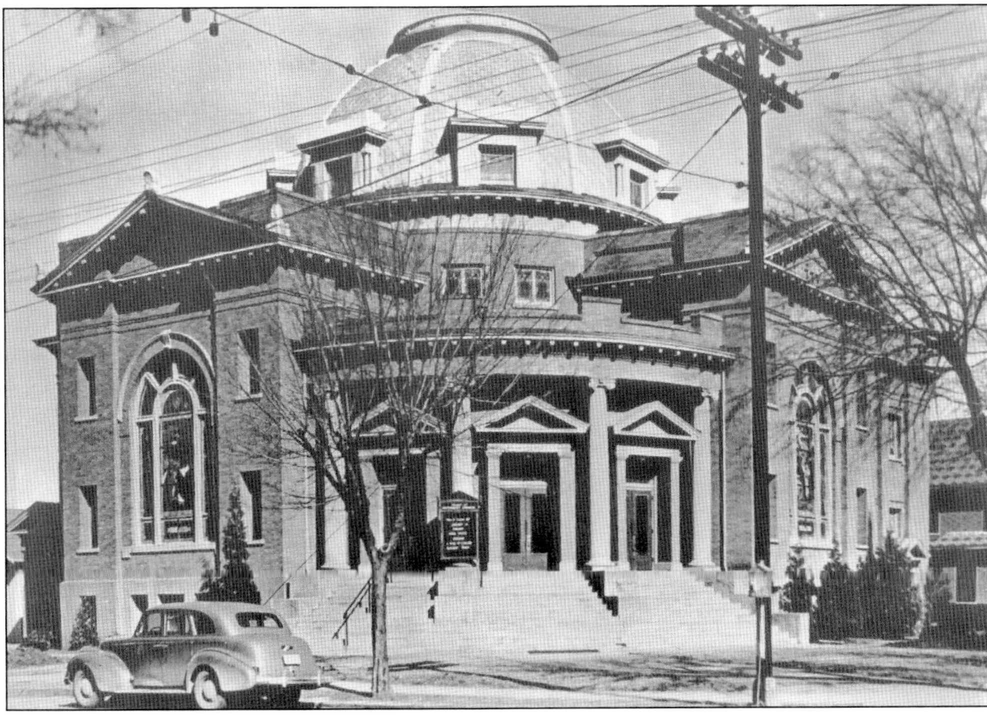

TRAVIS STREET METHODIST CHURCH. Travis Street Methodist Church was built in 1909 at the northeast corner of Travis and Mulberry Streets. The church grew, and on a Sunday in 1955, the members marched in a group to the new building at the northeast corner of Elm and Mulberry Streets. The congregation became known as First United Methodist Church. (Courtesy of the City of Sherman.)

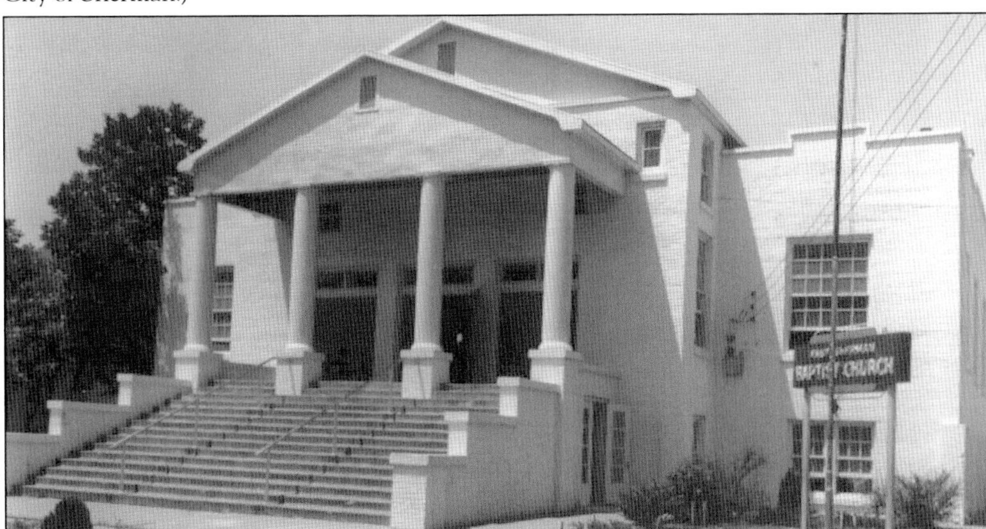

EAST SHERMAN BAPTIST CHURCH. East Sherman Baptist Church was first organized in 1892 with 13 members and was known as Carpenter's Chapel. In 1905, the church moved to King and Hazelwood Streets and changed its name to East Sherman Baptist Church. A brick structure was built in 1926 but was almost destroyed by fire in 1943. The auditorium was finally completed in 1948. (Courtesy of the Sherman Museum.)

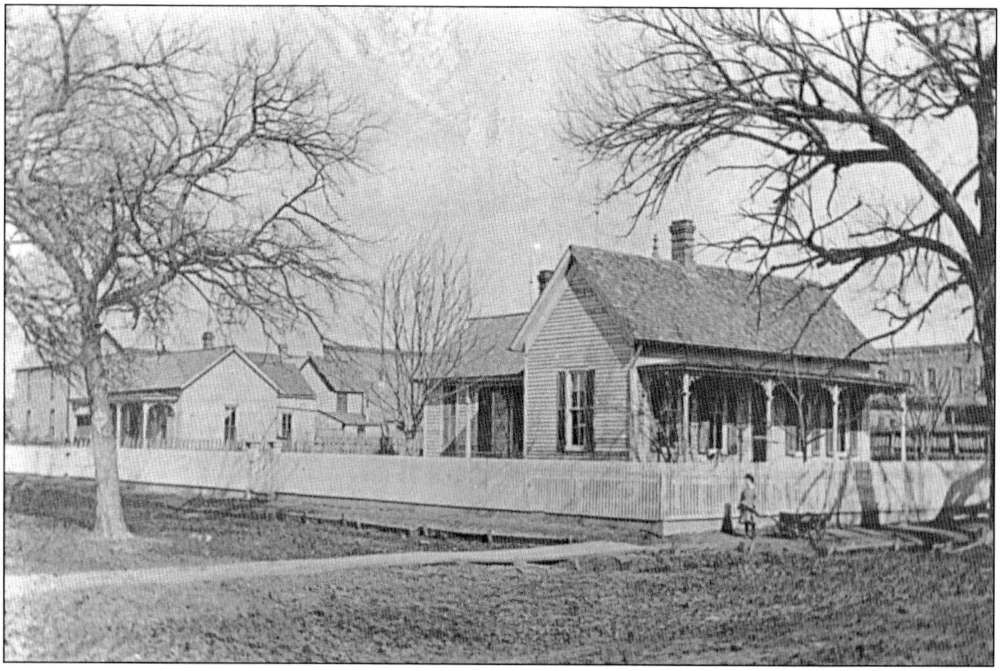

Hattie Kimball Home. The top photograph shows the original home of Hattie Kimball, built in the late 19th century by her father, H.S. Kimball. The 10-room house was located at 221 West Jones Street but was moved to the lot east of that location. She lived her entire life in the house except for a few years when she taught college and the last few months of her life, which were spent in a nursing home. The bottom photograph is of Miss Hattie in the early 1970s. She died in May 1979, and the house was razed by the City of Sherman. (Both courtesy of A Touch of Class Antique Mall.)

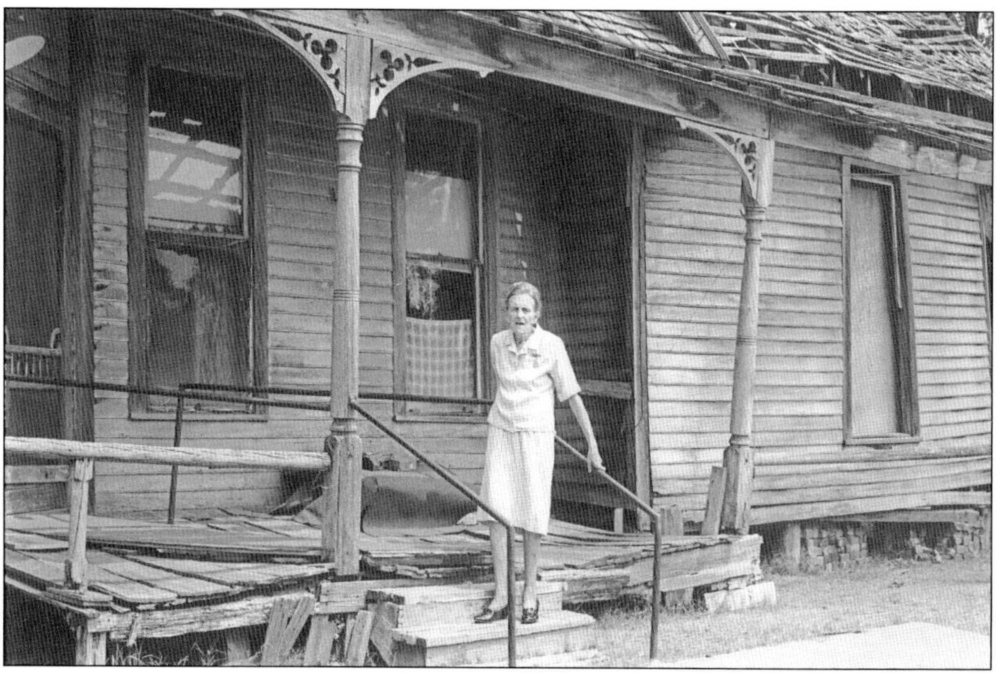

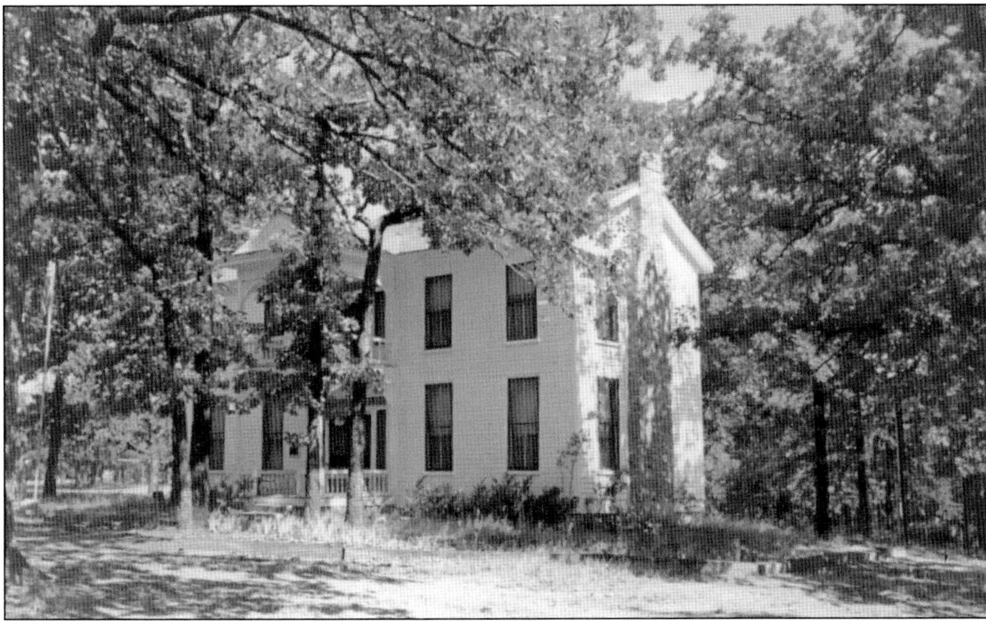

Nettie Bass House. The house at 216 West Houston was built in the 1850s by Dr. R.L. Bullock and was reportedly the first house in Sherman with glass windowpanes. Around 1867, Mary Jane Hocker purchased the house, and her daughter Ada married T.C. Bass. Their daughter Nettie Bass spent her entire life in the house, except the years she attended eastern schools. (Courtesy of Missy Sofey-Andrews.)

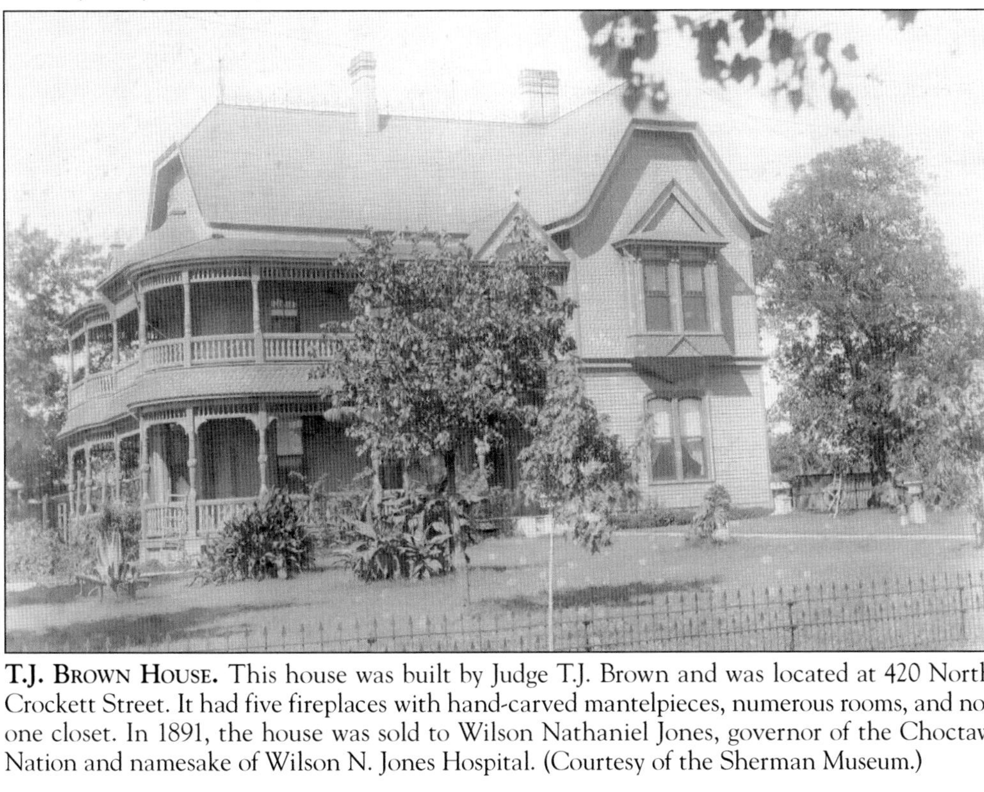

T.J. Brown House. This house was built by Judge T.J. Brown and was located at 420 North Crockett Street. It had five fireplaces with hand-carved mantelpieces, numerous rooms, and not one closet. In 1891, the house was sold to Wilson Nathaniel Jones, governor of the Choctaw Nation and namesake of Wilson N. Jones Hospital. (Courtesy of the Sherman Museum.)

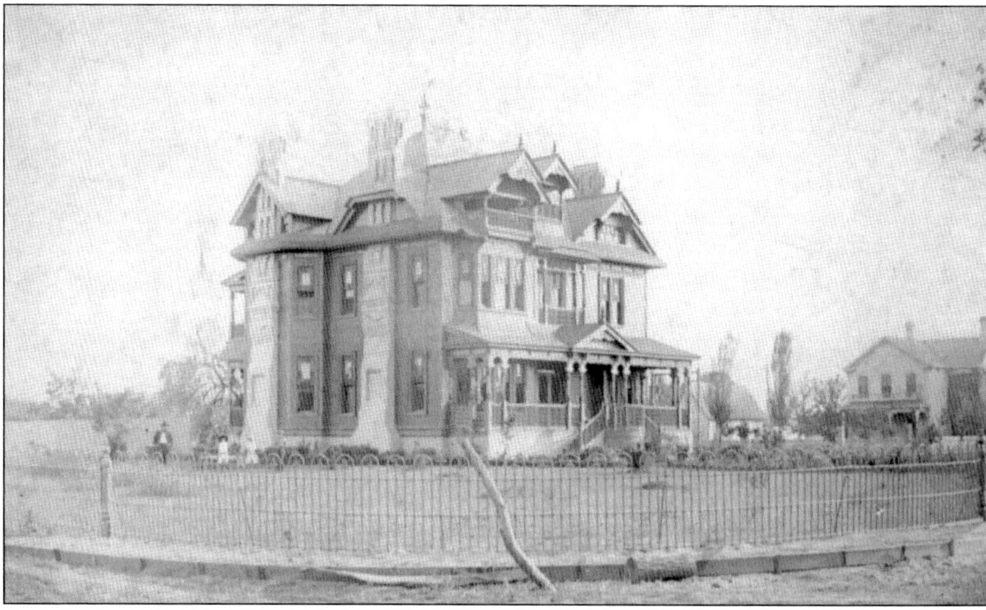

Capt. O.T. Lyon House. Capt. O.T. Lyon, founder of the Lyon Lumber Company and father of Col. Dupont Lyon and Cecil Lyon, built this house in 1887 at Crockett and King Streets. The Sherman School Board purchased the home, and in 1917 a new high school was erected on the site. Later it served as the Sherman Independent School District Administration Building. (Courtesy of the Sherman Museum.)

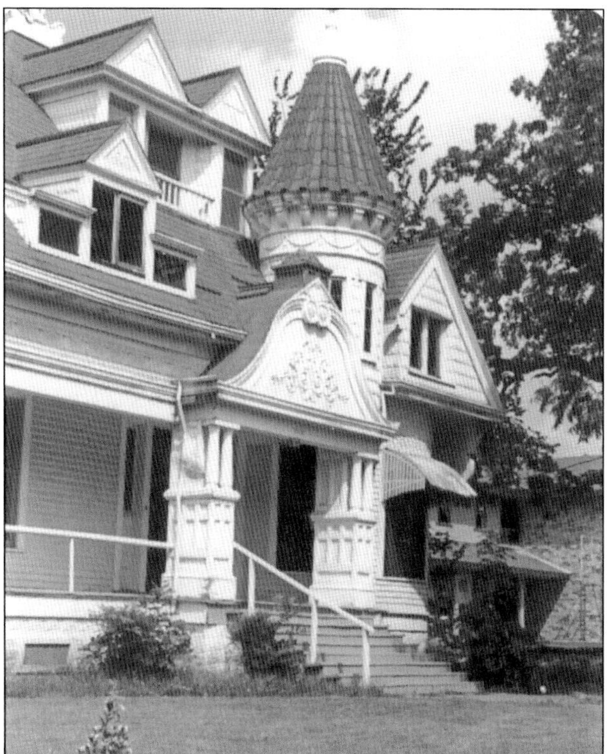

Col. Dupont Lyon House. The house at 516 North Crockett Street was originally built in 1897 for hardware merchant George E. Hardwicke, who occupied the house until 1899. It was purchased in 1902 by Col. Dupont Lyon, dairy farmer, lumberman, and mayor of Sherman from 1913 to 1915. Robert J. Tate purchased and restored the house in 1974. (Courtesy of Missy Sofey-Andrews.)

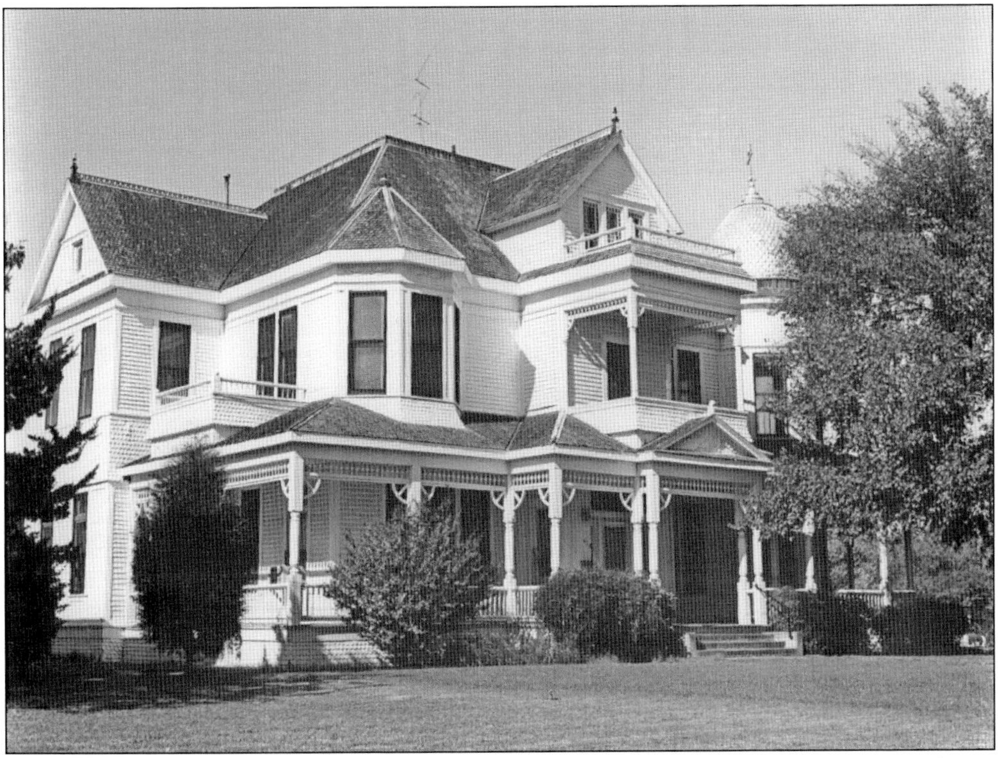

Thompson House. Capt. John M. Thompson, a sawmill owner and lumber dealer, built this house in 1895. It was located at 618 North Grand Street. Thompson moved his family to Sherman so his children could attend Austin College. He served on the college's board of trustees in the 1890s and financed the construction of the college's Thompson Hall Science Building in 1913. (Courtesy of A Touch of Class Antique Mall.)

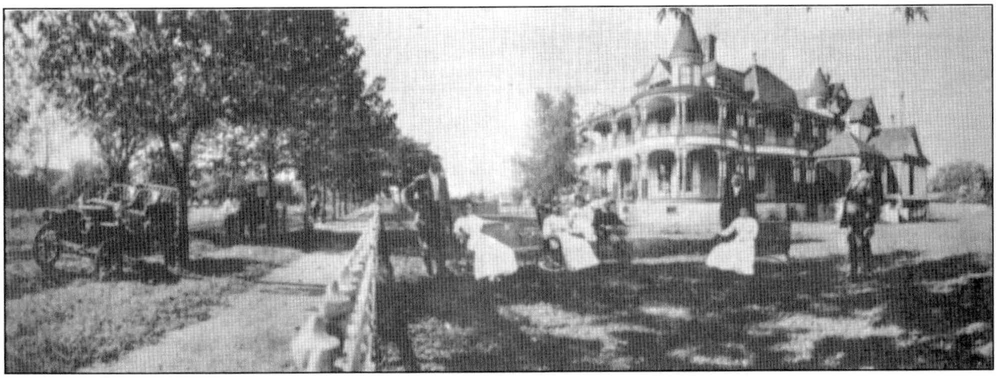

Arnoldi House. This house, located at Grand and Pecan Streets, was the second house in Sherman built by German Baron Ernest Arnoldi, the treasurer and general manager of the Sherman Packing Company and the Sherman Ice Company. Pictured in front of the home are, from left to right, James P. and Nell Arnoldi Everheart, Ernest and Minnie Arnoldi, Gladys Arnoldi, Ernest Arnoldi Jr. and Wood Arnoldi, and photographer George Chapman. (Courtesy of the Sherman Museum.)

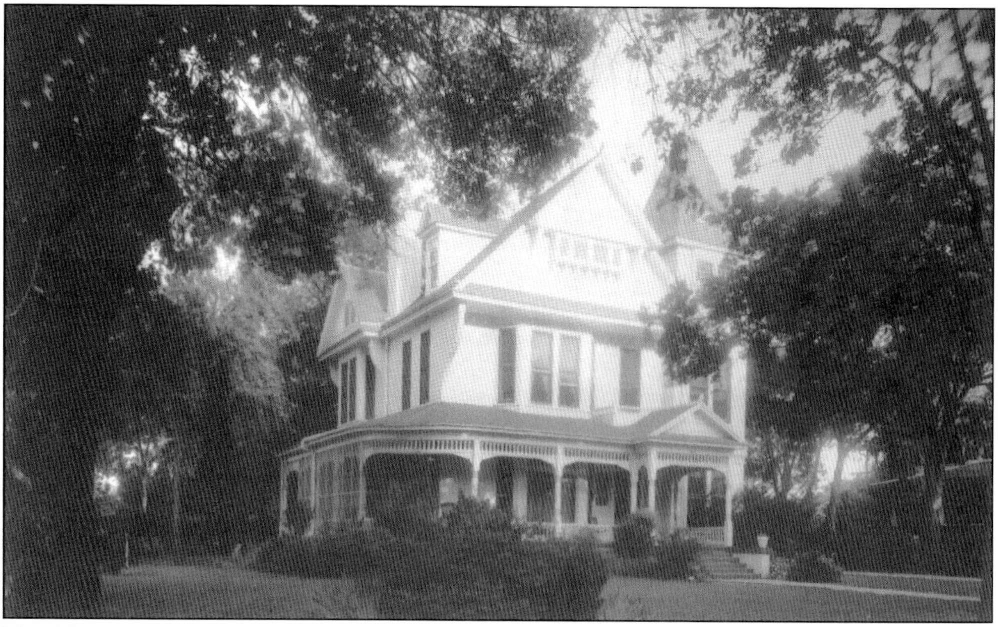

HAY-HARRINGTON HOUSE. Around 1895, W.W. Sturgis, a lumber dealer, built this house at 910 South Crockett Street. The house sold several times and in 1917, was purchased by W.L. Hay, an attorney. In the 1920s, he became chairman of the Texas Democratic Party. The home remained in the Hay-Harrington family until the death of Hay's daughter, Dorothy Lynn Harrington, in 2001. (Courtesy of the Sherman Museum.)

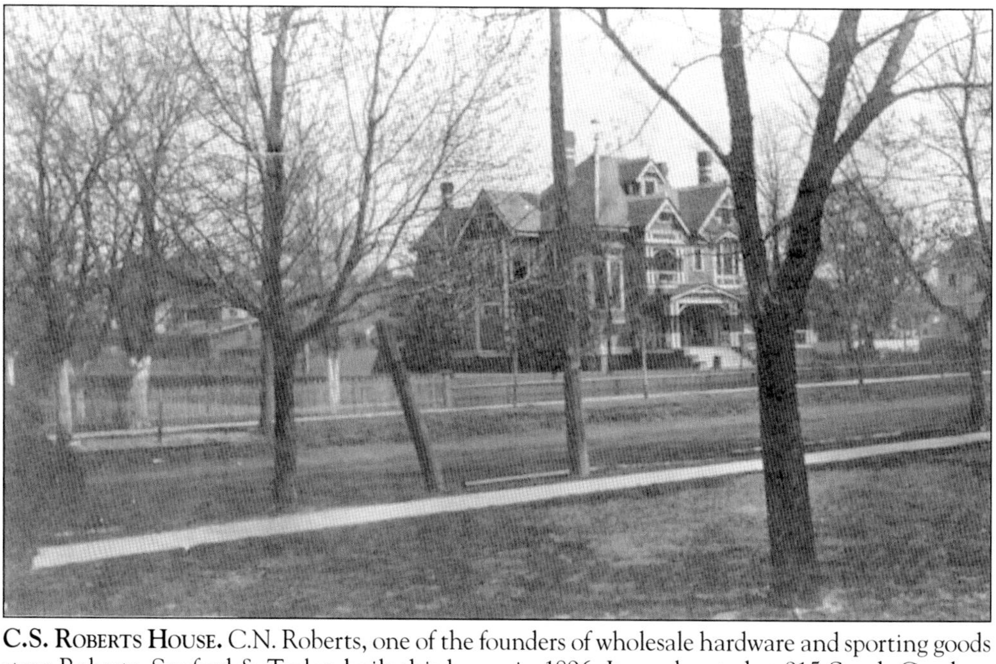

C.S. ROBERTS HOUSE. C.N. Roberts, one of the founders of wholesale hardware and sporting goods store Roberts, Sanford & Taylor, built this house in 1896. It was located at 915 South Crockett Street. Three generations of the Robert's family lived in the home until it was purchased by the Sherman Preservation League as a house museum in the 1980s. (Courtesy of the Sherman Museum.)

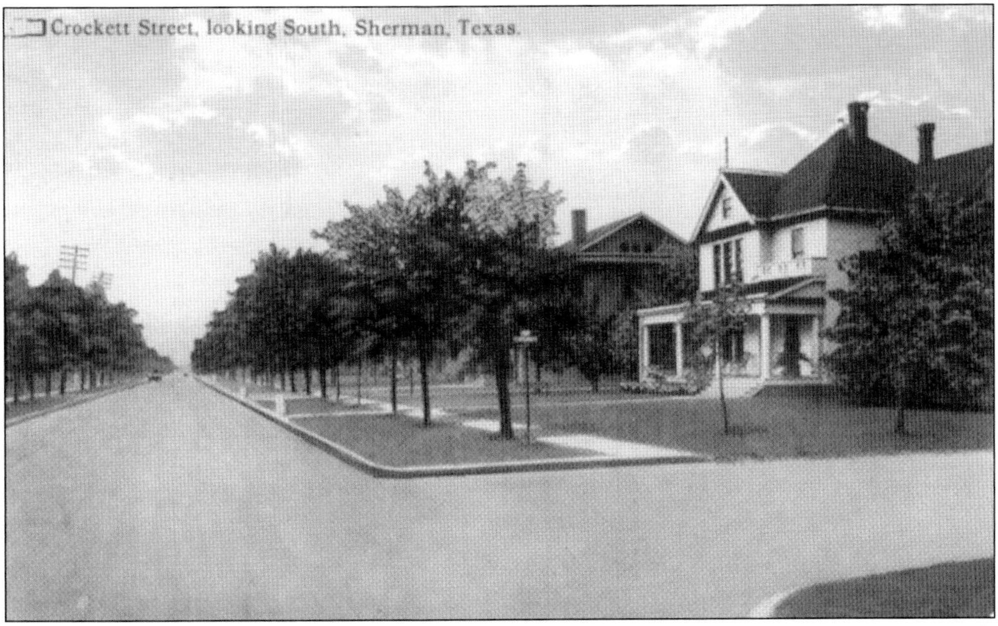

Crockett Street Looking South. Many large, commanding homes were located on South Crockett Street. Even today many of these homes have been restored in what is now Sherman's Historical District. Concrete hitching posts are still visible in front of some of the homes. (Courtesy of Greg Ashby.)

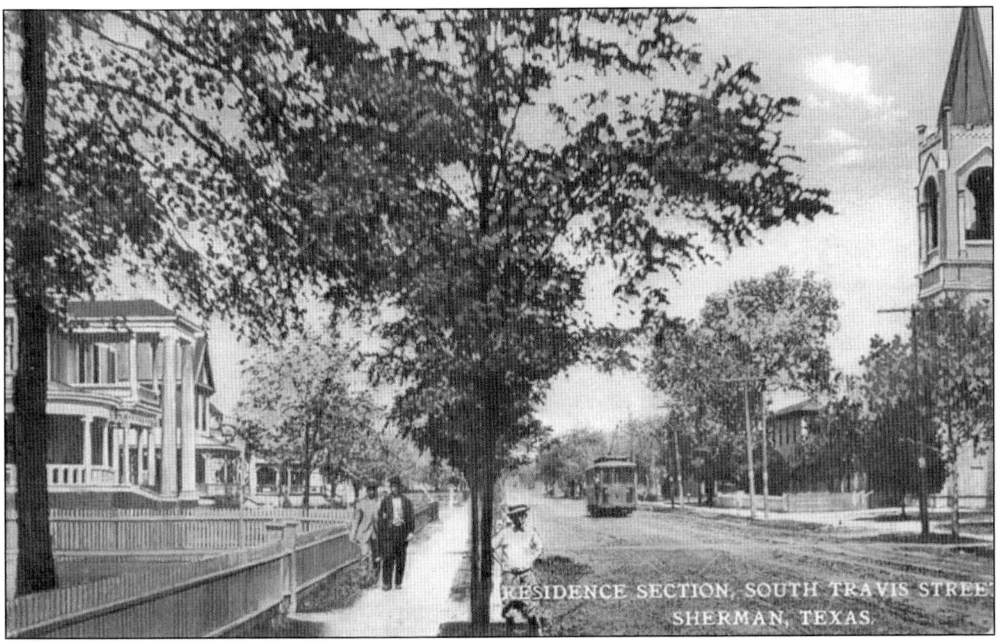

Travis Street Looking North. This postcard shows Sherman's residential district on South Travis Street looking north. Just visible is St. Mary's Catholic Church (right) and homes typical of the day. This postcard was taken during the early-to-mid-1940s. The Interurban is also seen on the street. (Courtesy of Greg Ashby.)

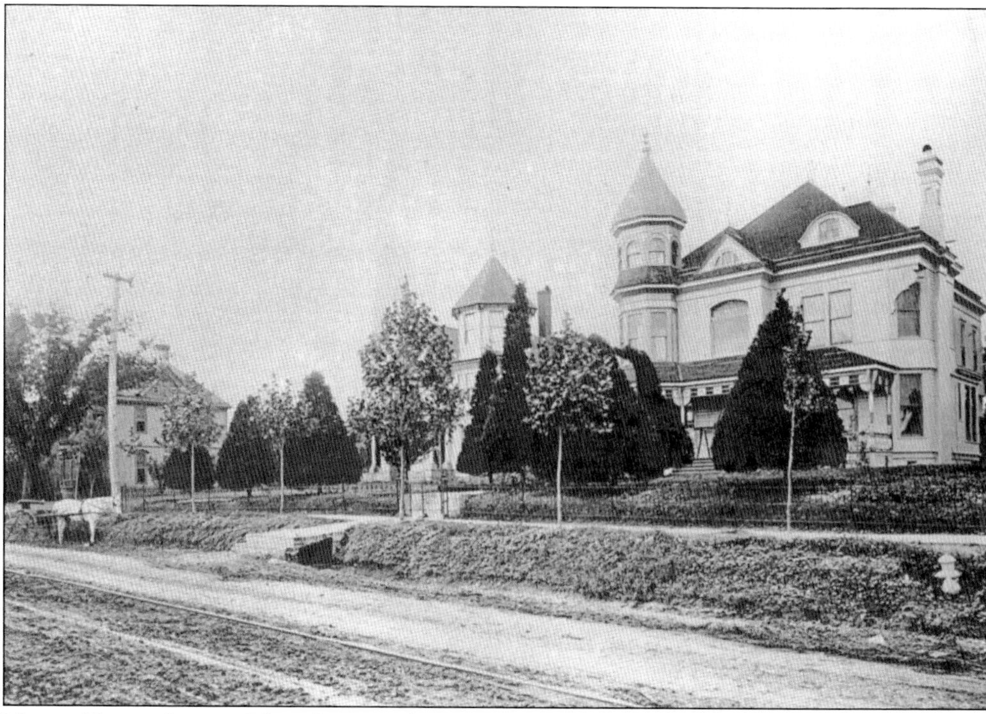

North Travis Street. This photograph was taken in the 400 block of North Travis Street. The buildings are, left to right, Fielder Lumber Yard, Rev. James Binkley's home, and the home of C.A. Andrews. Fielder also served five consecutive terms as mayor of Sherman. Rev. Binkley was the organizer and the first pastor of the church later known as First United Methodist Church. (Courtesy of A Touch of Class Antique Mall.)

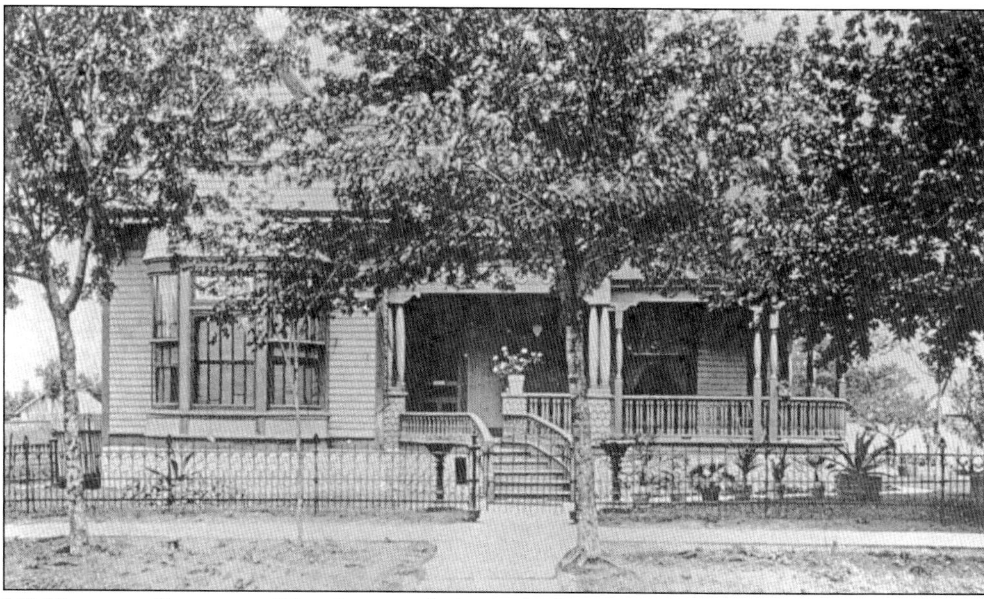

J.P. Harrison Residence. The photograph shows the J.P. Harrison residence as it appeared about 1903. It was located at 419 North Travis Street, north of the railroad tracks. Notice the curved staircase and the bay window on the left. (Courtesy of A Touch of Class Antique Mall.)

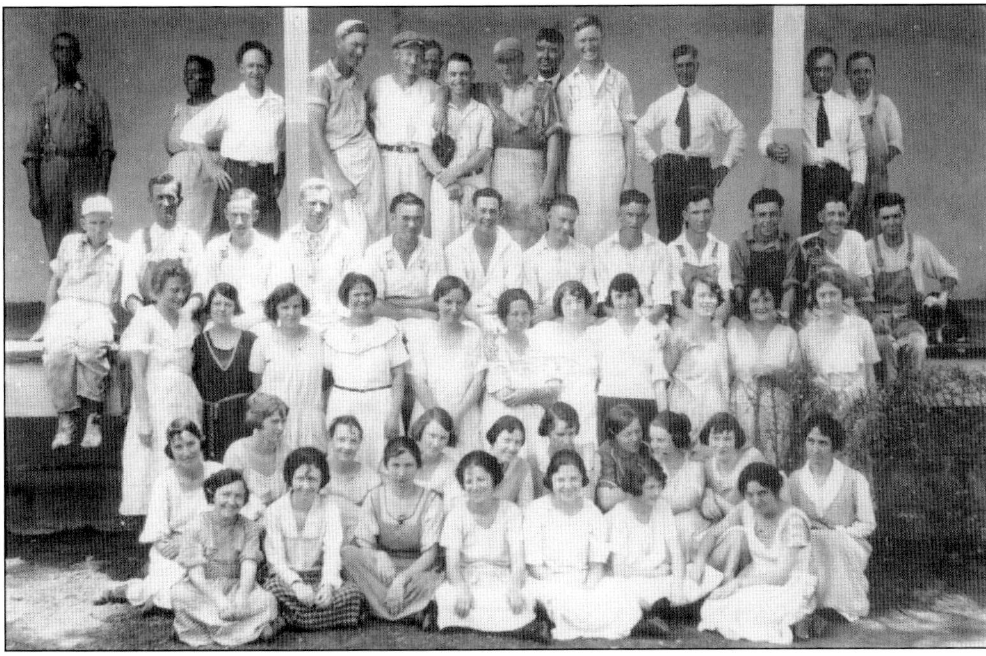

ABC Candy Company. Employees of the ABC Candy Company pose for a photograph in 1923. The company was located on Branch Street and was in business from about 1916 through the late 1930s. ABC Candy boasted seven salesmen on the road, selling candy throughout the south, north, and west. They also shipped to foreign lands, one order being shipped to the Sandwich Islands. (Courtesy of the Sherman Museum.)

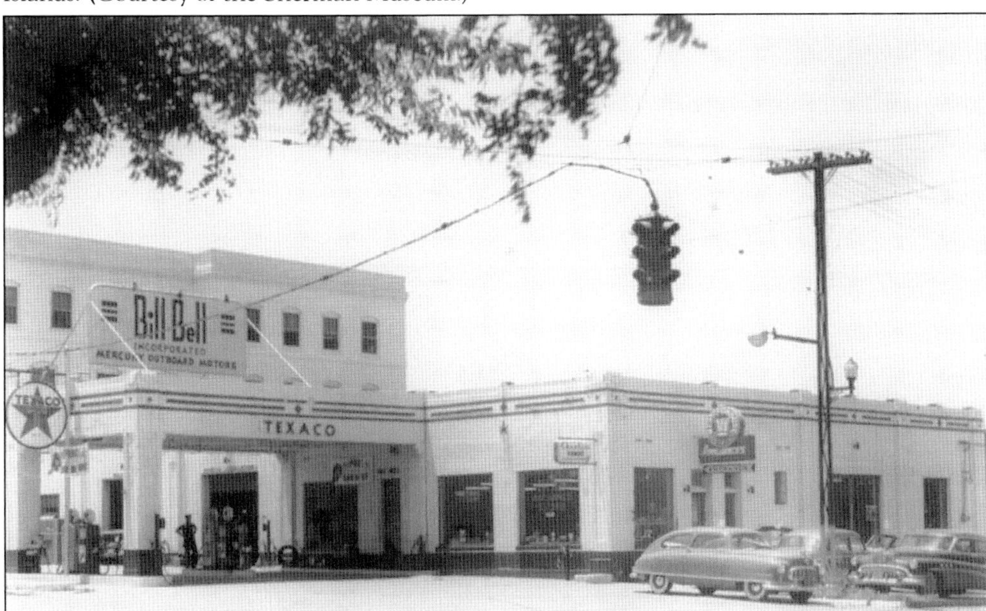

Bill Bell Incorporated. From the late 1940s to the early 1950s, William C. Bell operated the Texaco Filling Station and Bill Bell Appliance Store at 324 North Travis Street. The sign on the front of the building also advertises Mercury outdoor motors. (Courtesy of the Sherman Museum.)

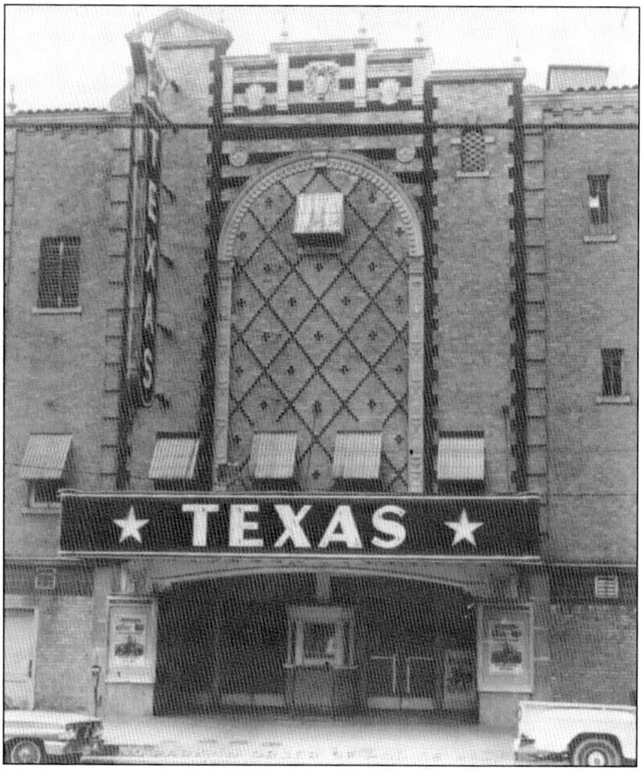

Texas Theater. The Texas Theater opened in 1931 at 112 East Houston Street. The first film shown in the new theater was *Dishonored*, starring Marlene Dietrich. The theater drew large crowds during the Depression years and was called "the pride of Sherman." The original cost of the theater was $100,000, and it seated 1,000 people on the main floor and in the balcony. (Courtesy of the Sherman Museum.)

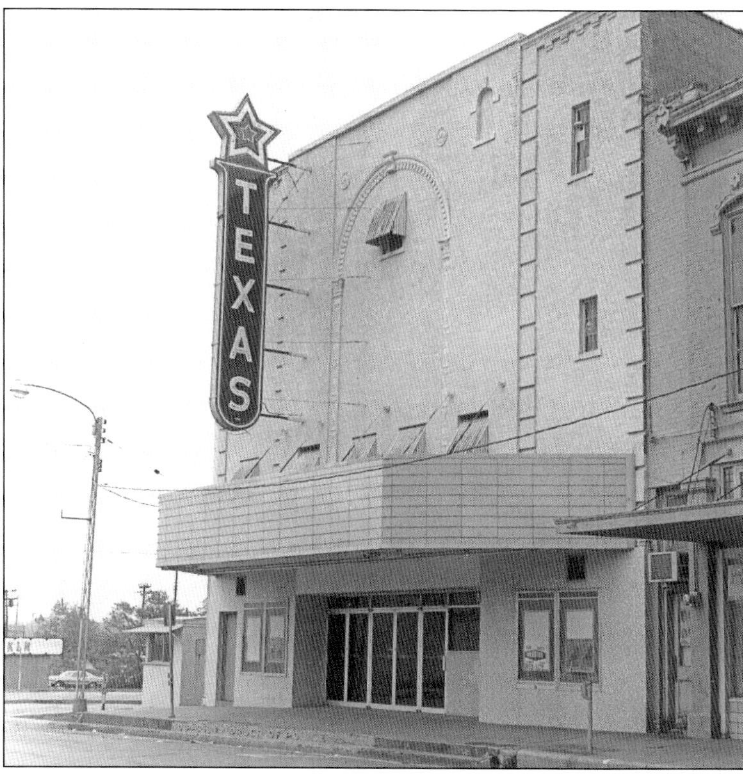

Texas Theater Sign. The Texas Theater closed on November 5, 1972, with the final double feature *Billy Jack* and *Man in the Wilderness*. The building was purchased in 1988 by a local attorney. The old Texas Theater sign was donated to the Bob Bullock Texas History Museum in Austin and stands as a testament to the memory of the Texas Theater. (Courtesy of A Touch of Class Antique Mall.)

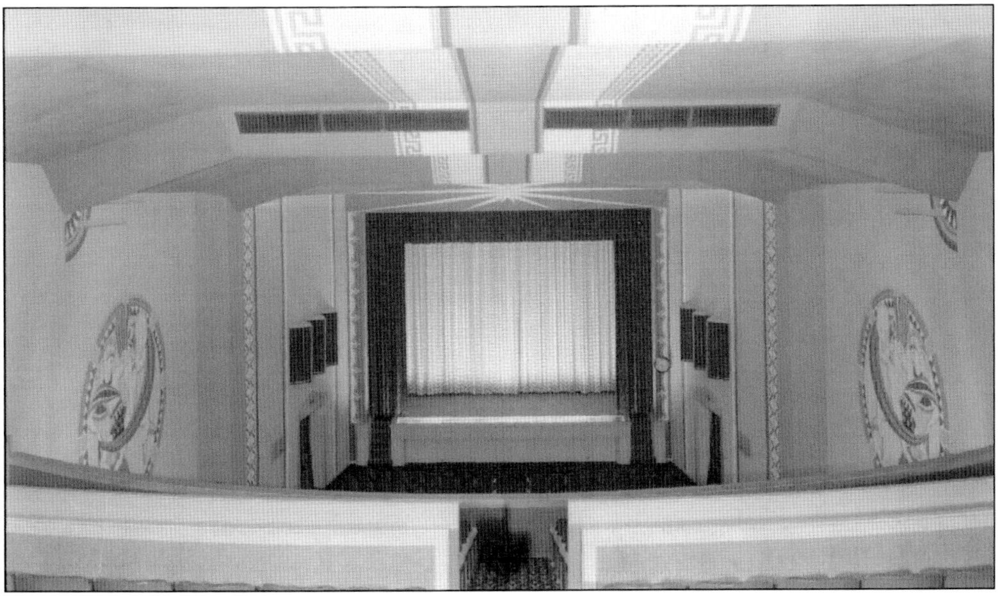

INSIDE THE TEXAS THEATER. In January 1939, a fire caused $50,000 worth of damage to the Texas Theater, but it reopened six months later and continued operating until 1972. Most of the walls and balcony were left standing after the fire, but it had to be remodeled. The newly remodeled interior, looking toward the front of the theater from the balcony, is pictured. (Courtesy of the Sherman Museum.)

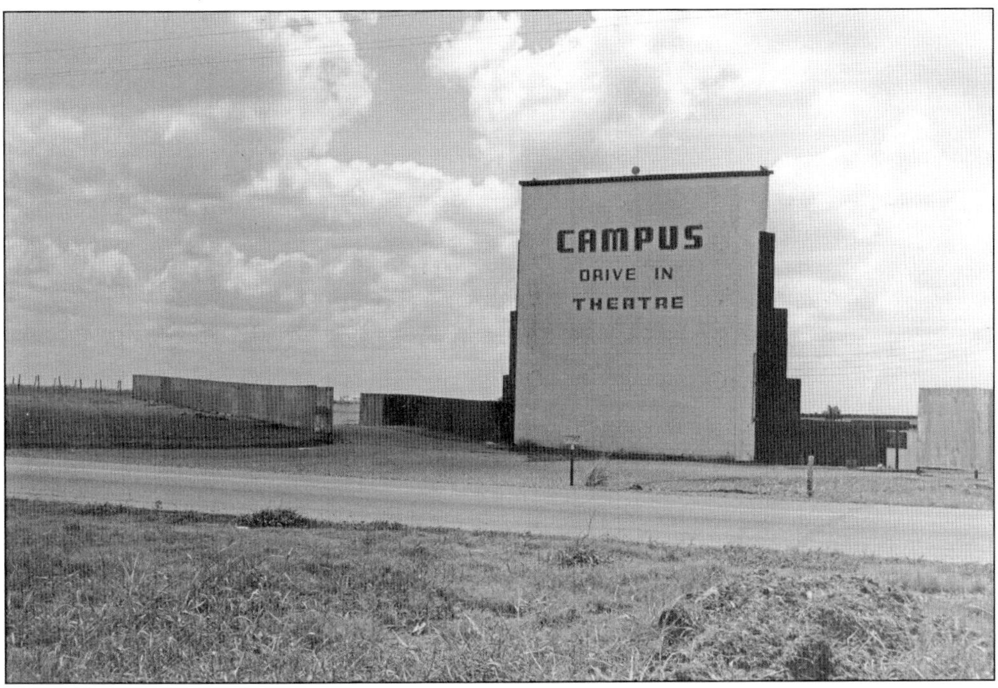

CAMPUS DRIVE-IN THEATER. The Campus Drive-In Theater opened in the late 1940s or early 1950s and was located at 2500 East Lamar Street. It advertised an air-conditioned snack bar, bottle warmers for the babies, centrally located restrooms, and the latest drive-in theater production equipment. (Photograph by Jack Goodwin; courtesy of Roger and Kay Goodwin.)

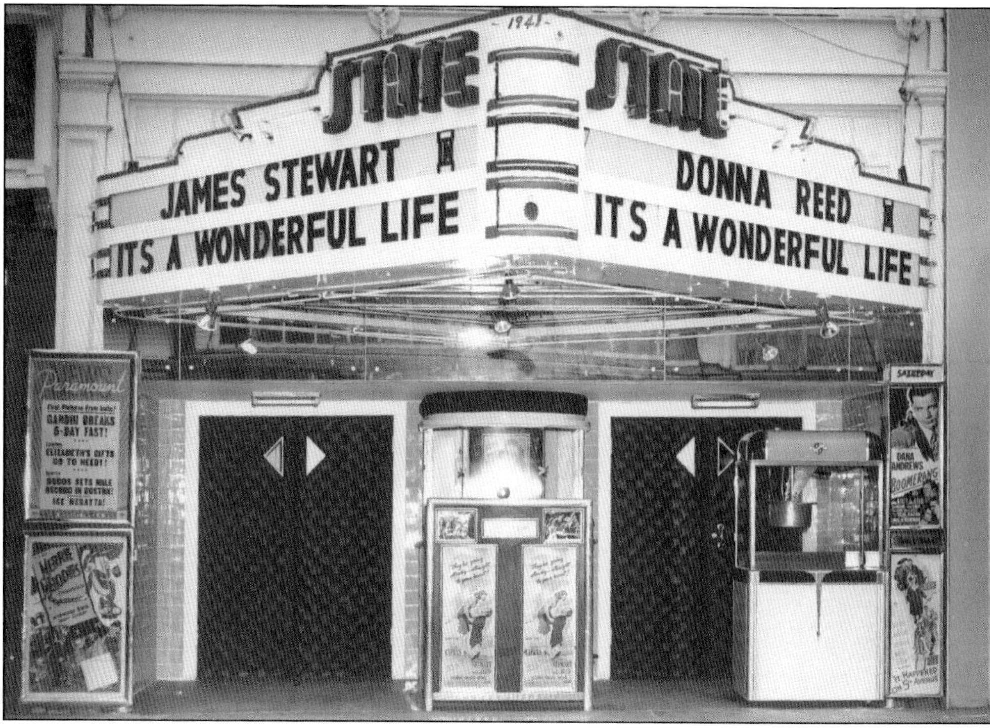

State Theater. The State Theater originally opened on June 29, 1939, as the Fox Theater, but closed on July 3, 1940. It reopened a few days later as the State Theater. It was located at 122 North Travis Street. The top photograph shows the State Theater in 1946 while showing *It's a Wonderful Life*. The bottom photograph was taken in 1948 when Western star Tim Holt appeared at the theater. The State Theater finally closed in 1961. (Both courtesy of the Sherman Museum.)

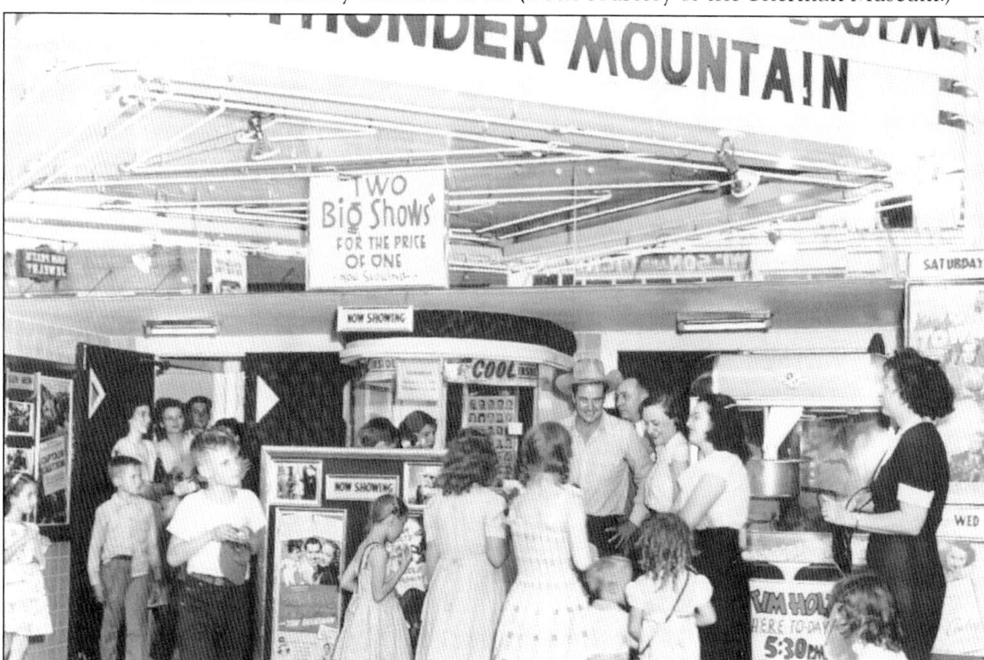

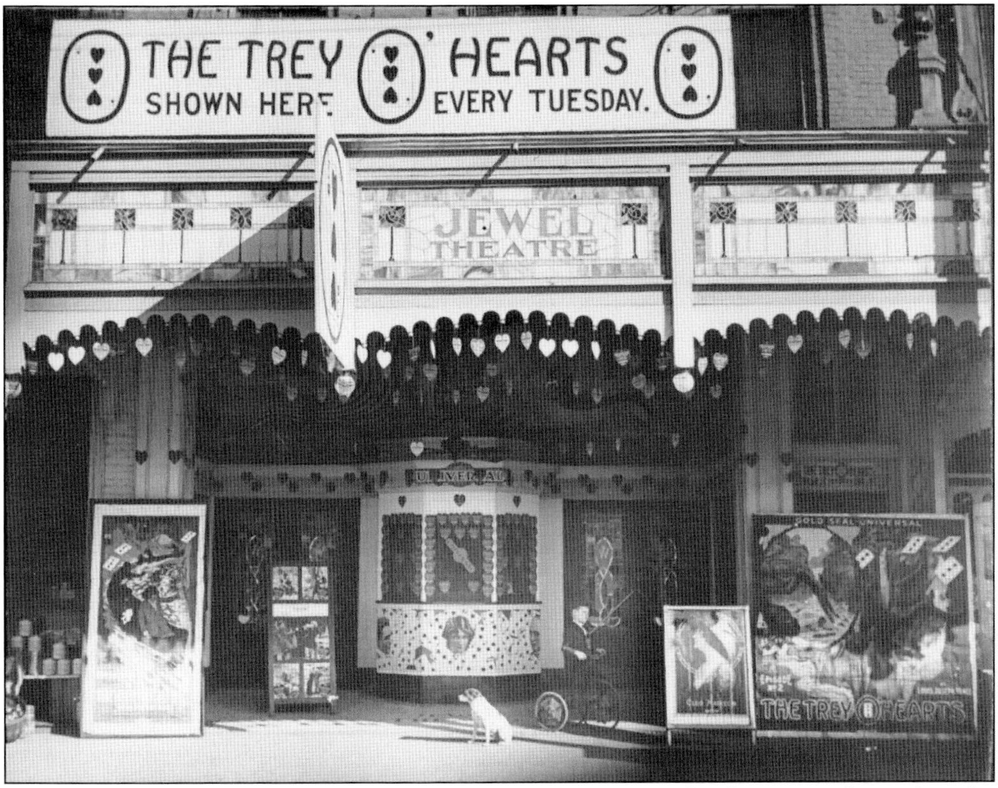

The Jewel Theater, c. 1910. Originally known as the Empire, the theater was located on the north side of the square at 115 West Houston Street and operated from 1909 to 1918. The theater later became known as the Washington and the Plaza. Admission was 10¢ for children and 25¢ for adults. The boy on the tricycle is Cecil Wilson, whose father, Jim, owned the theater. (Courtesy of the City of Sherman.)

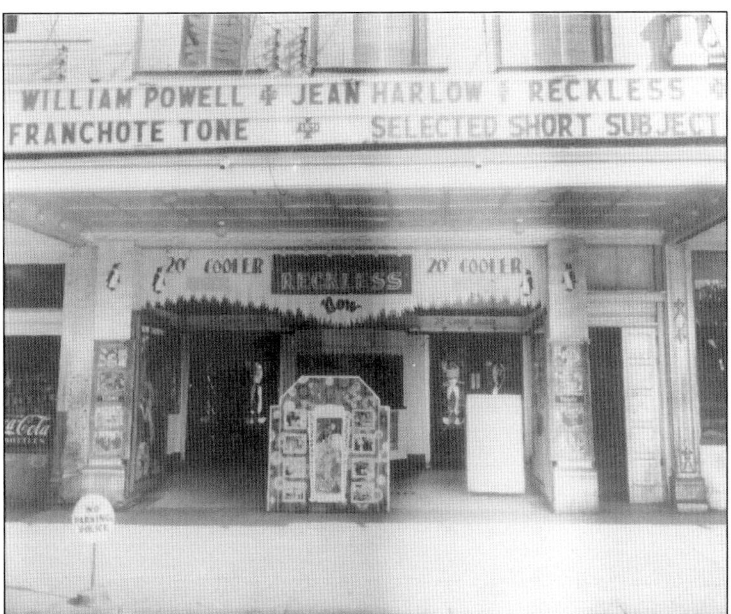

Washington Theater. Originally the Jewel Theater, the Washington Theater was located at 115 West Houston Street from about 1919 to 1935. The Plaza Theater was built in the same location in 1936 and was torn down in 1970. *Reckless*, starring Jean Harlow and William Powell, was released in 1935. (Courtesy of the Sherman Museum.)

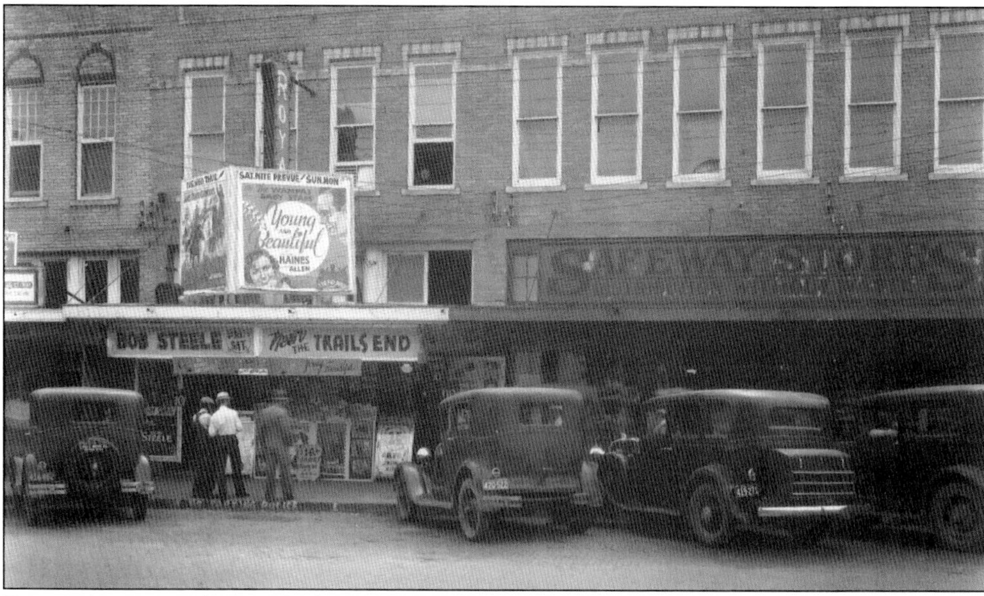

Royal Theater. The Royal Theater was located at 112 South Crockett Street. The photograph was taken in the mid-1930s. *The Wampas Baby Stars* was a 1926 short. The marquee advertises the 1934 movie *Young and Beautiful*. The Safeway Store is located to the right of the theater. The street in front of the theater is paved with brick. (Courtesy of the Sherman Museum.)

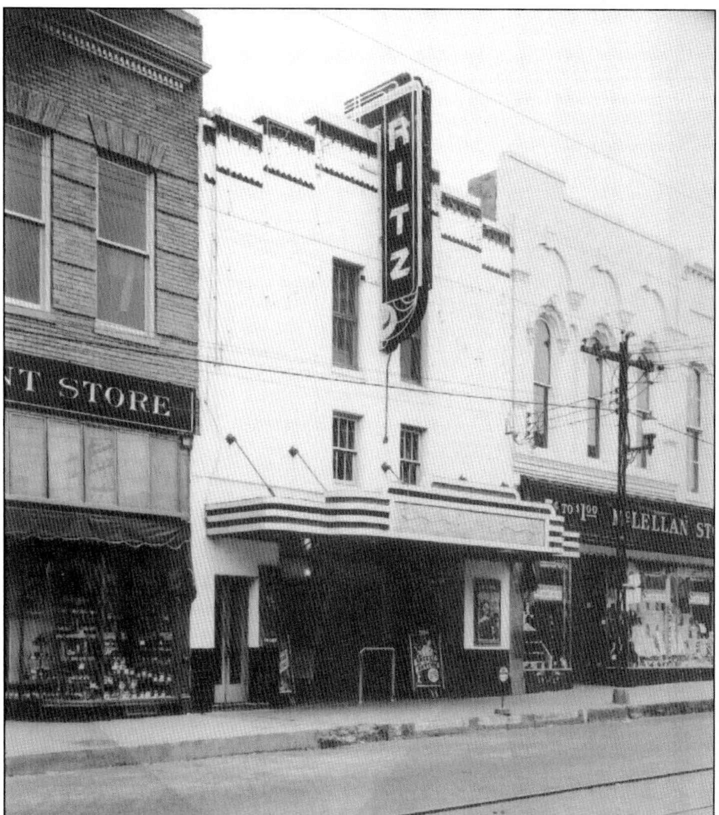

Ritz Theater. The Ritz Theater, located at 116 North Travis Street, opened in 1935 and was active until 1956. The store to the right is McLellan's, a five-and-dime store. S.H. Kress and Company, another five-and-dime, is located to the left of the theater. (Courtesy of the Sherman Museum.)

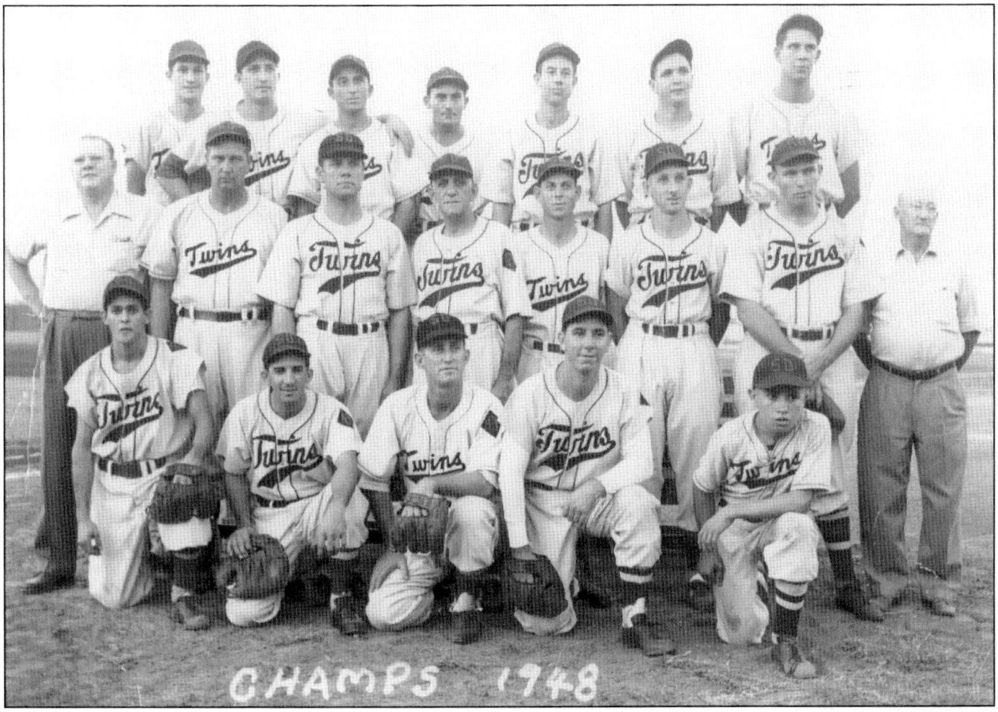

SHERMAN-DENISON TWINS. The Sherman-Denison Twins baseball team won the Big State League in 1948. Baseball was very popular in Texoma in the 1940s, and the Twins played teams from Greenville, Paris, and Texarkana. One game against Austin lasted four hours and set a league record by running 19 innings. (Courtesy of the Sherman Museum.)

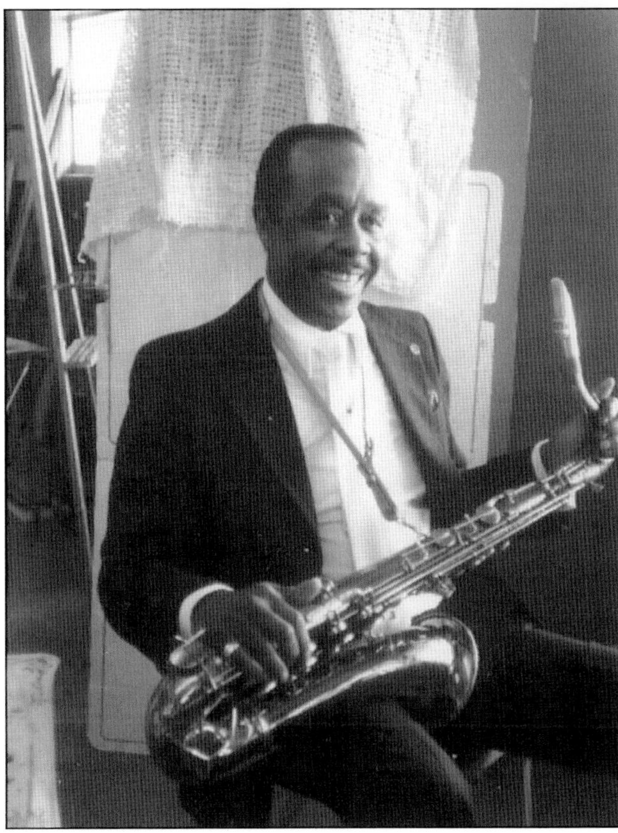

BUDDY TATE. George Holmes "Buddy" Tate was born in Sherman on February 22, 1913. At the age of 12, his brother gave him an alto saxophone. He went on to be a talented blues saxophonist and was a member of the Count Basie orchestra. Tate died on February 10, 2001. (Courtesy of the Sherman Museum.)

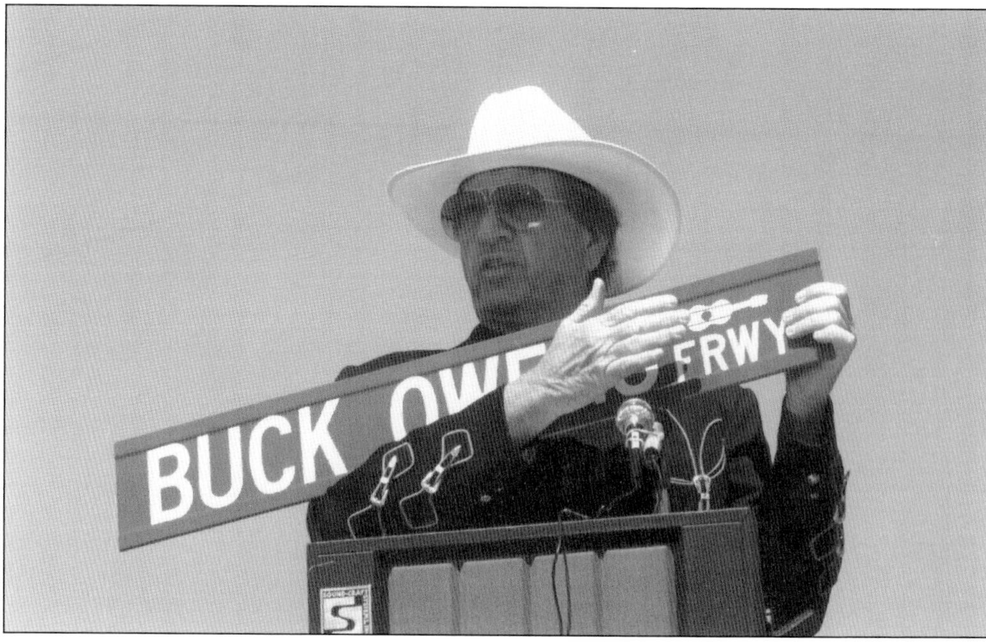

BUCK OWENS VISITS SHERMAN. Alvis Edgar "Buck" Owens Jr. was born in Sherman in 1929. In 1996, the City of Sherman honored him with the dedication of a portion of US Highway 82 as "Buck Owens Freeway." Owens attended the dedication and also performed a concert to kick-off the fundraising for the restoration of the Kidd-Key Auditorium. In the top photograph, Owens displays a street sign during the dedication ceremony. In the bottom photograph, he shows Mayor Julie Ellis Starr the signature red, white, and blue guitar that he donated to the city. Restoration of the auditorium was completed in 2001, and the guitar is on display in the balcony foyer. (Both courtesy of Julie Ellis Starr.)

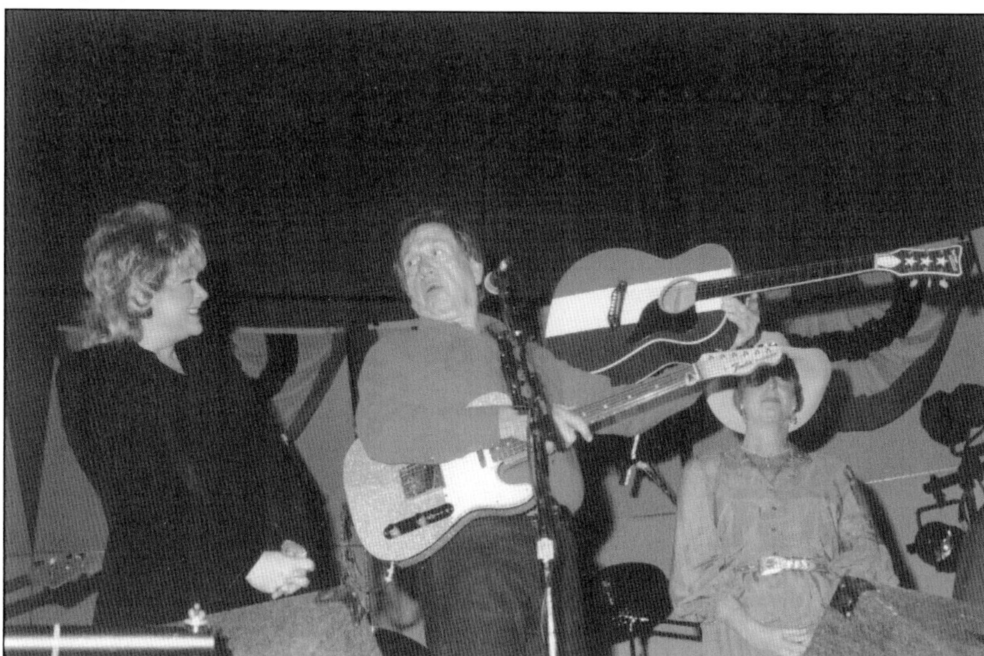

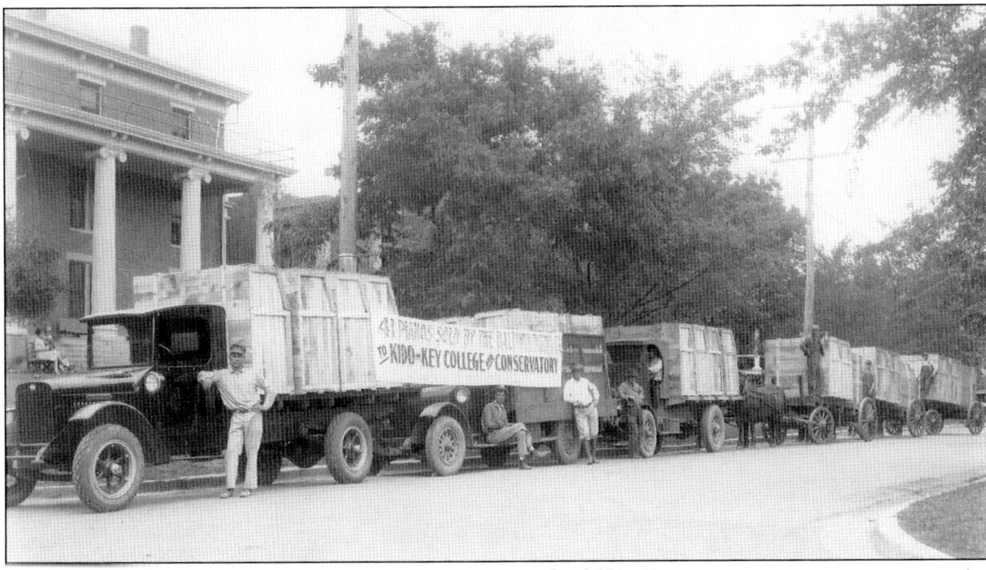

DELIVERY OF PIANOS TO KIDD-KEY CONSERVATORY. In 1928, Kidd-Key Conservatory expanded with a new auditorium and an administration building. Vestal Music Company delivered 41 new Baldwin pianos to the school. The expansion housed classrooms, laboratories, music practice rooms, an art studio, an auditorium, library, assembly room, music studios, and administrative offices. (Courtesy of the Sherman Museum.)

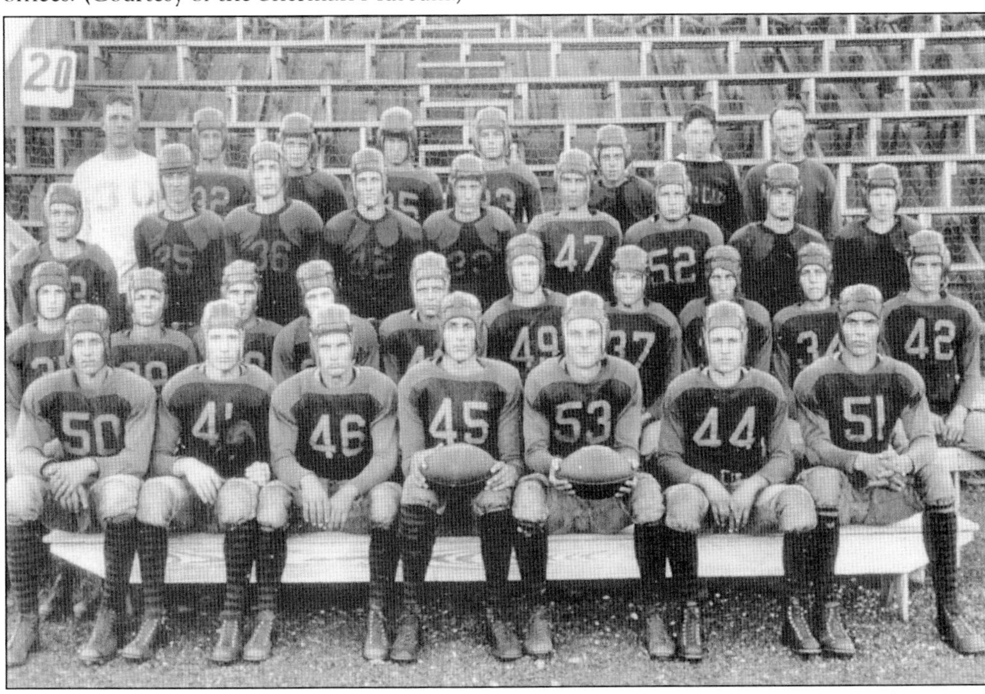

SHERMAN BEARCATS. The Sherman Bearcat Football Team posed for a photograph about 1925. They had their nickname decided on September 25, 1923, by a committee representing the student body. Each student turned in a name they liked and O.C. Burgess suggested the Bearcats. The Sherman Bearcats and the Denison Yellow Jackets have the longest continuous football rivalry among all Texas high schools. (Courtesy of the City of Sherman.)

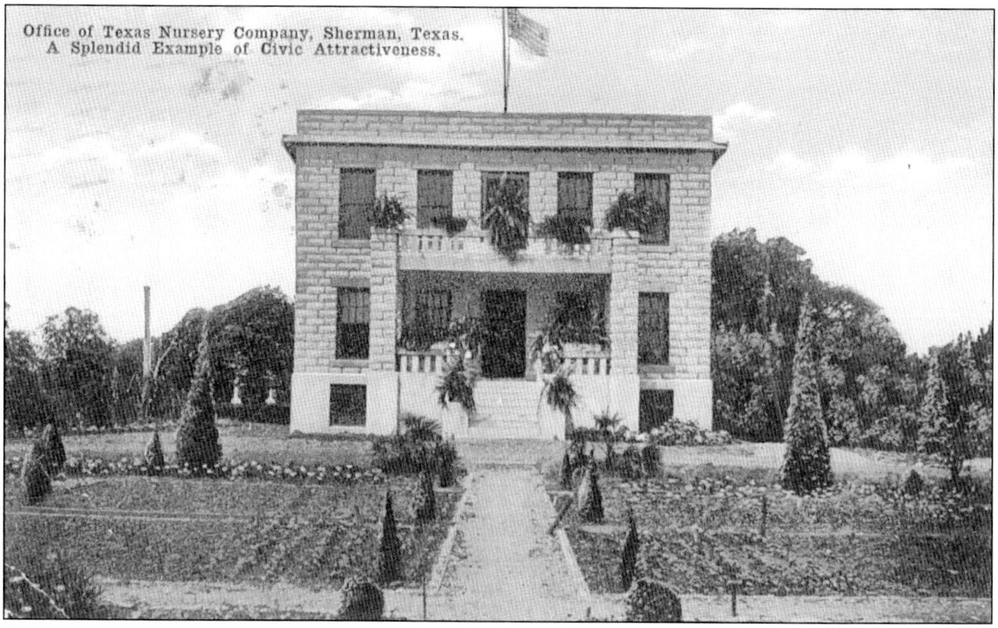

TEXAS NURSERY COMPANY. This company grew from a nursery business established in 1874 in McKinney by Col. E.W. Kirkpatrick. In 1899, C.C. Mayhew joined the firm, and the plant was moved to Sherman because of its excellent railroad facilities. Texas Nursery Company was located at the south end of Walnut Street and closed around 1970. (Courtesy of Greg Ashby.)

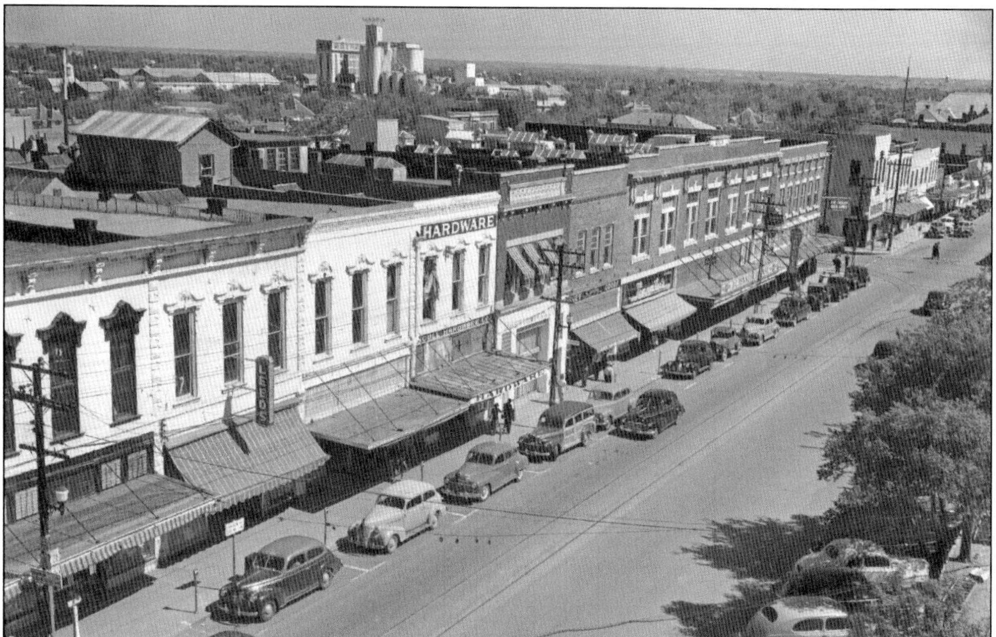

TRAVIS STREET. This photograph was taken looking south on Travis Street toward the railroad tracks. Taken around the late 1940s, businesses pictured include, from left to right, Keith's Drugs, Leed's Women's Clothing, Scull Hardware, Grayson County State Bank, Loe's Sporting Goods, Linxwiler's Store for Men and Boys, and J.C. Penney. The Interurban tracks are also visible in the street. (Photograph by Jack Goodwin; courtesy of Roger and Kay Goodwin.)

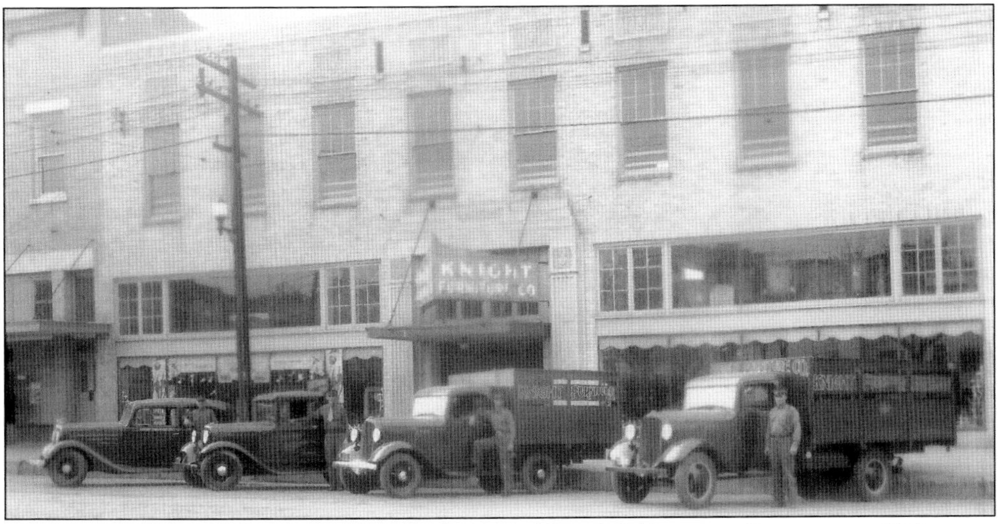

Knight's Furniture Company. J.B. Knight started Knight's Furniture Company in 1912; it was located on East Houston Street. In 1915, the store moved to the south side of the square into a part of the O.L. Bailey Furniture Store. Two years later, they purchased the remaining Bailey business, but the building was destroyed by fire in 1931. The new store was completed in May 1932 on the same site. (Courtesy of the Sherman Museum.)

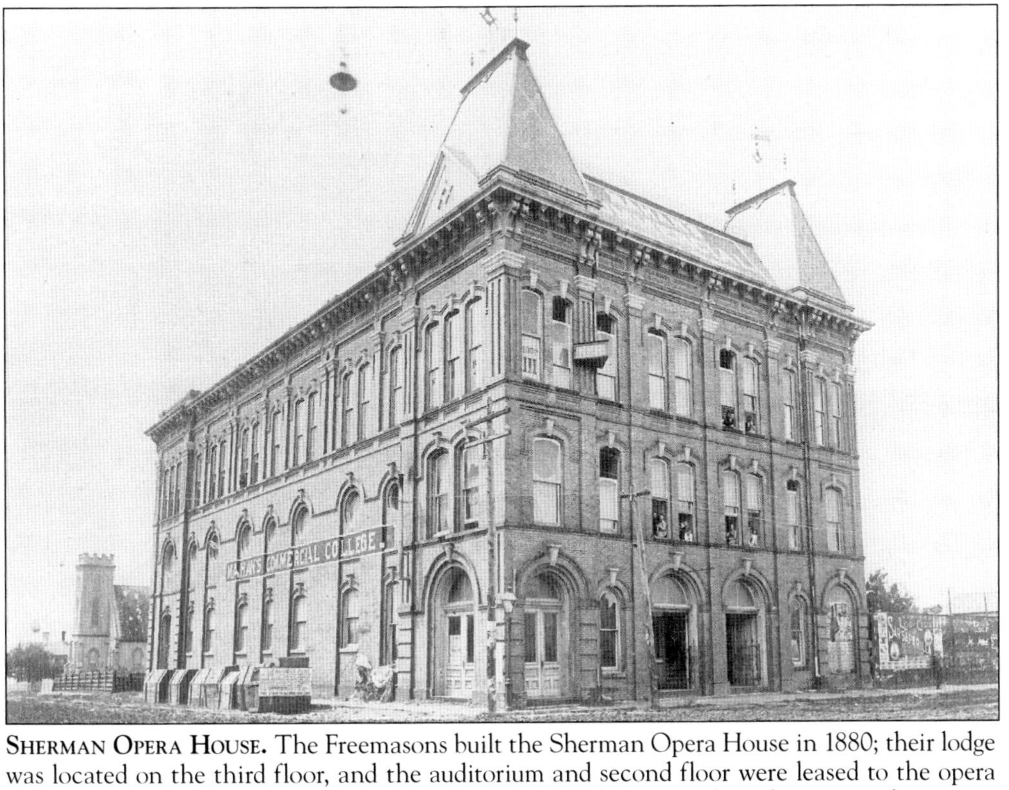

Sherman Opera House. The Freemasons built the Sherman Opera House in 1880; their lodge was located on the third floor, and the auditorium and second floor were leased to the opera company. The opera house helped make Sherman a cultural center with performances of operettas, Shakespearean plays, musical reviews, temperance lectures, trained animal acts, and church revivals. The opera house closed in 1918. (Courtesy of the Sherman Museum.)

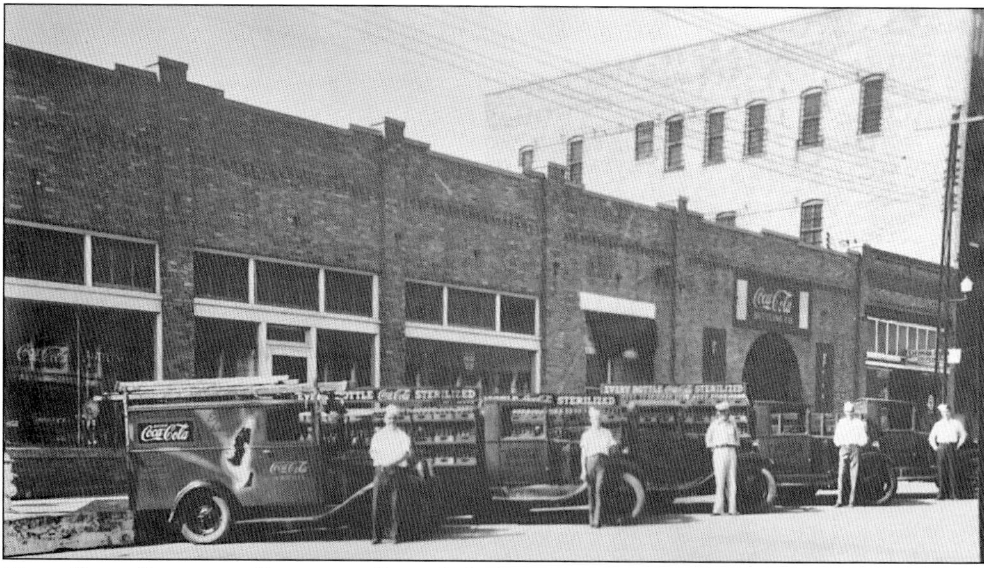

Coca-Cola Bottling Company. Coca-Cola Bottling Company began in Sherman in 1907 and was located on West Houston Street. In 1915, Sam Woodson bought the plant from Dr. J.C. Bouge, and in 1917, he moved it to the southwest corner of Walnut and Pecan Streets. In 1963, the plant moved to Frisco Road. A 1925 newspaper article said the plant was bottling "145,000 cases of Coca-Cola a year." (Courtesy of the City of Sherman.)

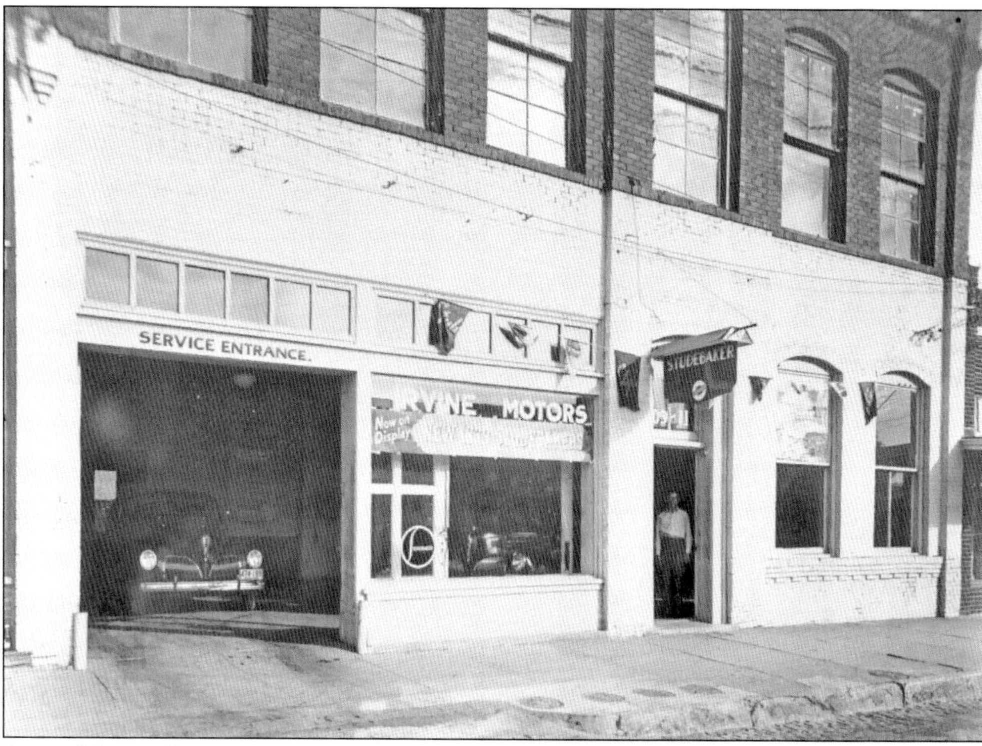

Irvine Motor Company. In 1938, Irvine Motor Company was located in the 100 block of East Pecan Street. The sign advertises "now on display 1938 Studebakers." The company later became Wood Auto Company and then Tom Roach Motors. (Courtesy of the City of Sherman.)

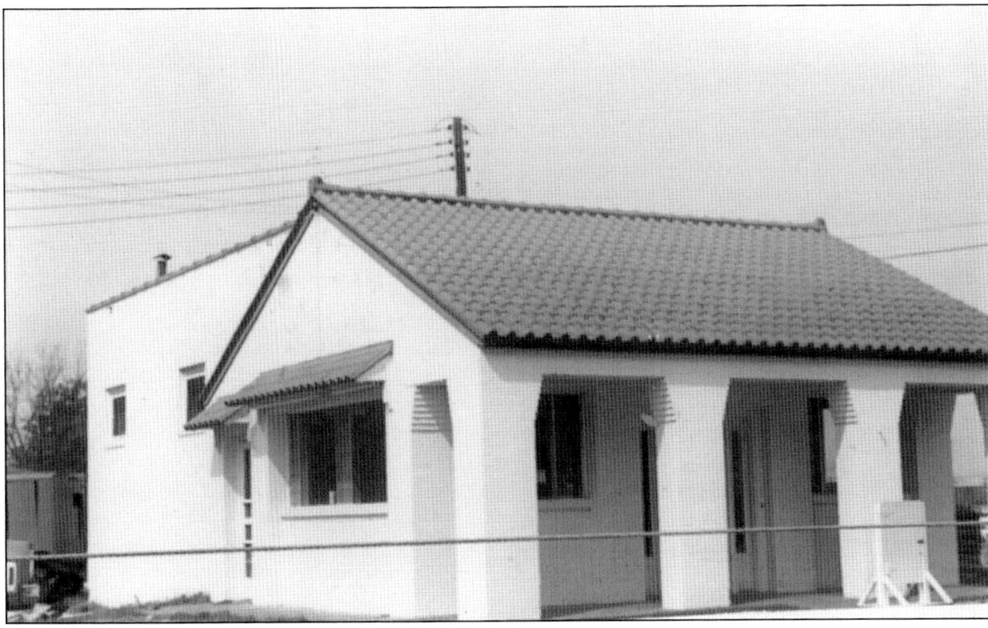

ASHBURN'S ICE CREAM. W.L. Ashburn started Ashburn's Ice Cream in 1906 in Denison. His son Frank Ashburn opened the Sherman store in 1930 at 212 South Crockett Street. From 1969 until it closed in the early 1980s, it was operated by W.L. Ashburn III. Ice cream was sold at two dips for 5¢. The building was razed to make way for the Grayson County Justice Center. (Courtesy of Missy Sofey-Andrews.)

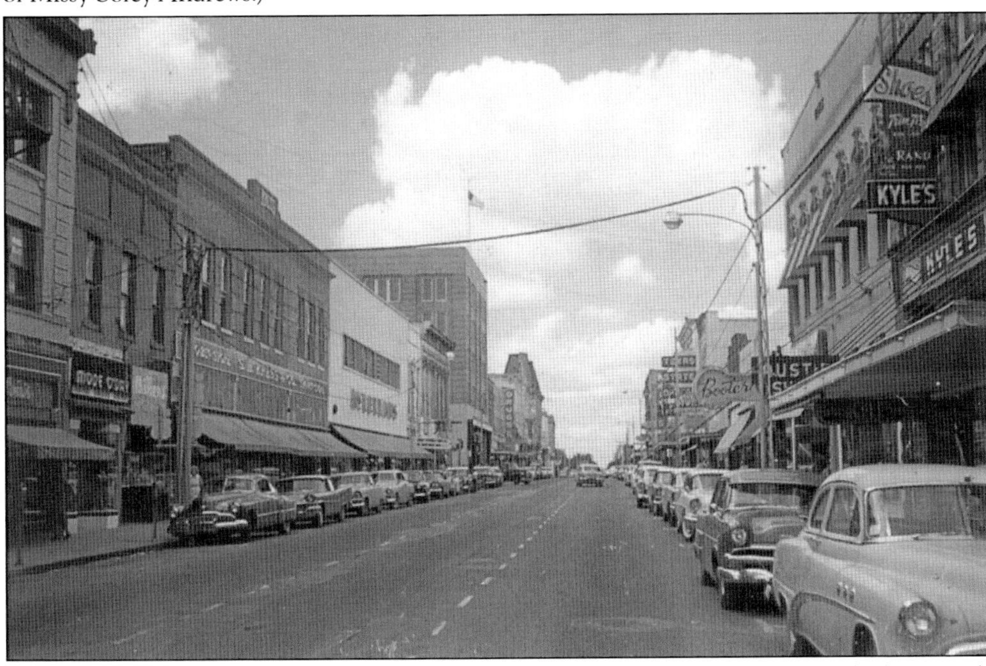

NORTH TRAVIS STREET, 1950S. This photograph is of the 100 block of Travis Street looking north, as it looked in the 1950s. On the west side of the street are, from left to right, Kress and McLellan's discount stores; on the east side of the street are, from left to right, Texas State Optical, Booterie Women's Shoes, Austin's Shoes, and Kyle's Shoes. (Courtesy of Greg Ashby.)

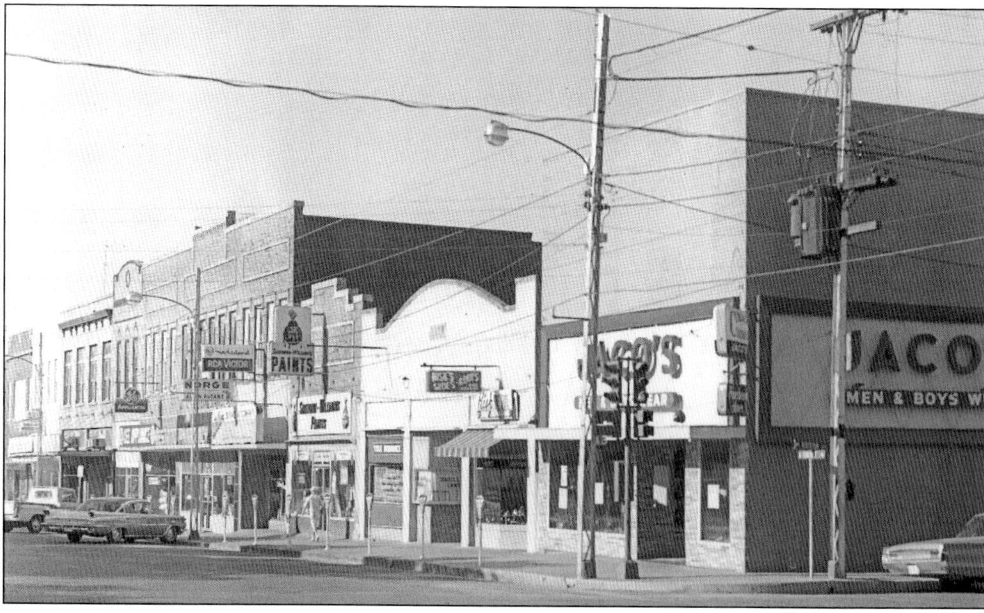

West Side of the Square, 1967. This photograph shows Crockett Street on the west side of the square, looking south, as it looked in 1967. Visible buildings are, left to right, Medical Rentals, Lee Appliances, Hestand Pharmacy, Allen Butane Gas and Equipment, Sherwin-Williams Company, Security Abstract and Title Company, Charles Hughes Attorney, Risk Shoe Store, and Jaco's Men & Boys Wear. (Courtesy of A Touch of Class Antique Mall.)

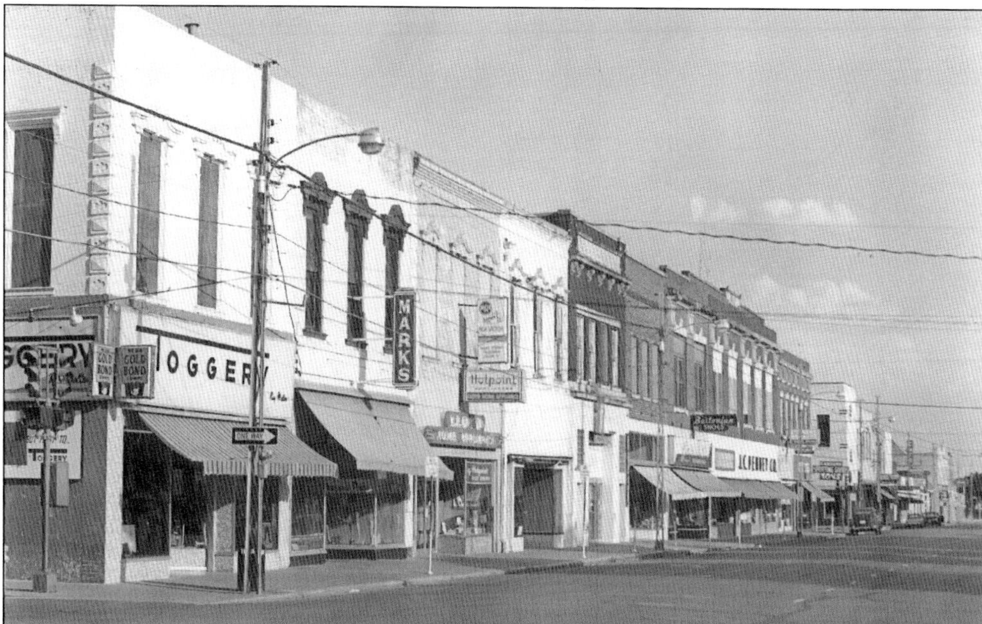

East Side of the Square, 1967. This photograph shows Travis Street on the east side of the square, looking south, as it looked in 1967. Visible buildings are, left to right, Toggery Men's Clothing, Marks Ready to Wear (women's clothing), Lloyd Home Appliances, vacant, Toyland, Linxwiler's Store for Men, J.C. Penney Company, and Mentzel's Appliance Household. (Courtesy of A Touch of Class Antique Mall.)

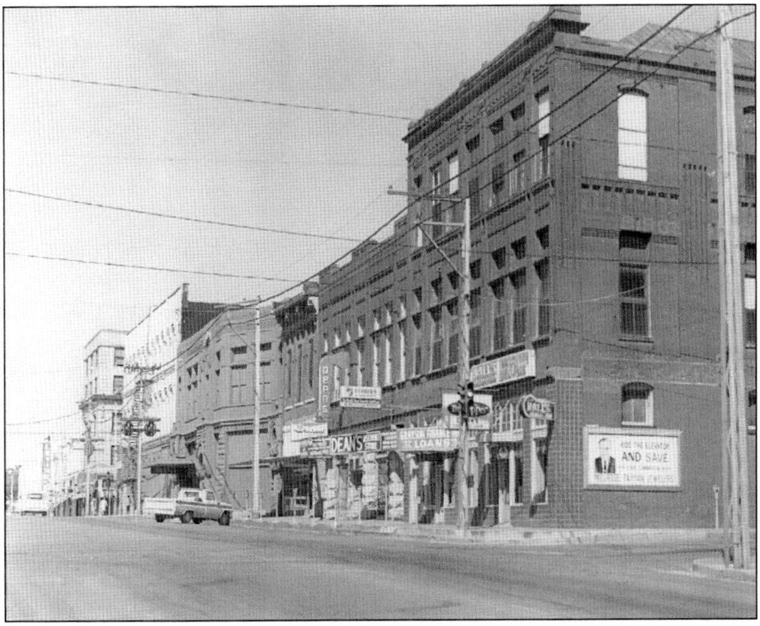

East Houston Street, 1967. This photograph shows the 100 block of Houston Street looking west as it looked in 1967. Visible buildings are, left to right, the Legionnaire Club, Dean's Discount Store, and Grayson Finance. Melrose Tappan Jewelers also has a billboard on the side of the building facing Walnut Street. (Courtesy of A Touch of Class Antique Mall.)

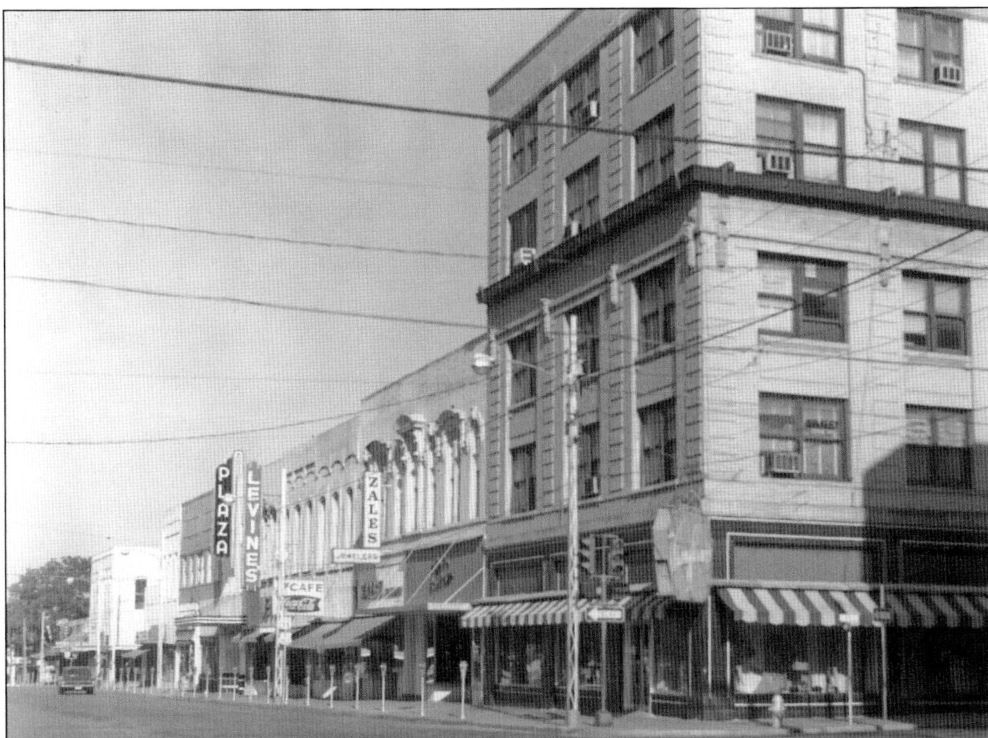

North Side of the Square, 1967. This photograph shows Houston Street on the north side of the square, looking west, as it looked in 1967. Visible buildings are, left to right, the Sewing Basket, Williams Furniture, the Plaza Theater, Levine's Department Store, M&M Cafe, Zales Jewelers, and Toppers Menswear. (Courtesy of A Touch of Class Antique Mall.)

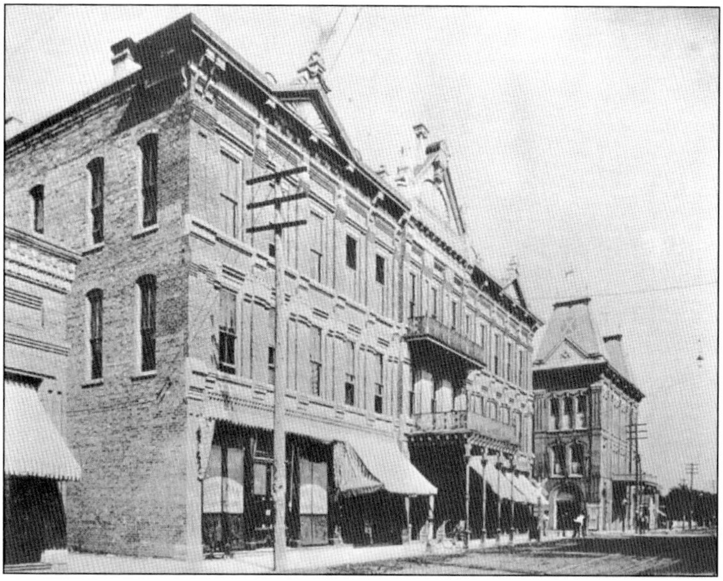

BINKLEY HOTEL, C. 1908. The Binkley Hotel was originally erected in 1877 and named for Judge C.C. Binkley. The hotel burned in 1887 and was rebuilt on the same site. It burned again in the mid-1890s. The name of the Binkley Hotel was changed to the Texas Hotel in later years, and it burned for the last time in 1967. (Courtesy of the City of Sherman.)

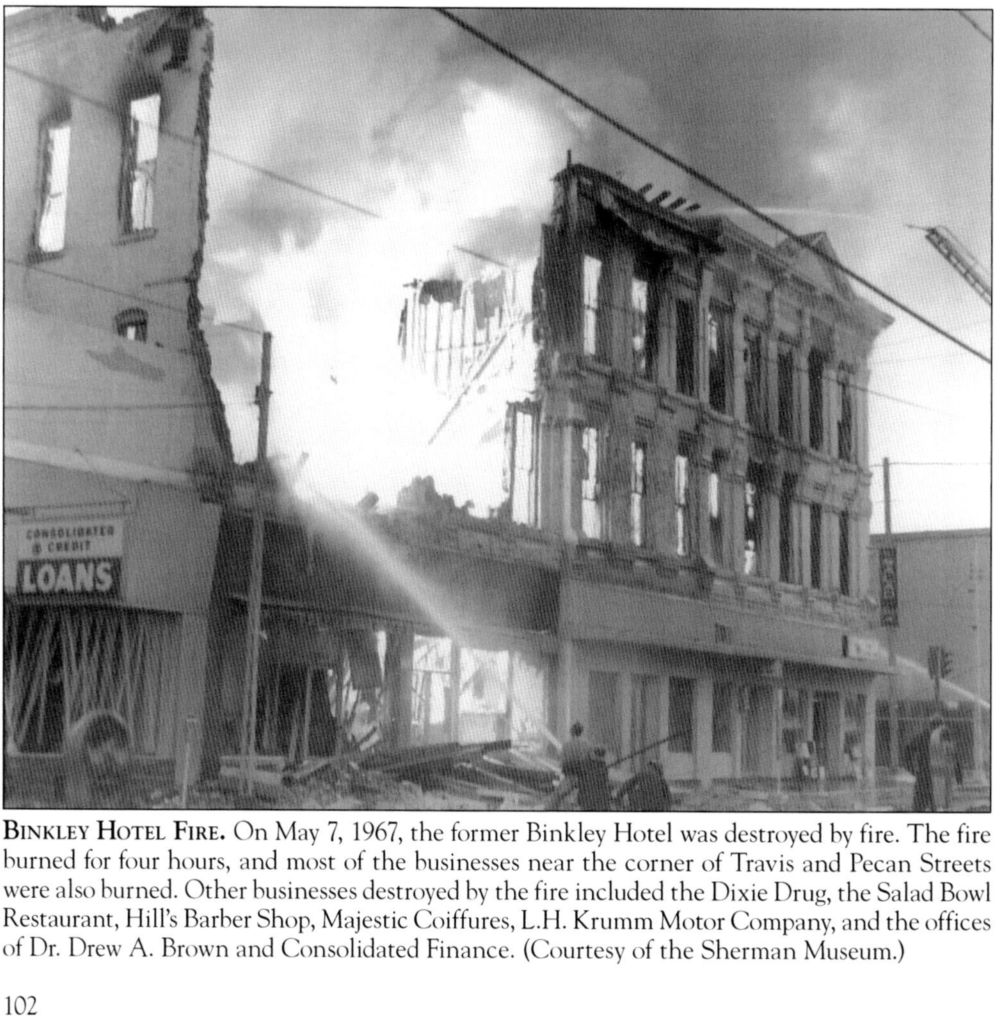

BINKLEY HOTEL FIRE. On May 7, 1967, the former Binkley Hotel was destroyed by fire. The fire burned for four hours, and most of the businesses near the corner of Travis and Pecan Streets were also burned. Other businesses destroyed by the fire included the Dixie Drug, the Salad Bowl Restaurant, Hill's Barber Shop, Majestic Coiffures, L.H. Krumm Motor Company, and the offices of Dr. Drew A. Brown and Consolidated Finance. (Courtesy of the Sherman Museum.)

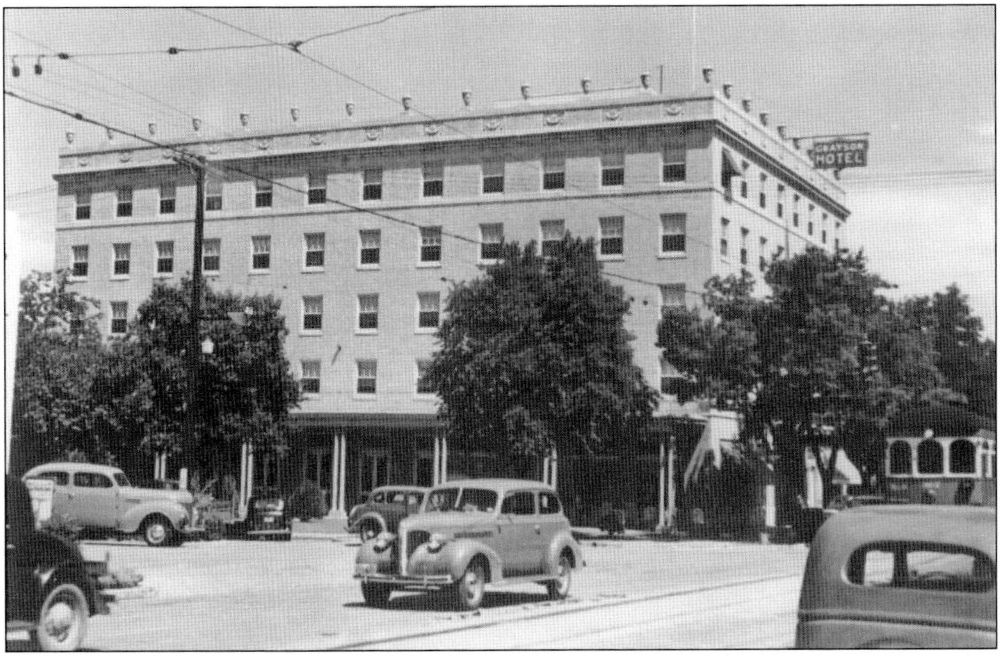

GRAYSON HOTEL. The Grayson Hotel was built in 1927 at a cost of $350,000. It was located at the corner of Travis and Mulberry Streets, and a 1929 newspaper opinion piece called it "the envy of the city." In 1961, Dr. Rhea L. Nichols of Dallas purchased the hotel. A 1965 fire closed the hotel briefly, and it was razed in 1966. (Courtesy of the Sherman Museum.)

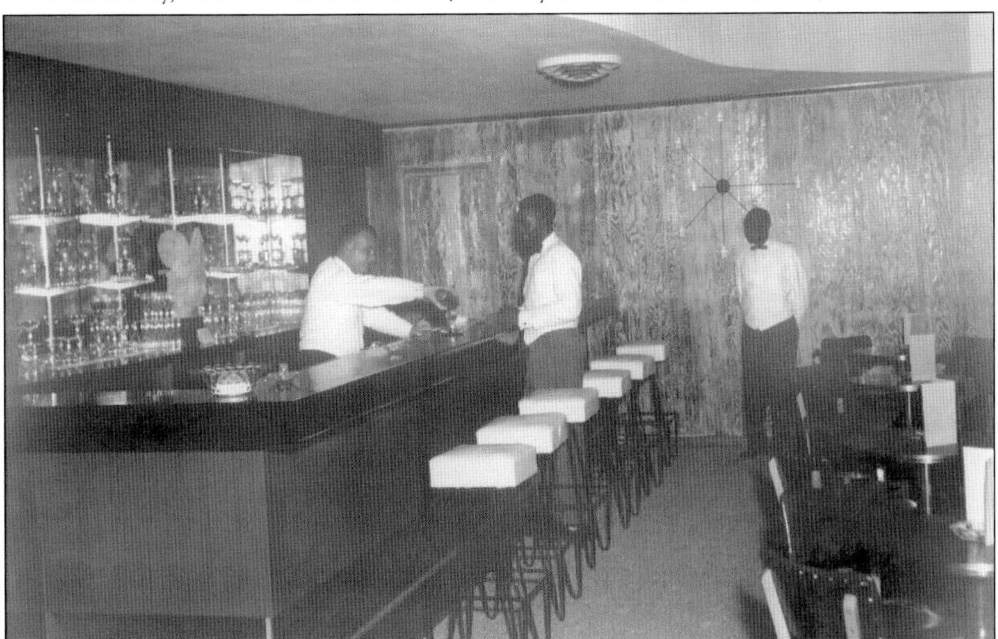

GRAYSON HOTEL'S OIL AND INDUSTRY CLUB. The Grayson Hotel also featured the Oil and Industry Club with a fashionable bar area, a coffee shop that seated 80, and a first class soda fountain. During the time of prosperity, the Grayson Hotel boasted full registers, but in the late 1950s the hotel business in downtown Sherman begin to fail. (Courtesy of the Sherman Museum.)

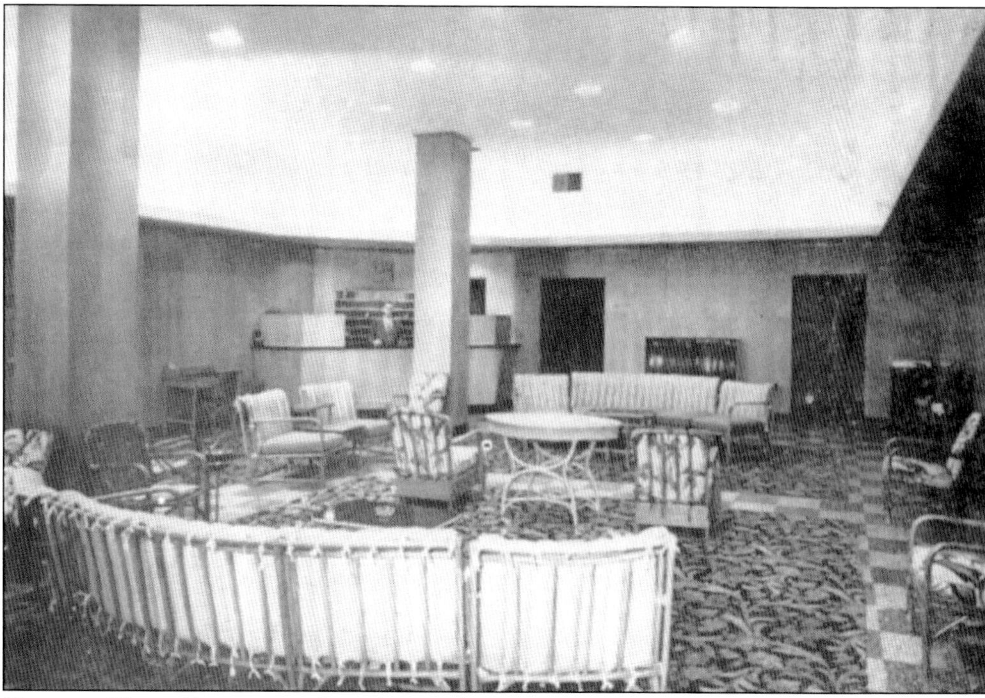

Grayson Hotel Lobby and Gift Shop. The Grayson Hotel was a luxury hotel that featured five stories and 100 rooms. It was said that the hotel offered service that was second to none. The top photograph shows the grand entrance and seating area. The lobby had a terrazzo floor inlaid with strips of copper. There were fashionable dining and meeting rooms to accommodate clubs, schools, and businesses. The bottom photograph shows the hotel gift shop. (Both courtesy of Greg Ashby.)

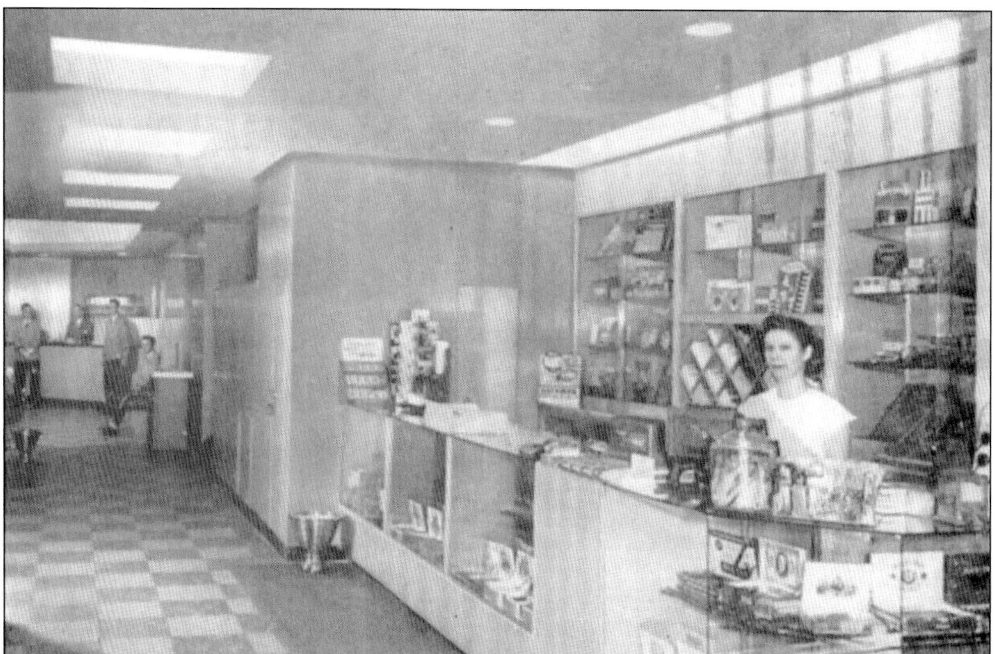

Five

THE ATHENS OF TEXAS

By the late 1890s and into the new century, Sherman was being touted as the Athens of Texas because of its schools, cultural centers, hotels, and hospitals. Some felt that Sherman lost out in the 1870s when the Missouri, Kansas, and Texas Railway, or the "Katy," located in Denison. Others said Sherman deliberately chose culture over the Katy.

Whichever version is true, Sherman did seem to attract the educational and more cultured citizenry. The first college founded in the community was the Sherman Male and Female Academy in 1870. It later became the North Texas Female College and still later the Kidd-Key Conservatory.

Lucy Kidd took over the Sherman Male and Female Academy in 1888, after it had been closed for two years. The college reopened and grew to include seven brick buildings, several cottage units, and a gymnasium. Kidd married Bishop Joseph S. Key in 1892, and the school's charter was amended to read "North Texas College and Kidd-Key Conservatory of Music." The college continued to grow.

The second college in Sherman was the Sherman Female Institute, which began in 1877 and was renamed Mary Nash College in 1901. It was located across the street from Kidd-Key College. In 1905, the Mary Nash College and its four buildings were absorbed into the Kidd-Key organization. Lucy Kidd-Key died in 1916, and the college finally closed in 1935.

Other schools were also active in Sherman from an earlier time, including professor LeTellier's Academy founded in 1871, St. Joseph's Academy founded in 1877, and Carr-Burdette College, which opened in 1894.

Carr-Burdette College was started by O.A. and Mattie Carr to teach girls the importance of Christian womanhood. The school was located on an eight-acre site on North Burdette Street in east Sherman. After the death of Mattie Carr in 1907, the Christian Church of Texas operated the college until it finally closed in 1930.

Another college that called Sherman home was Austin College. Originally founded in 1849 in Huntsville, Austin College moved to Sherman in 1876 and is the oldest college in Texas operating under its original charter. Today Austin College boasts a 60-acre campus in the heart of Sherman and remains a recognized leader in higher education.

Sherman's rich educational heritage, coupled with the opera houses, theaters, magnificent hotels, and the feelings of community leaders that a community with high moral standards and good educational opportunities would attract businesses and industries, helped contribute to sound economic development in Sherman.

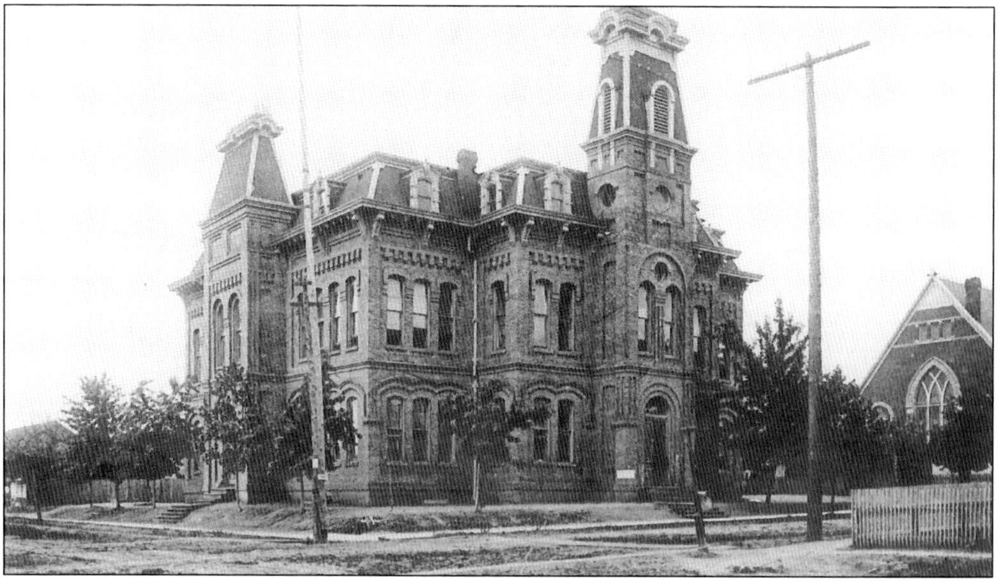

Franklin School, 1905. Located at the southwest corner of Walnut and Mulberry Streets, the Franklin School was erected in 1884 and was the first brick school building in Sherman. It originally housed elementary and high school students. Franklin School was torn down in 1925. (Courtesy of the Sherman Museum.)

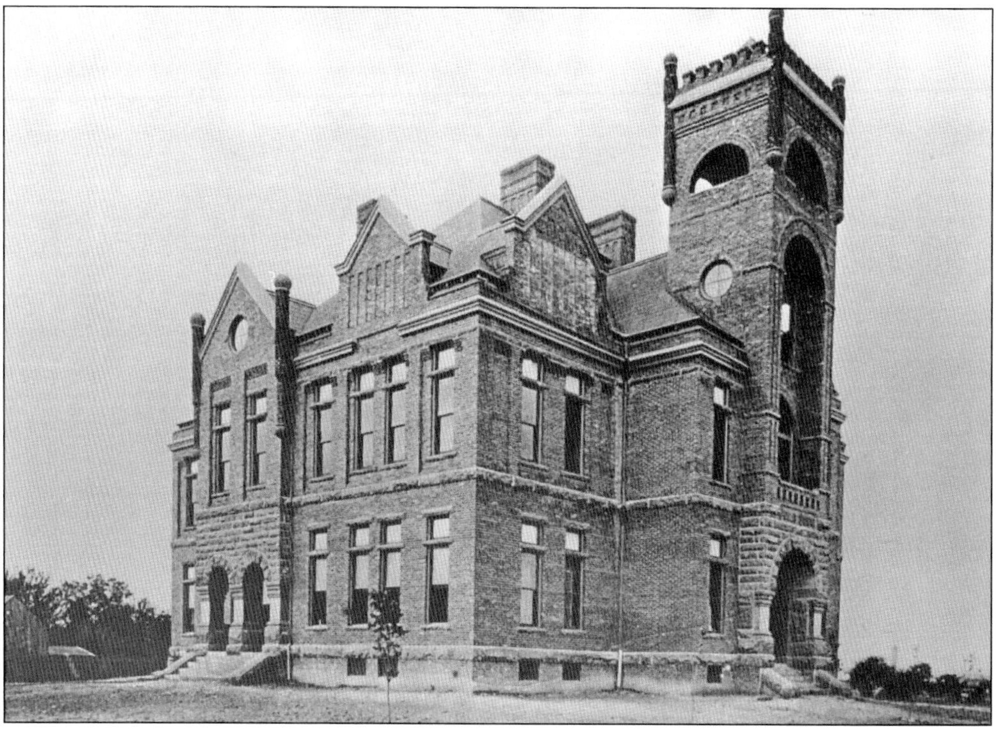

Jefferson Elementary School, c. 1900. Jefferson Elementary School was built in 1896 on East Chaffin Street, behind the Fifth Ward Fire Station. The building was used until 1931 when a new school was constructed at the southwest corner of Lee and Brockett Streets. Lizzie Dulin was the first principal of Jefferson Elementary School. (Courtesy of the City of Sherman.)

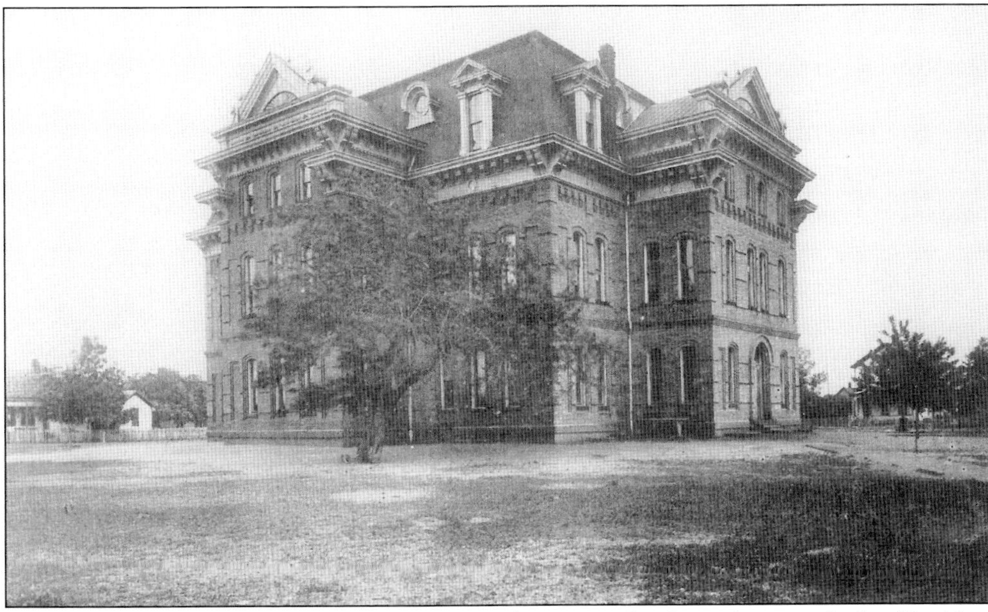

WASHINGTON SCHOOL. Constructed in 1885, Washington School was the second school building in Sherman created specifically as a school. It housed the first six grades and the eighth grade. The seventh grade was located at Franklin School. The original building was razed in 1928, and the second building was erected on the same site with bricks from the old structure. (Courtesy of the Sherman Museum.)

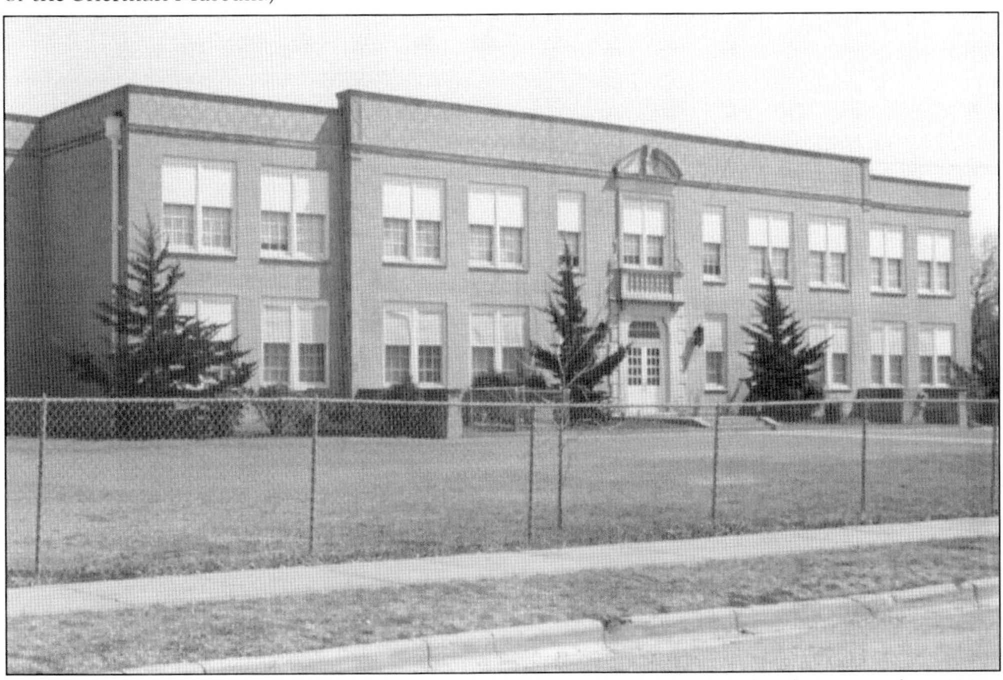

WASHINGTON GRAMMAR SCHOOL. The first Washington Grammar School was razed in 1928, and this building was opened in 1929. It is located at 815 South Travis Street. Before the school had a regular cafeteria, mothers of students brought soup and chili to school and heated it on a "monkey" stove. (Courtesy of the Sherman Museum.)

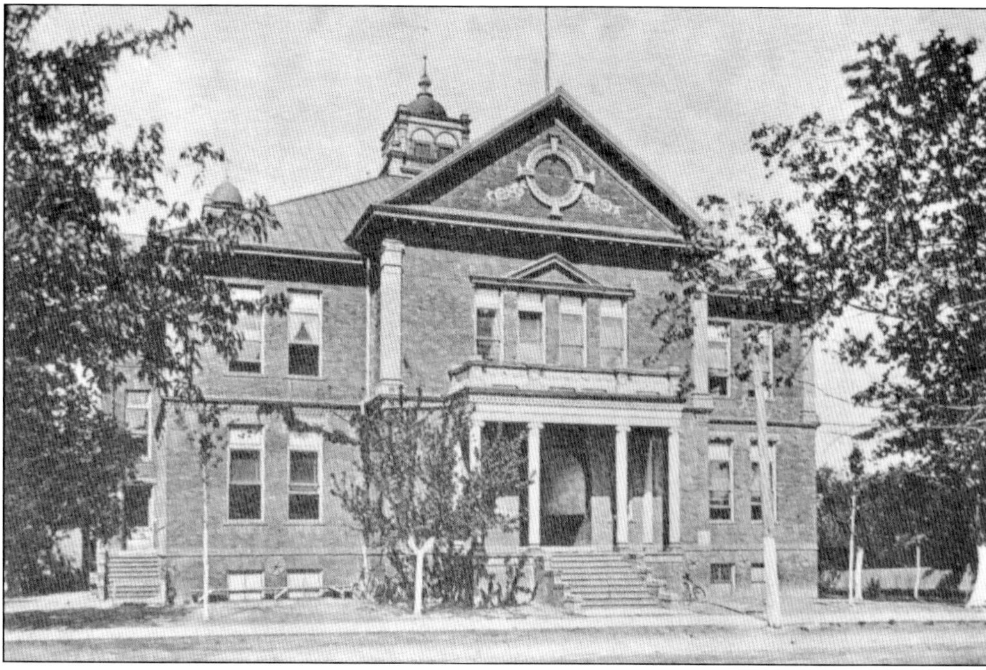

Sherman High School. The second Sherman High School was erected in 1908 on the site of the one that burned the previous year. This building was used as a high school until 1917, when a new building was constructed at Crockett and King Streets. Sixty-four students graduated from the high school that year. Afterwards, it became a junior high school. In 1929, the building was sold. (Courtesy of the City of Sherman.)

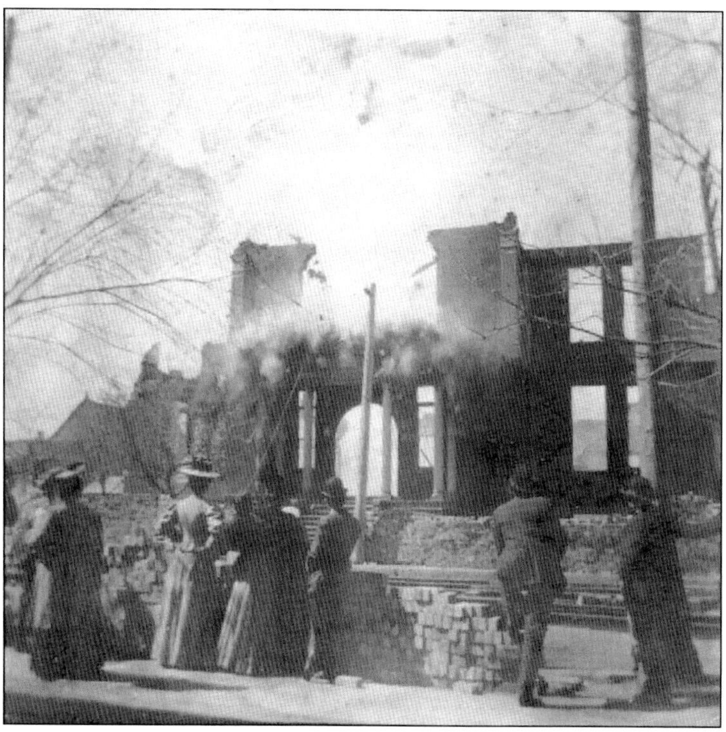

Sherman High School Fire. The first Sherman High School was built in 1899 on the southeast corner of Travis and Mulberry Streets. The school burned on March 7, 1907, and was rebuilt the following year. Eleven students graduated in 1899. (Courtesy of the Sherman Museum.)

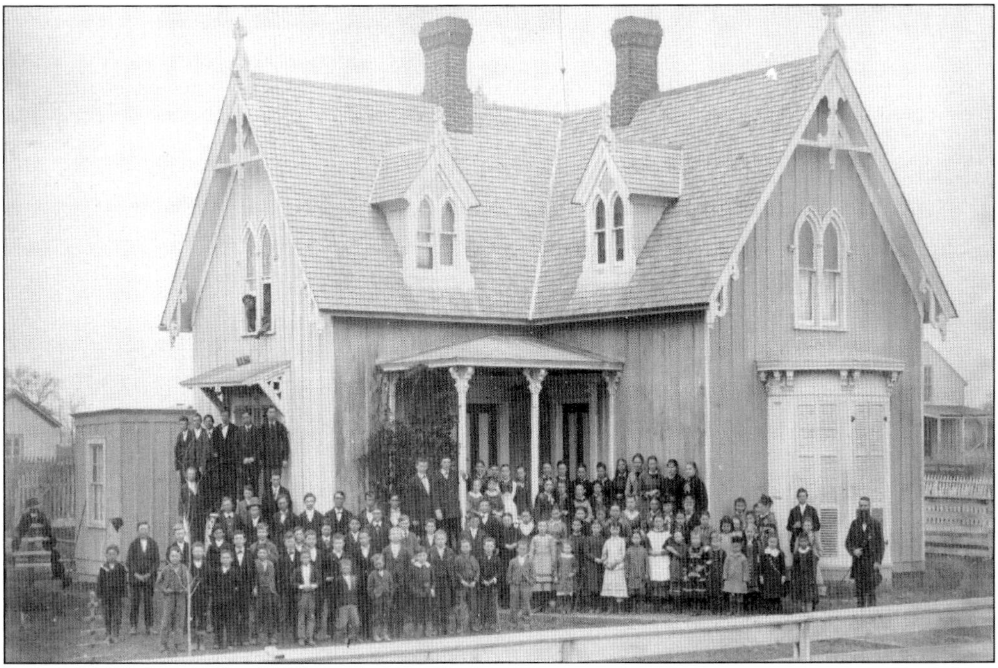

Capt. LeTellier's Private School. The Sherman Private School was established in 1871 by Capt. John Henry LeTellier and was located at 1723 South Travis Street. The school primarily educated boys, however a few girls were occasionally admitted. Tuition was $3 per month when the school opened. Sherman Private School operated until the death of Captain LeTellier on July 24, 1913. (Courtesy of the Sherman Museum.)

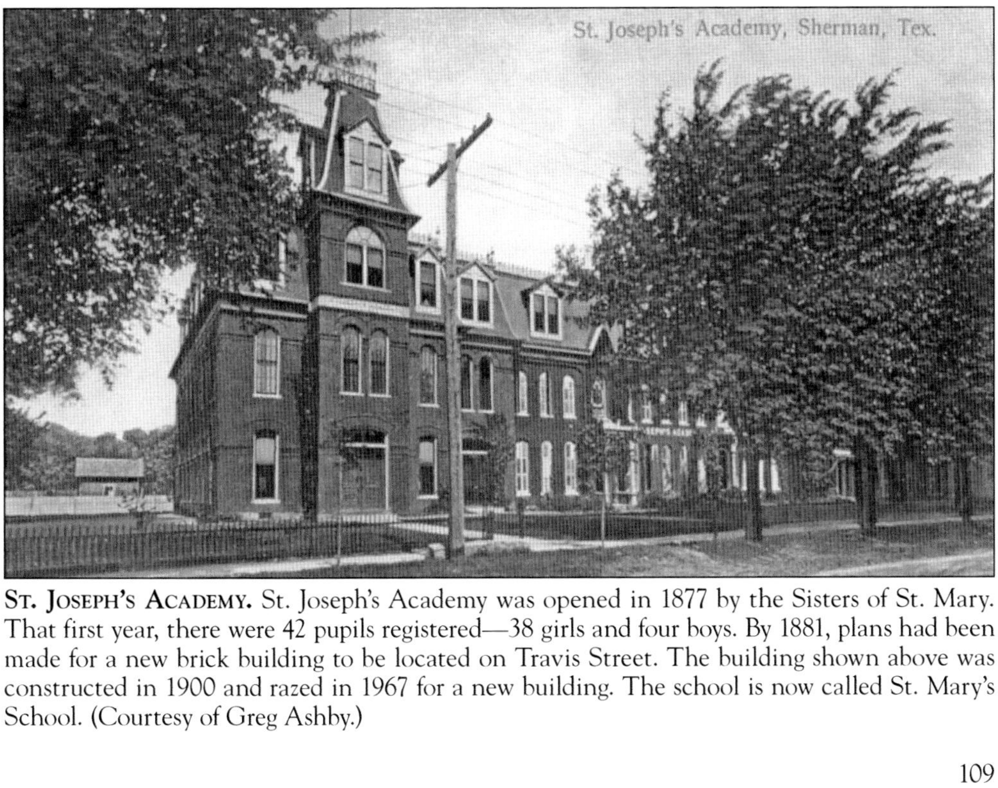

St. Joseph's Academy. St. Joseph's Academy was opened in 1877 by the Sisters of St. Mary. That first year, there were 42 pupils registered—38 girls and four boys. By 1881, plans had been made for a new brick building to be located on Travis Street. The building shown above was constructed in 1900 and razed in 1967 for a new building. The school is now called St. Mary's School. (Courtesy of Greg Ashby.)

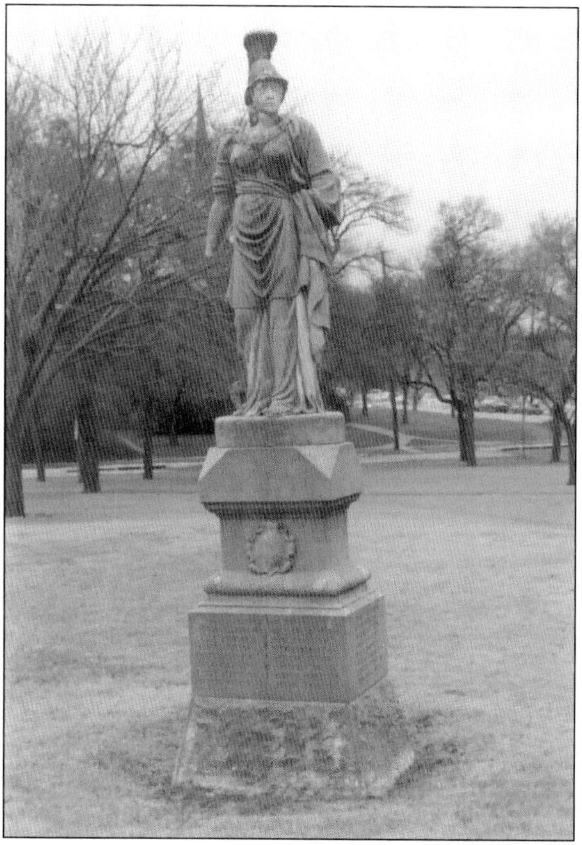

Minerva Statue. This statue, located in front of the municipal building, is the last remaining statue from the Kidd-Key Conservatory campus. The statue is missing one hand, and etched at the base is "Class of 1898." The college closed in 1935. (Courtesy of the City of Sherman.)

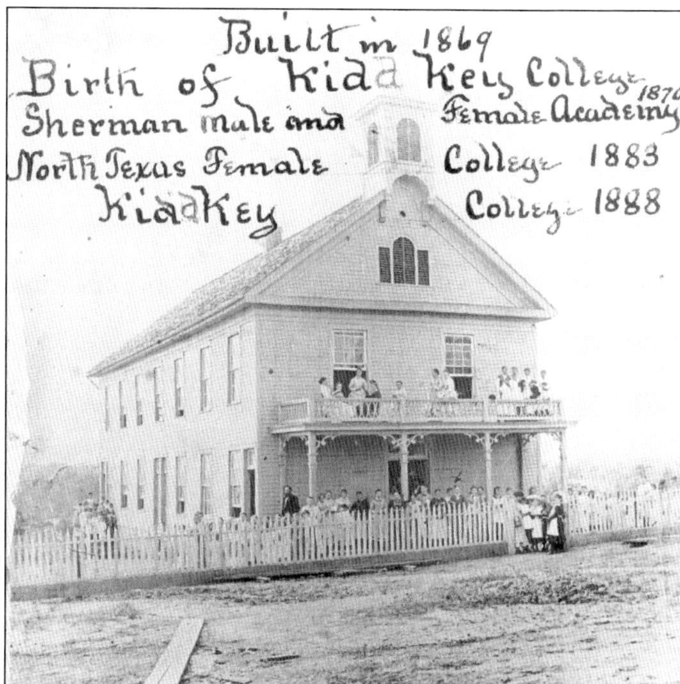

Kidd-Key Conservatory. This was the first building erected on the site that would eventually house Kidd-Key Conservatory. Founded in 1870, Sherman Male and Female Academy also held the first public school classes in Sherman. In 1888, Lucy Kidd took fragments of the first college and developed a program for young women, known as Kidd-Key Conservatory. In 1905, Kidd reclaimed parts of the Mary Nash College to incorporate into the conservatory. (Courtesy of the Sherman Museum.)

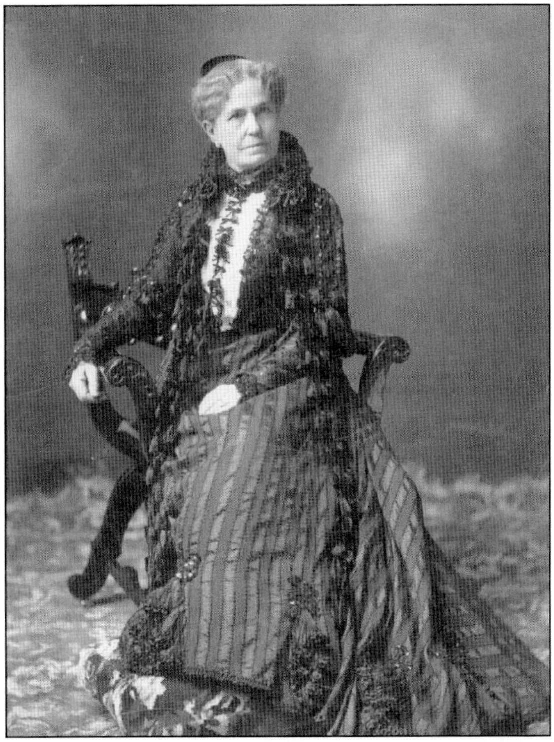

Lucy Kidd-Key. Lucy Thornton Kidd came to Sherman in 1888 to become president of a college originally known as Sherman Male and Female Academy and later North Texas Female College. In 1892, she married Bishop Joseph S. Key and the college gained fame as the Kidd-Key Conservatory. Kidd-Key directed the schools growth from an enrollment of 100 to more than 500. She died in 1916. (Courtesy of Greg Ashby.)

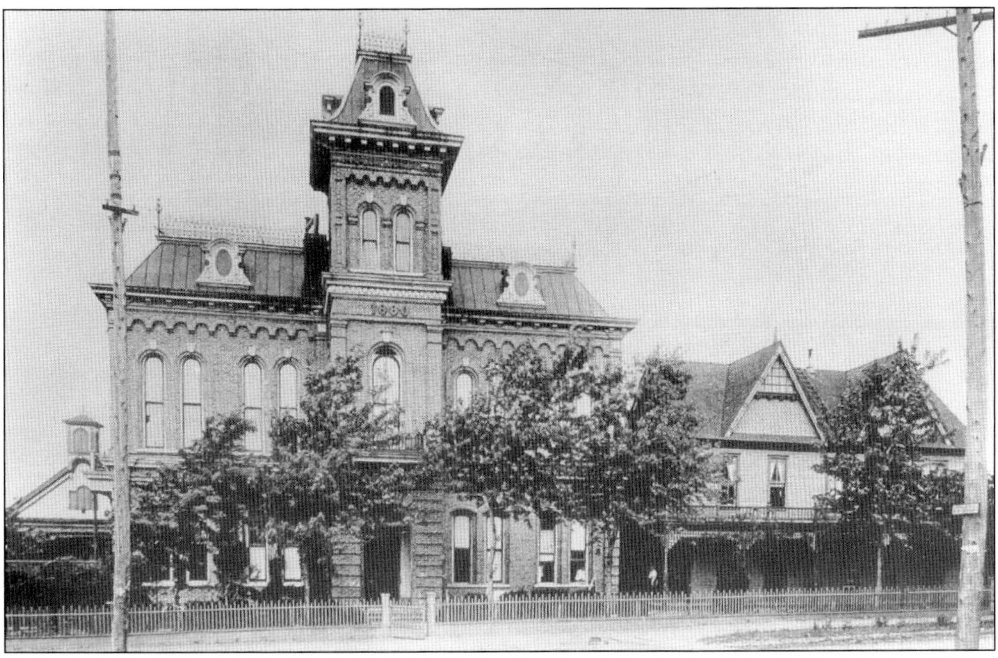

North Texas Female College. This building housed the North Texas Female College and was later the main building for Kidd-Key College. It was located where the municipal building now sits. The city purchased the administration building during construction and completed it as the municipal building to house city offices. The surrounding buildings were torn down. (Courtesy of the City of Sherman.)

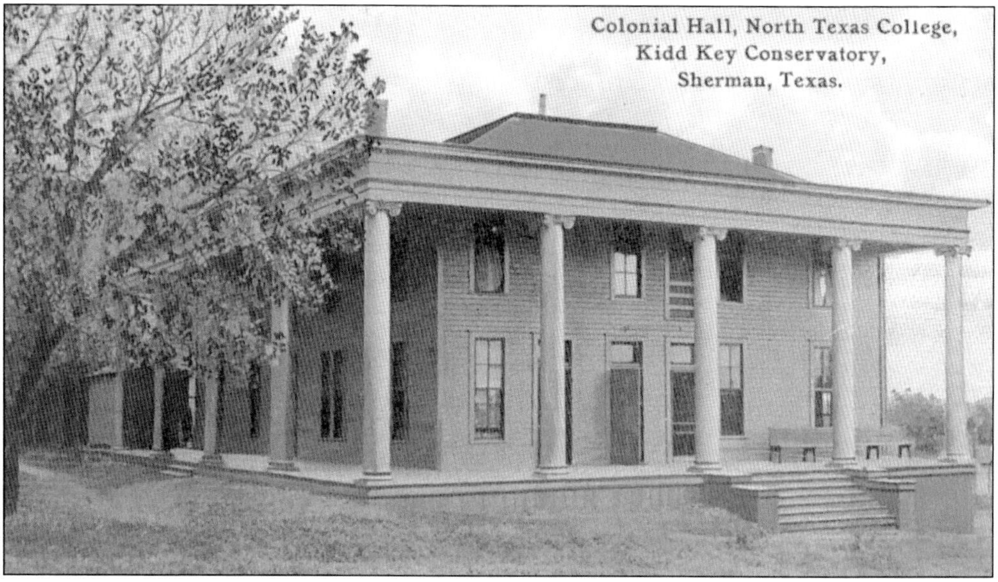

Colonial Hall at Kidd-Key College. Colonial Hall was an early building at North Texas College, which later became Kidd-Key College. In 1888, when Lucy Kidd took over the school, it had been closed for two years. At that time the only buildings left were the original academy building, an uncompleted frame just south of it, and the first unit of the chapel. (Courtesy of Greg Ashby.)

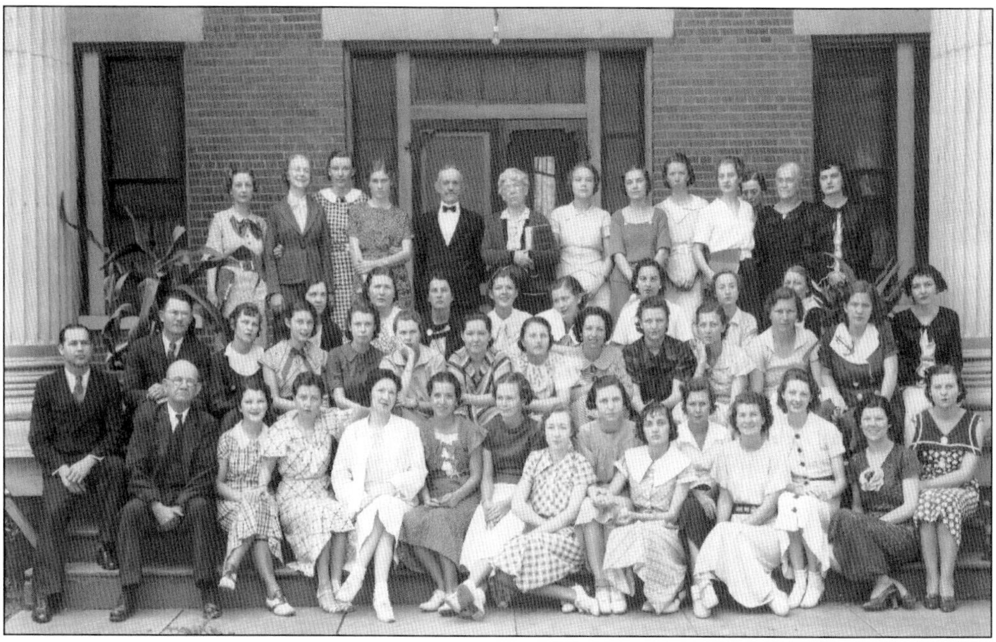

Students and Faculty of Kidd-Key Conservatory. Students and faculty pose on the steps of Kidd-Key Conservatory. Originally known as North Texas Female College, the school was renamed in honor of Lucy Kidd-Key, three years after her death. Kidd-Key insisted on strict standards of propriety for her young women and admonished them to be devout and ladylike and to cherish their future duties as wives and mothers above all other pursuits. (Courtesy of the Sherman Museum.)

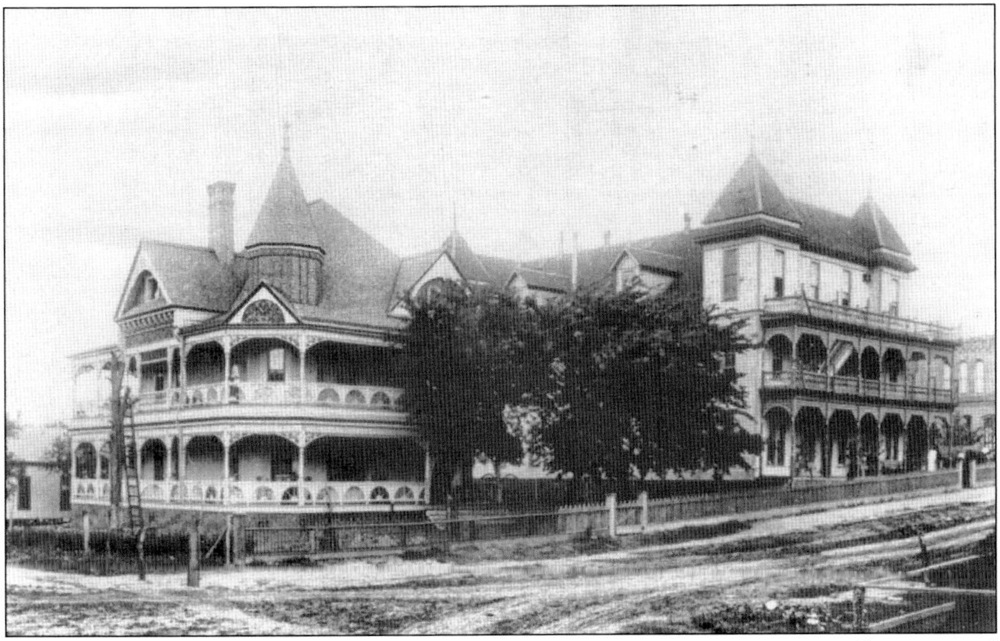

Residence of Lucy Kidd-Key and the Anna Nugent Hall. Anna Nugent Hall was erected in 1891 and served as the residence of Lucy Kidd-Key and a three-story dormitory. It burned in 1905 and was replaced with Annie Green Hall in 1906. Sherman Male and Female Academy was reopened in 1888 by Kidd-Key after it had been closed for two years. (Courtesy of the Sherman Museum.)

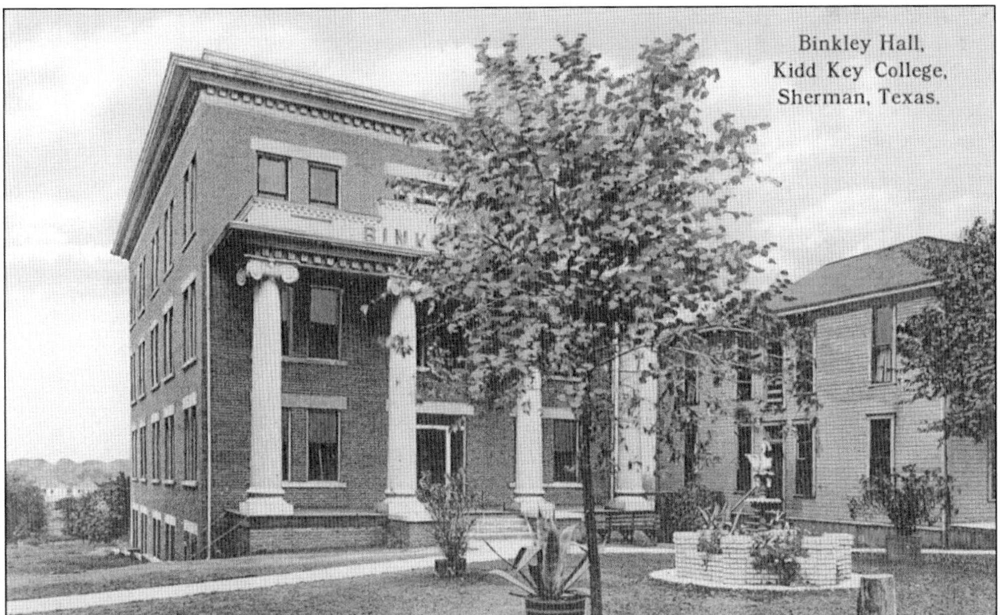

Binkley Hall at Kidd-Key College. Binkley Hall was erected in 1887 and was named for Rev. James M. Binkley, a pioneer Methodist minister. Reverend Binkley was president of the clerical members of the college board—the Methodist North Texas Conference—that was responsible for bringing Lucy Kidd to the North Texas Female College. (Courtesy of Greg Ashby.)

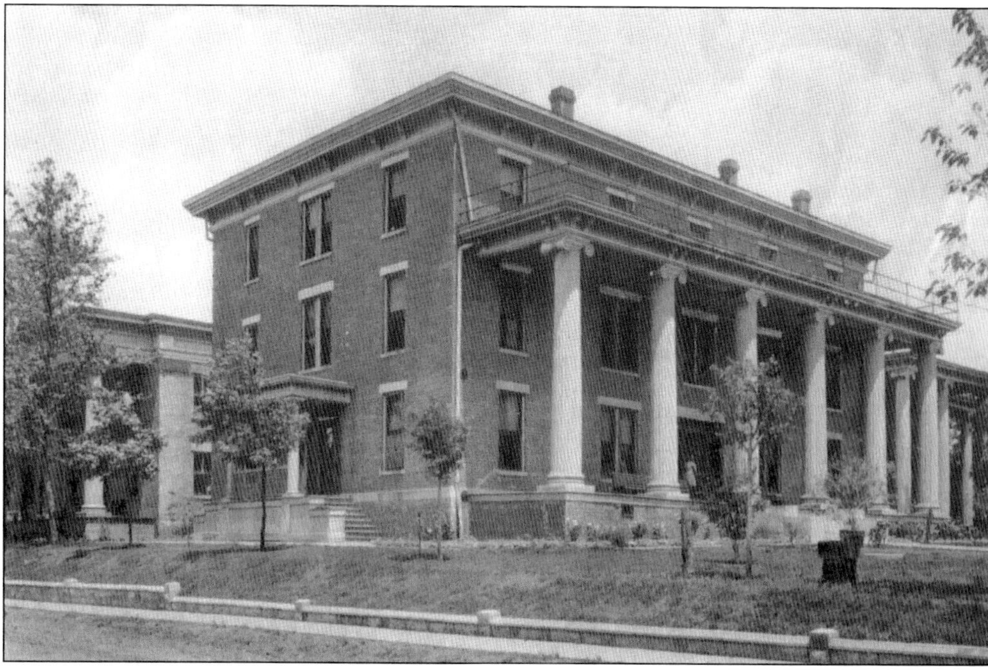

MARY NASH COLLEGE. Mary Nash College was a school for girls founded in 1877 by Baptist minister Jesse G. Nash and his wife, Mary L. Nash. The college was originally called the Sherman Female Institute. Mary Nash College closed in 1901 during a smallpox epidemic, and the property was purchased by the Kidd-Key College and Conservatory and became part of that campus. (Courtesy of the Sherman Museum.)

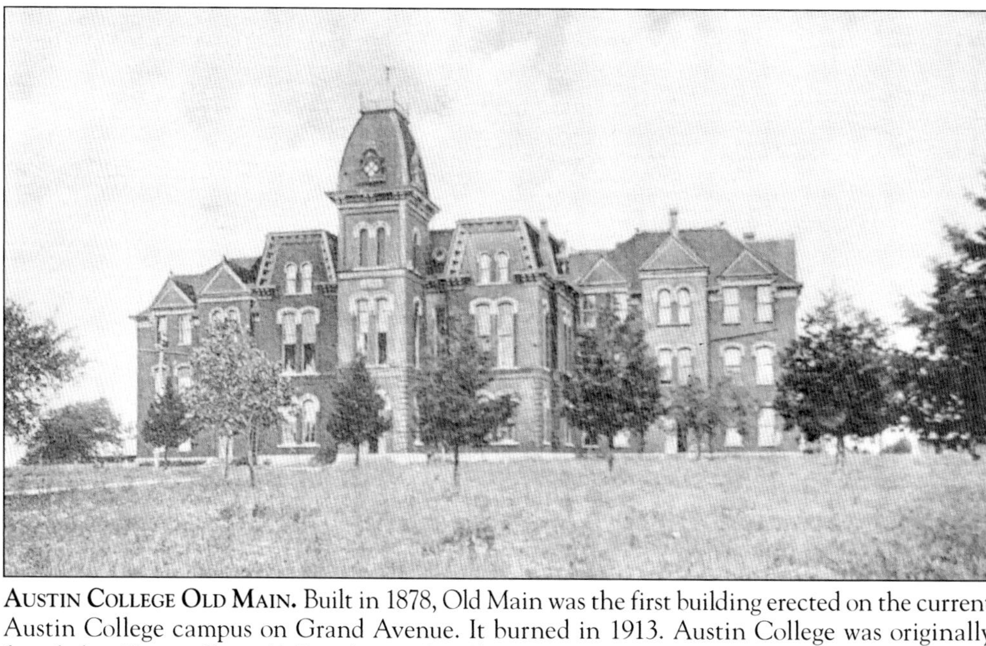

AUSTIN COLLEGE OLD MAIN. Built in 1878, Old Main was the first building erected on the current Austin College campus on Grand Avenue. It burned in 1913. Austin College was originally founded in Huntsville in 1849 and moved to Sherman in 1876. Today, it is the oldest institution of higher education in Texas operating under its original name and charter. (Courtesy of the City of Sherman.)

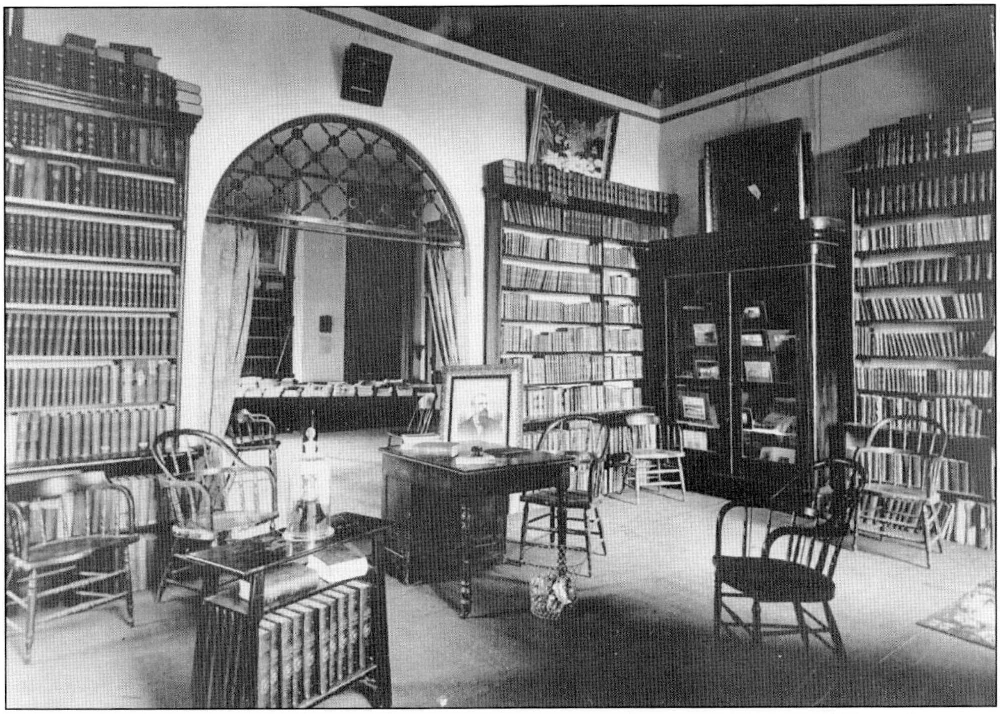

Old Main Library and Chemistry Laboratory. Austin College's first library and their chemistry laboratory were both located in the Old Main administration building, constructed between 1876 and 1878. The top photograph was taken in 1895 and shows the library after it had been renovated. An arch was cut between the library room and the north room, and the entire area was called Chadwick Memorial Hall. The bottom photograph shows the chemistry laboratory in 1912. The building was again being renovated when a 1913 fire destroyed the Old Main. It was said that the fire was caused by a "disgruntled student's wrath." (Both courtesy of the City of Sherman.)

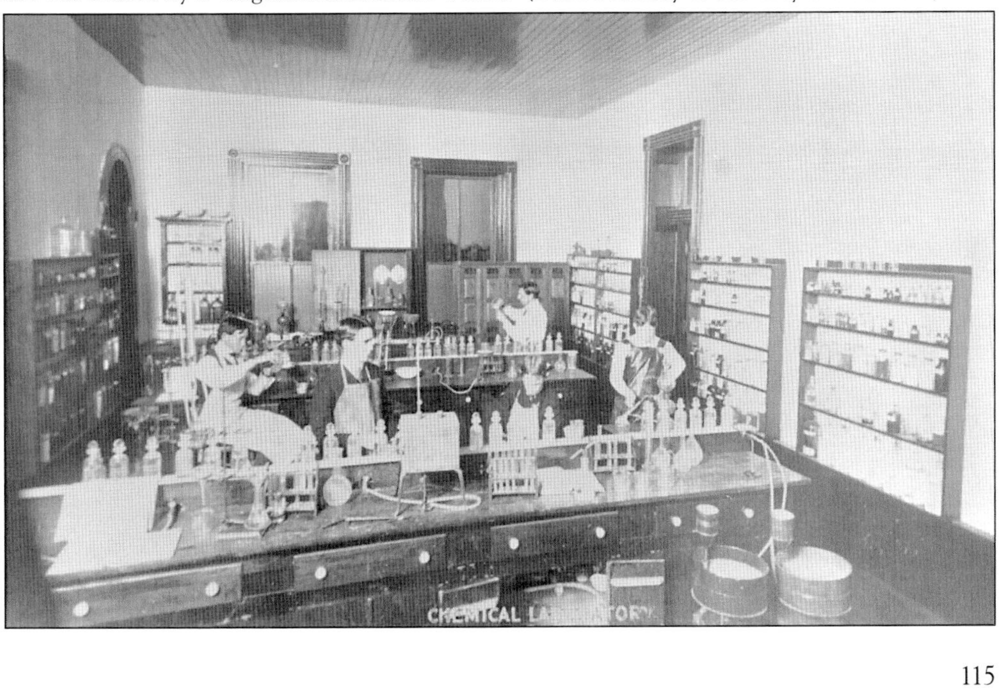

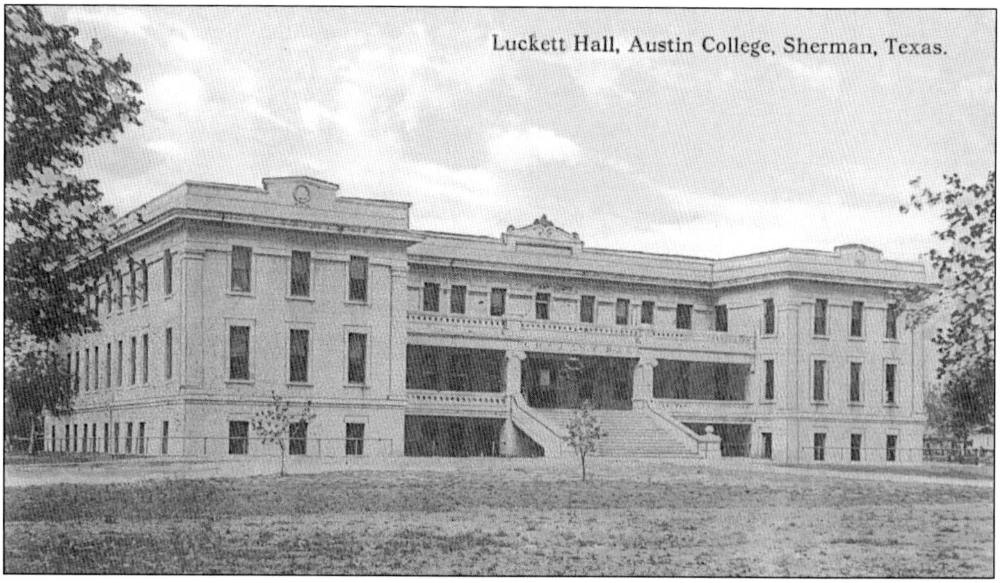

Austin College's Luckett Hall. Luckett Hall was built in 1907 and was the first men's dormitory at the college. It was named for Dr. S.M. Luckett, Austin College president from 1871 to 1878 and from 1887 to 1897. Dr. Luckett was president at the time Austin College moved to Sherman and favored relocating the school to a "town with better prospects." (Courtesy of Greg Ashby.)

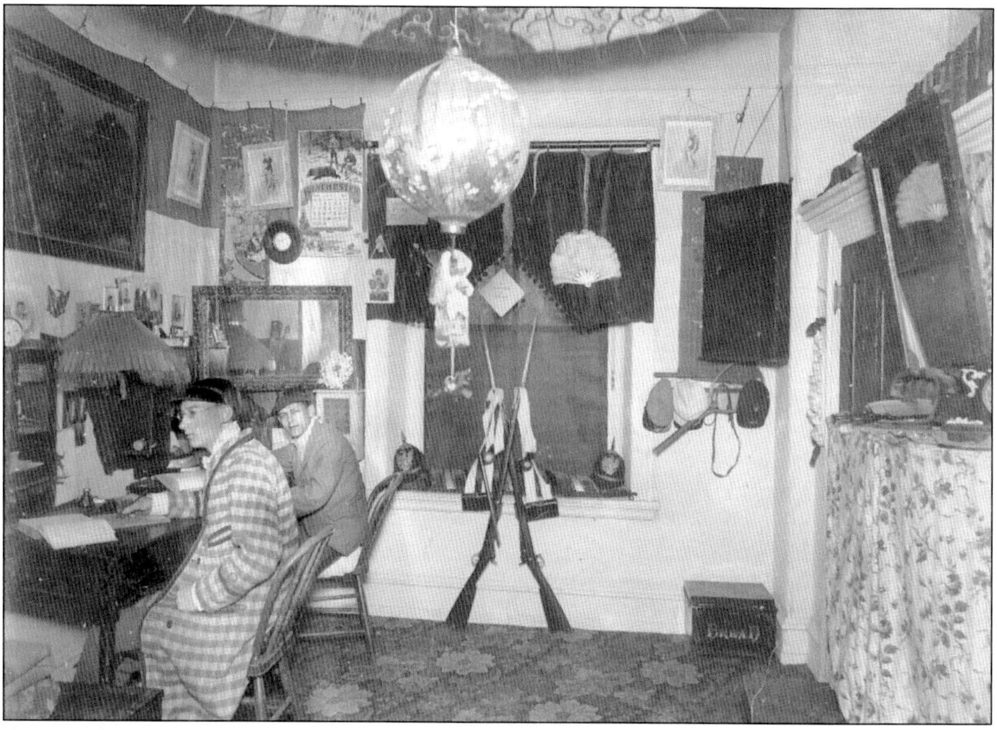

Austin College Dorm Room. This photograph shows a dormitory room at Austin College. Enrollment at Austin College increased with the return of war veterans in 1945 and temporary housing units were erected on the athletic field. The college became coeducational in 1918. (Courtesy of the Sherman Museum.)

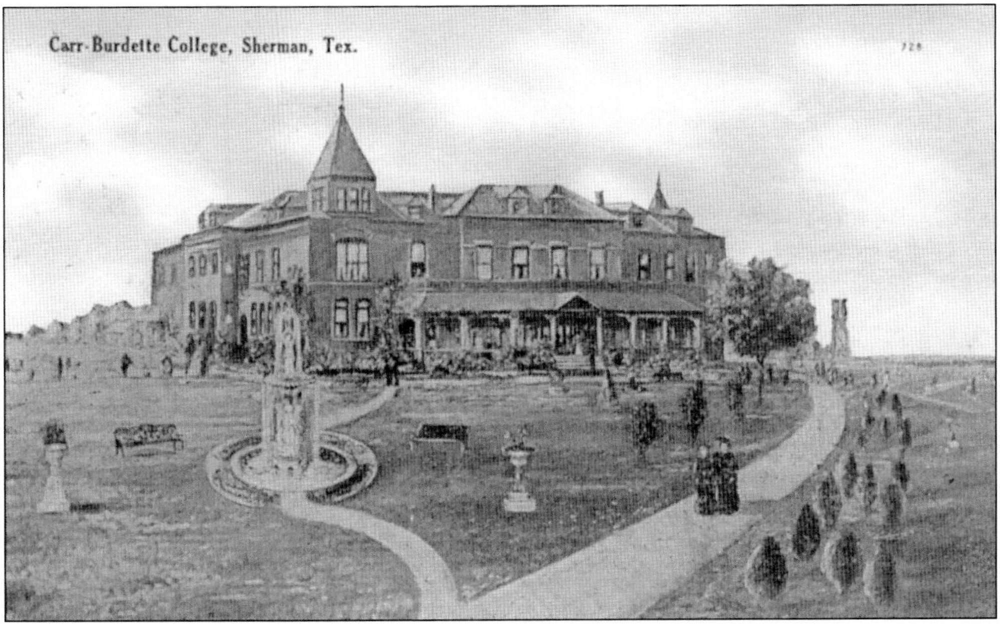

CARR-BURDETTE COLLEGE. Carr-Burdette College opened in 1894 as a home and school for girls. It was located on an eight-acre site on North Burdette Street and was founded by O.A. and Mattie Carr. The school catalogue described the orchard and garden that supplied the school with food. After Mattie Carr's death in 1907, the Christian Church of Texas took over the college. It closed in 1930. (Courtesy of Greg Ashby.)

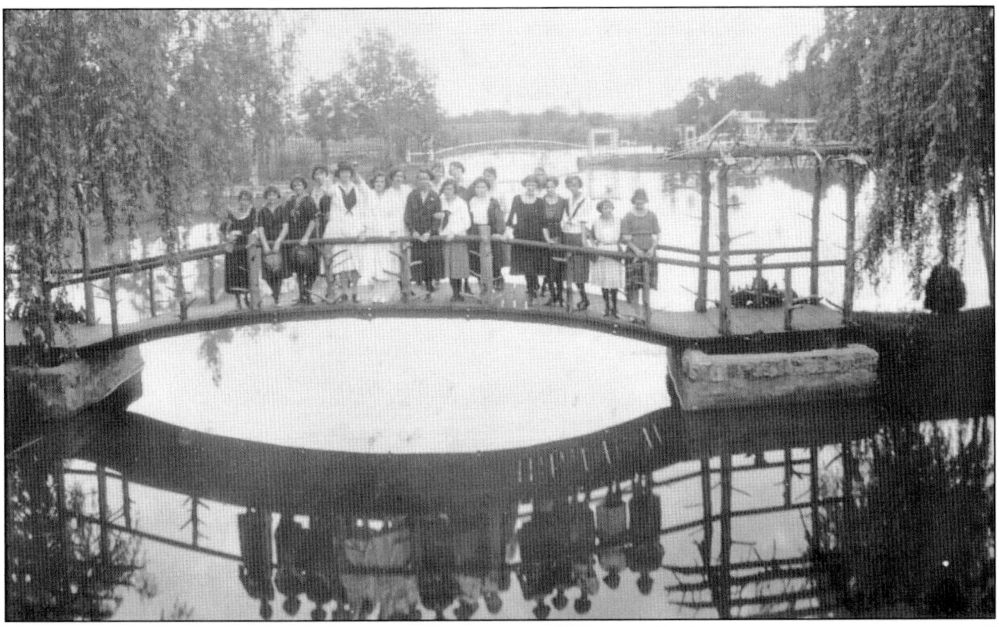

CARR-BURDETTE COLLEGE GIRLS AT CHAPMAN PARK. Chapman Park was a private preserve several miles southeast of Sherman and operated by the Chapman family, who also owned Chapman Milling Company. Brothers Richard and George Chapman opened the park to local college students, factory workers, and members of clubs to which they belonged. In 1921, students from Carr-Burdette visited the park. (Courtesy of the City of Sherman.)

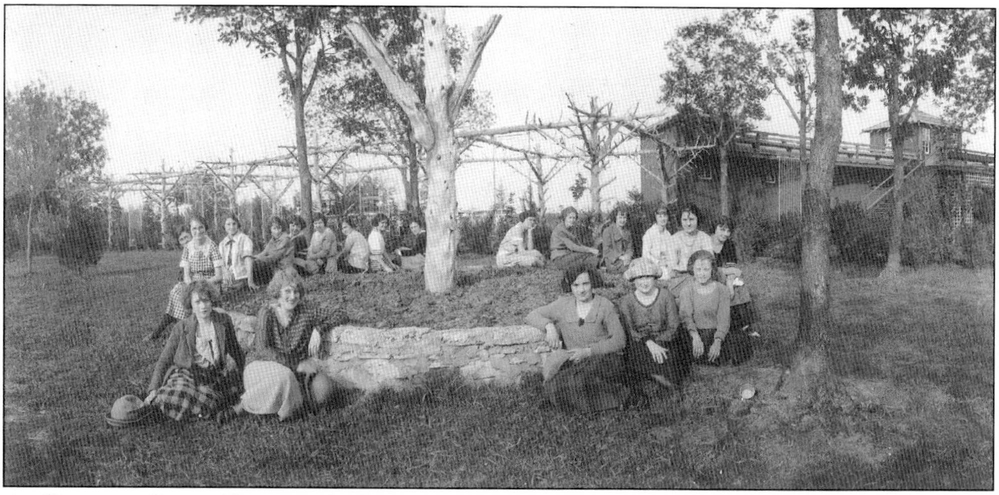

At Chapman Park. Chapman Park was a 26-acre tract of land that was never open to the public and featured a lake and a sizeable pond. Carr-Burdette College was established as a college that would promote a high cultural tradition for young women and train them in ladylike conduct and the social graces. Carr-Burdette students are shown visiting Chapman Park. (Courtesy of the Sherman Museum.)

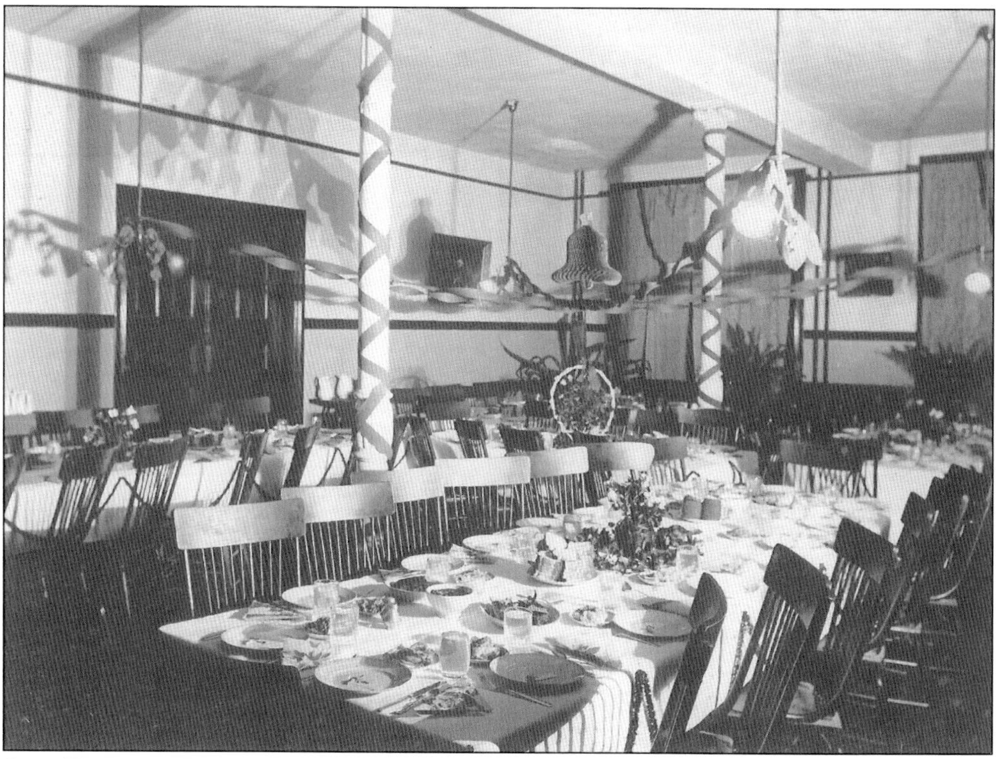

Carr-Burdette Dining Room. The eight-acre campus of Carr-Burdette College had fruit trees and raspberry, blackberry, and grapevines. According to the school's catalogue, vegetables from the garden would supply the summer and fall vegetables for the college tables. "They will recognize when they visit us that our table fare is above that of the average boarding school." (Courtesy of the Sherman Museum.)

Six

Industry Moves to Town

Economic Development had been a mainstay of Sherman, and by the 1950s, it became known as the "City of Diversified Industry." The population was about 26,804, and Sherman featured 64 manufacturing establishments with 3,300 workers.

Industrial growth continued with companies such as Sherman Steel and Wire, IBM, Johnson & Johnson, Olson Bodies Grumman, Kaiser Aluminum, and Texas Instruments. No longer was grain, cotton, or clothing the only industry leaders in Sherman. Now plants served the growing needs of data processing machines, surgical dressings, truck bodies, and semiconductors.

Sherman Card Plant was established in 1957 and was constructed to serve data processing machine customers in the Southwest. The plant produced the color coded cards that were used to input information into computers as well as the IBM Correcting Selectric typewriter and the IBM Sorter. Sherman's IBM plant closed in 1975.

Johnson & Johnson opened its Sherman plant in 1961 on a 440-acre tract in the Blalock Industrial District. At the time they marketed 40 different products including sponges, gauze pads, tapes, and cleaners. By 1976, the plant employed more than 900 people and made over 200 different products. The plant closed in 2003.

Texas Instruments opened in 1965 on more than 600 acres in the Blalock Industrial District and became Sherman's biggest employer. The company makes electronic equipment, defense equipment, and silicon products.

Sherman continued to grow with companies such as Oscar Mayer, Fisher Controls, Folgers, Libby-Owens-Ford, Sunny Delight, and Presco Products. By 1985, the community boasted 63 manufacturing establishments with 12,500 workers.

Oscar Mayer opened in 1976 as a processing plant for wieners and cold cuts. In 1990, the company employed more than 800 people, but closed in 1998. The facility was eventually sold to Tyson Foods.

Folgers Coffee Company also opened a plant in 1976 to produce coffee and chilled juice products. Sunny Delight opened in 1989 as part of the Folgers Coffee facility under the Procter & Gamble Company group. In 2008, Folgers was acquired by the J.M. Smucker Company and announced their closing in 2011. However, Sunny Delight purchased the building and will continue processing their juice drink in Sherman.

Even today Sherman boasts continued industry growth with companies such as GlobiTech, Progress Rail Services, CertainTeed Corporation, and Tyson Foods.

Between the rail service, Sherman's location at the crossroads of US Highway 75 and US Highway 82, and the steps taken to ensure that plenty of water is available, the location continues to be prosperous for local industry.

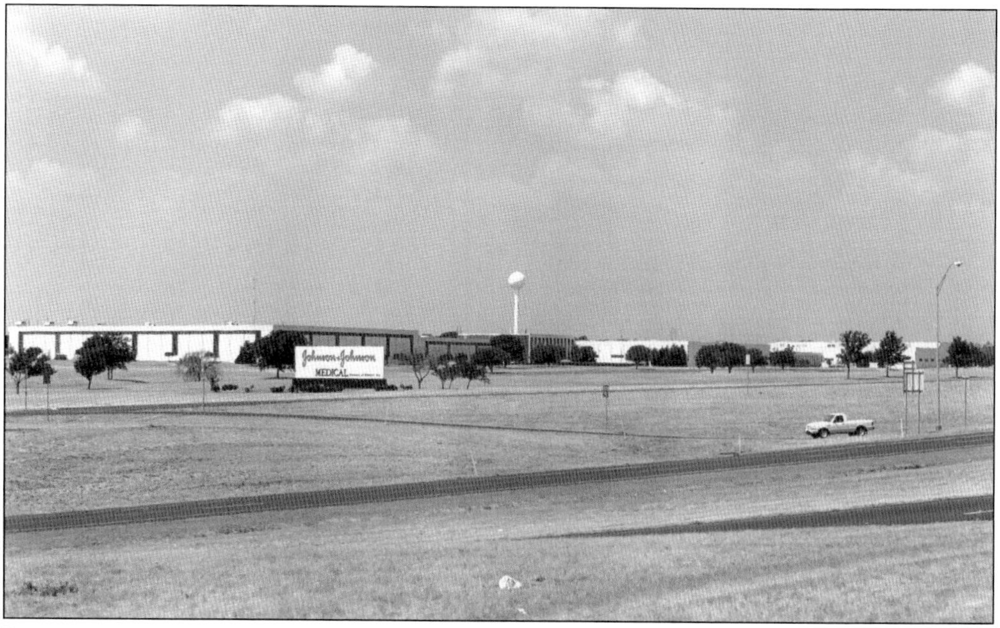

JOHNSON & JOHNSON. Johnson & Johnson opened in 1961 as a surgical dressings plant making sponges, gauze pads, tapes, and cleaners. By 1976, the company had more than 900 employees and produced more than 200 different products. In 1991, Johnson & Johnson Medical, Inc. of Sherman was named one of the 10 best manufacturing plants in the nation by *Industry Week* magazine. The plant closed in 2003. (Courtesy of the Sherman Economic Development Corporation.)

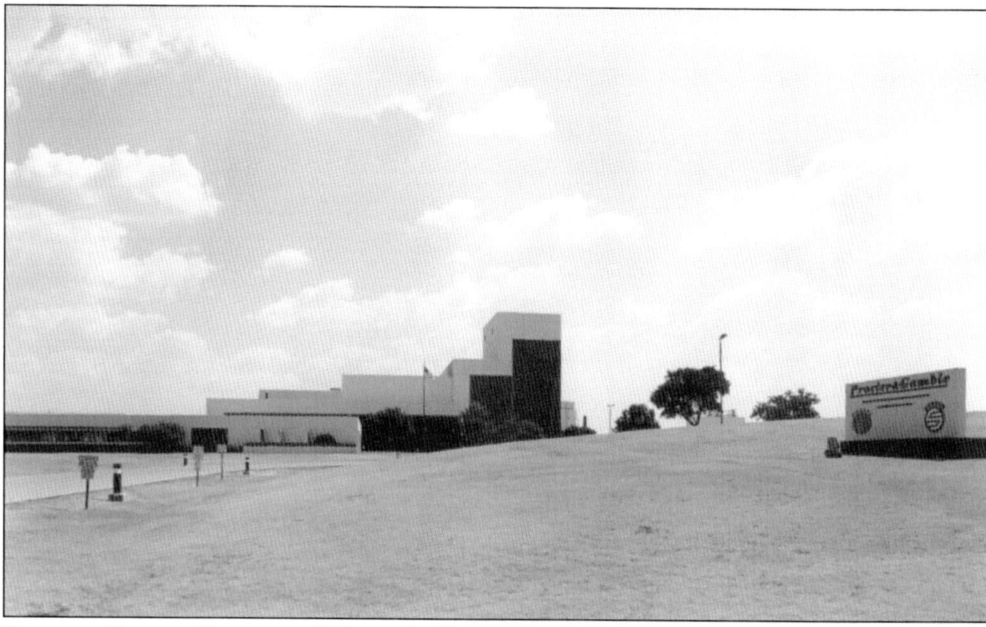

FOLGERS COFFEE COMPANY. Folgers Coffee Company, a subsidiary of Procter & Gamble, opened in Sherman in 1979, employing 400 people. In one hour, the plant could produce more than three million cups of coffee. Chilled juice products were also made there. In 2008, the company was acquired by the J.M. Smucker Company. (Courtesy of the Sherman Economic Development Corporation.)

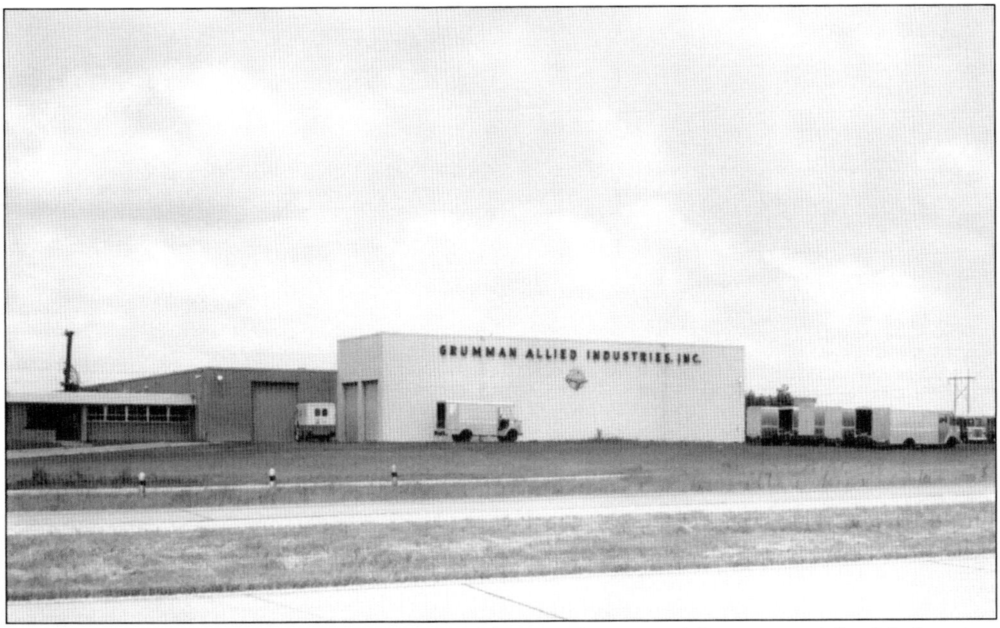

GRUMMAN ALLIED INDUSTRIES. Grumman Olson, a division of Grumman Allied Industries, opened their Sherman plant in March 1963, after purchasing the plant from the Glasspar Boat Company. Over the years, they produced truck bodies and pleasure boat hulls made of aluminum and fiberglass. The Sherman plant closed in 1990, due to decreased sales in the South and Southwest. (Courtesy of the Sherman Economic Development Corporation.)

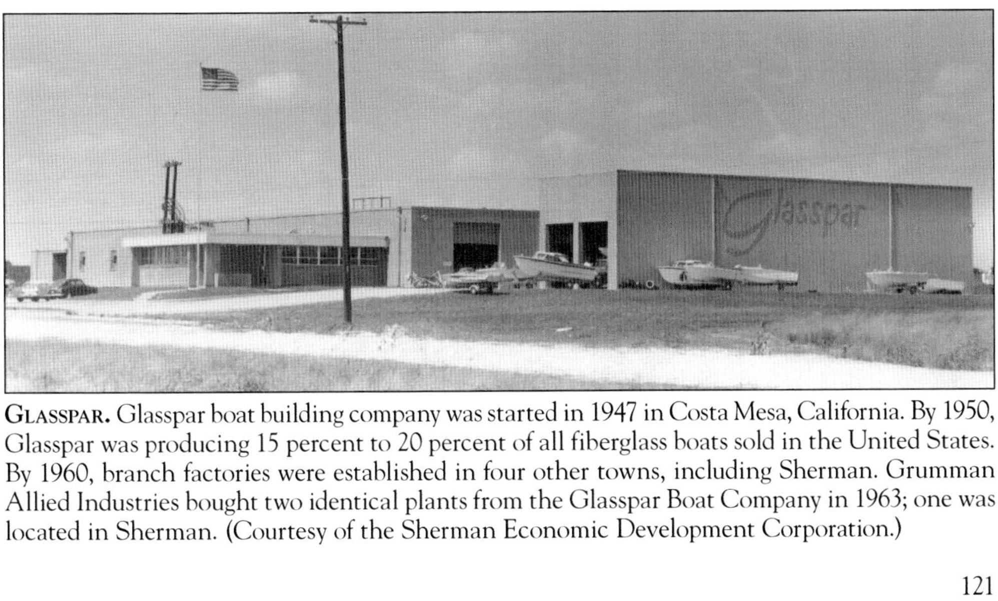

GLASSPAR. Glasspar boat building company was started in 1947 in Costa Mesa, California. By 1950, Glasspar was producing 15 percent to 20 percent of all fiberglass boats sold in the United States. By 1960, branch factories were established in four other towns, including Sherman. Grumman Allied Industries bought two identical plants from the Glasspar Boat Company in 1963; one was located in Sherman. (Courtesy of the Sherman Economic Development Corporation.)

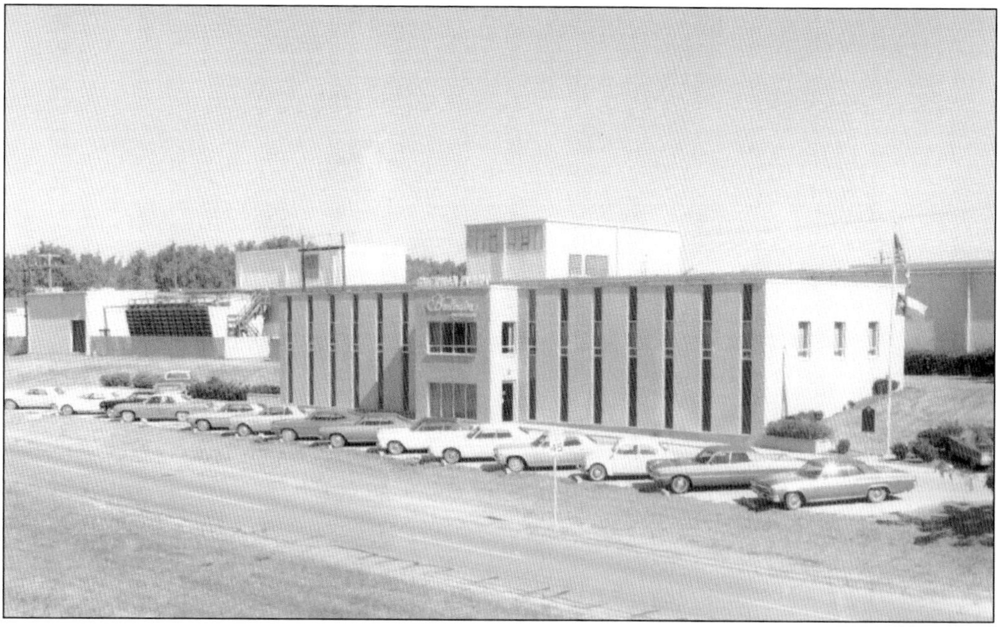

Burlington Industries. Sherman Seamless Bag Mill was constructed in 1891 for textile manufacturing. In 1955, Burlington Industries acquired controlling interest in the company from the Ely and Walker Company. At that time wide sheeting became their main product. When the plant closed in 1986, 550 employees worked there and they produced greige, or unfinished fabric used in the production of sheets and pillowcases. (Courtesy of the Sherman Museum.)

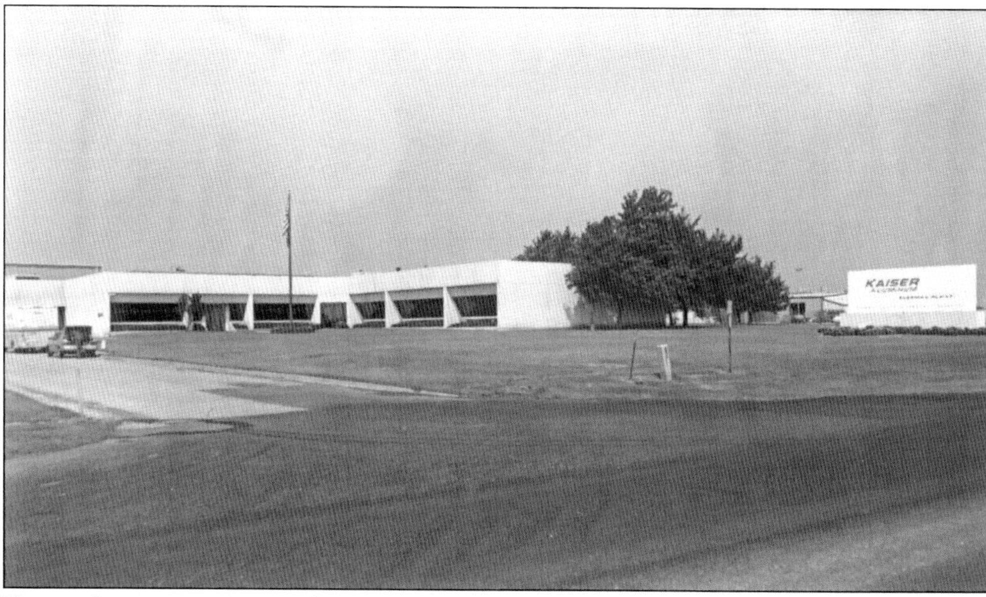

Kaiser Aluminum. Kaiser Aluminum opened in 1963 in the Blalock Industrial District. The company was the first aluminum extruding facility in the Grayson County area and supplies aluminum extrusions to the Southwest, Southeast, and Midwest markets. In 2010, Kaiser Aluminum employed 200 people. Prior to 1963, the plant building was a fabrication and distribution center for Capitol Products, a manufacturer of aluminum windows and doors. (Courtesy of the City of Sherman.)

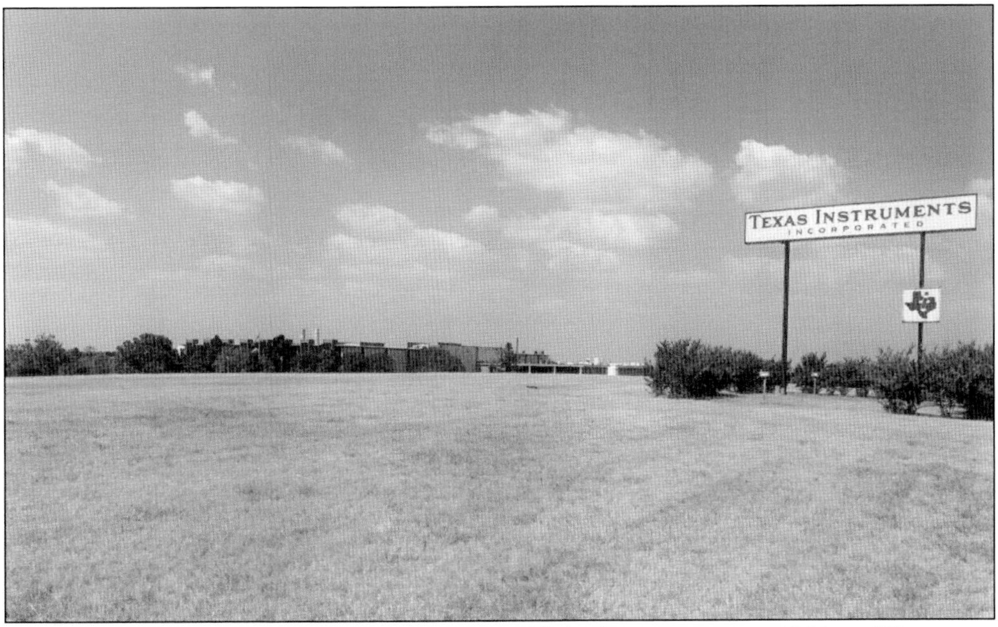

TEXAS INSTRUMENTS. Texas Instruments was established in Sherman in 1965 on 600 acres in the Blalock Industrial Park. The facility produces over 3,000 different products to fit a diverse base of applications. The first commercial silicon transistors, the first integrated circuits, and the first hand-held calculators are among Texas Instruments' inventions. (Courtesy of the Sherman Economic Development Corporation.)

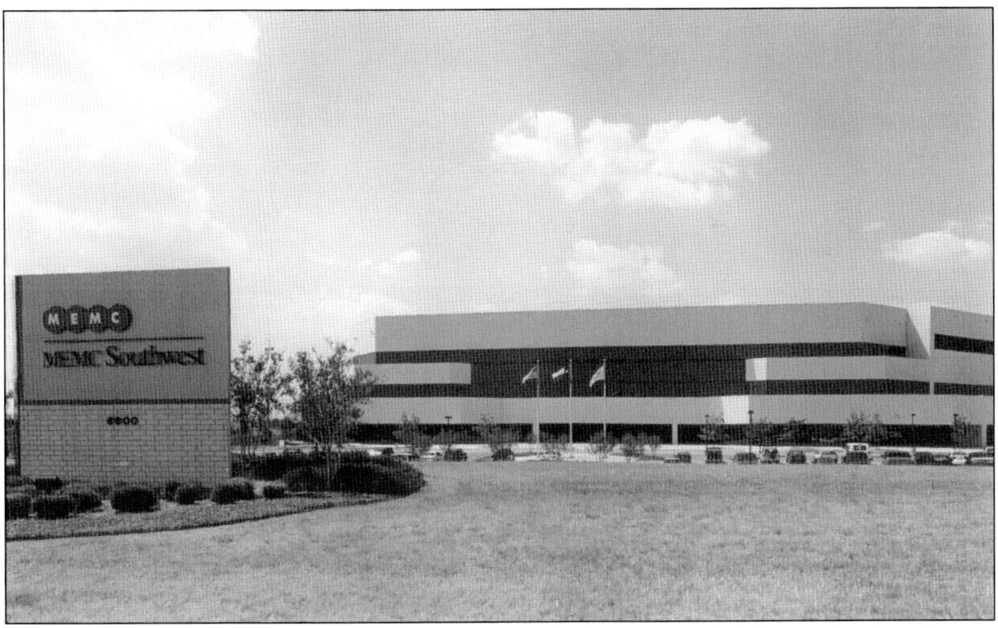

MEMC SOUTHWEST. MEMC Southwest opened in Sherman in 1997 and was a joint venture with the Texas Instruments plant. MEMC produced and manufactured wafers that were the foundation for semiconductors and solar cells, and the new plant would be the only producer for wafers in the Texas Instruments chain. MEMC added 500 to 800 more high-tech jobs to the local workforce. (Courtesy of the Sherman Economic Development Corporation.)

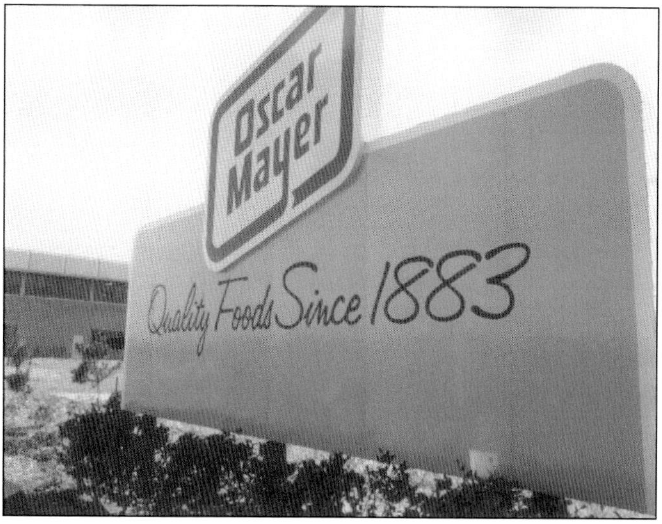

Oscar Mayer. Oscar Mayer opened in 1976 in a 537,000-square-foot facility in the Blalock Industrial District. Over 500 employees worked at the plant. In 1981, General Foods bought the company for $423,400,000 and changed the name to Oscar Mayer Foods Corporation. Later, it became part of Kraft General Foods, Inc. Oscar Mayer closed in 1998, and the plant was eventually sold to Tyson Foods, Inc. (Courtesy of the City of Sherman.)

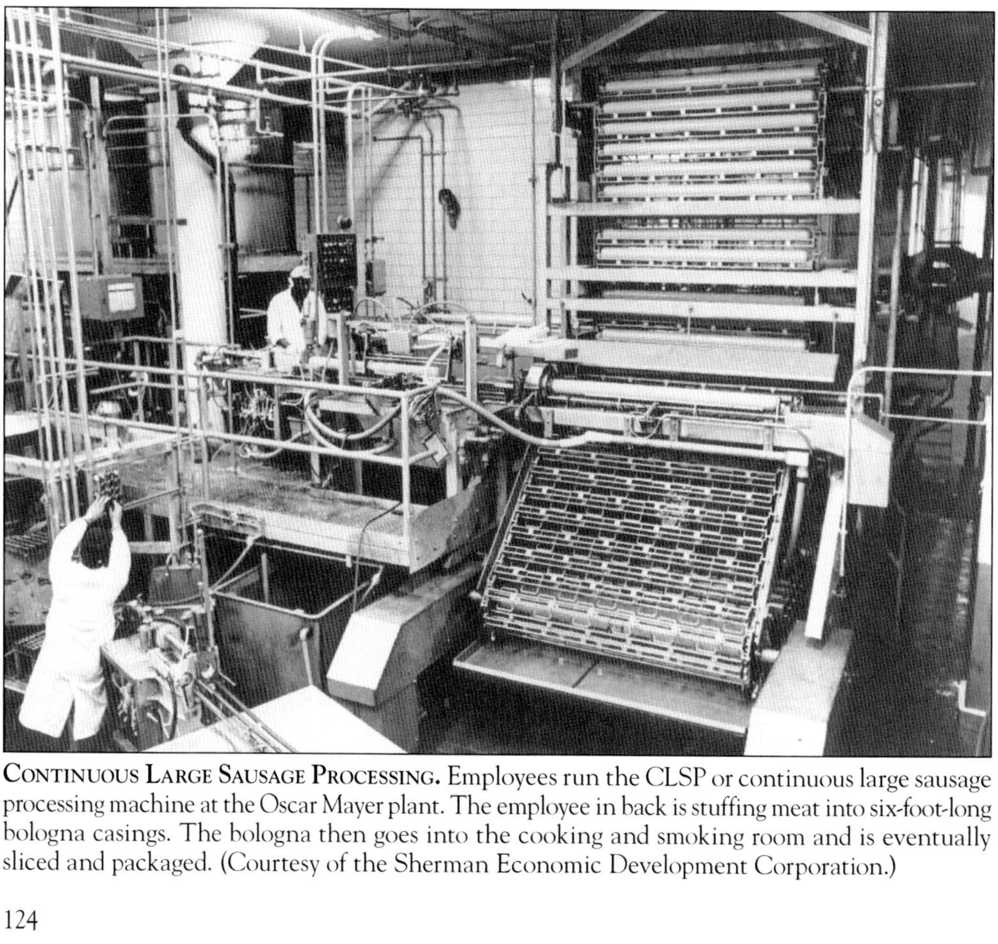

Continuous Large Sausage Processing. Employees run the CLSP or continuous large sausage processing machine at the Oscar Mayer plant. The employee in back is stuffing meat into six-foot-long bologna casings. The bologna then goes into the cooking and smoking room and is eventually sliced and packaged. (Courtesy of the Sherman Economic Development Corporation.)

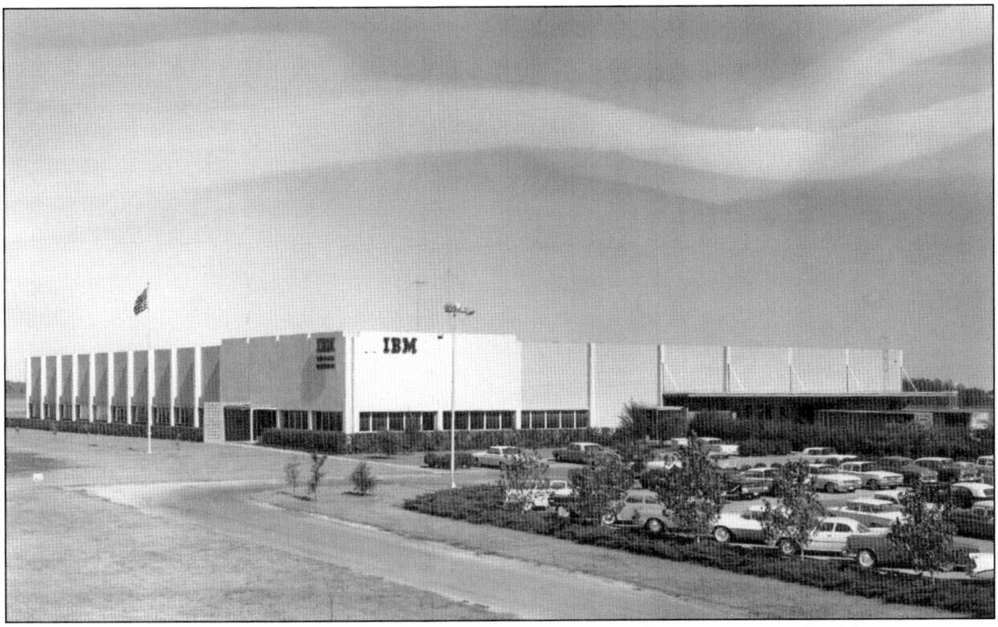

IBM. The Sherman Card Plant was established in 1957 to serve the growing needs of data processing machine customers in the Southwest. They produced color-coded cards that were used to input information into computers. The company also produced IBM Correcting Selectric typewriters and IBM sorters. The company closed in 1975 and was located in the building now occupied by Fisher Controls. (Courtesy of the Sherman Economic Development Corporation.)

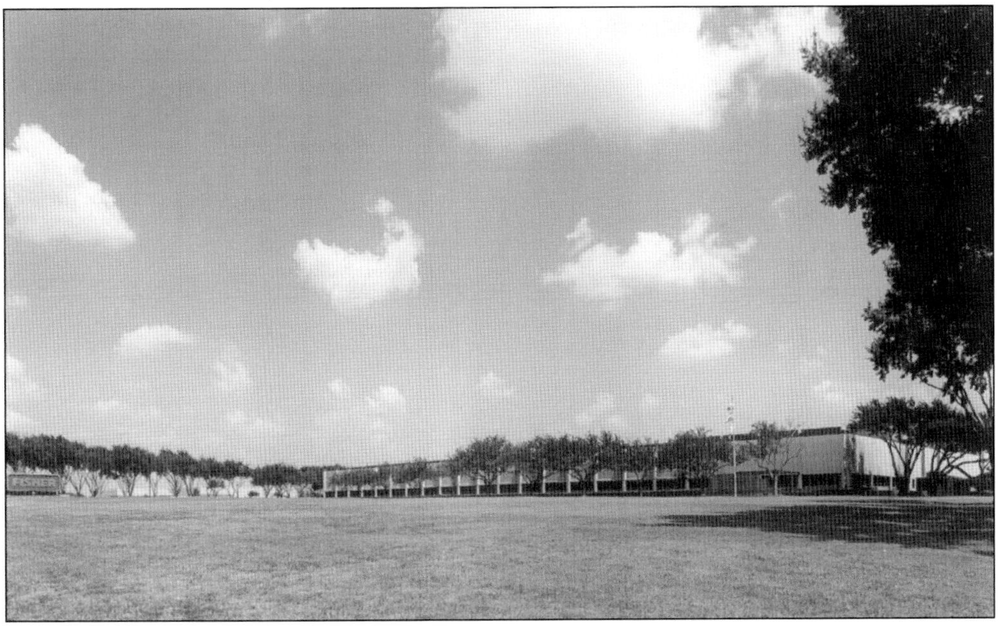

Fisher Controls. Fisher Controls opened in 1976 to produce a special line of rotary valves with tight shutoff capabilities. By 1995, the company manufactured rotary ball, high performance butterfly, and sliding stem globe valves. Emerson Process Management purchased Fisher Controls in 1992, and by 2010 the company employed 300 people. (Courtesy of the Sherman Economic Development Corporation.)

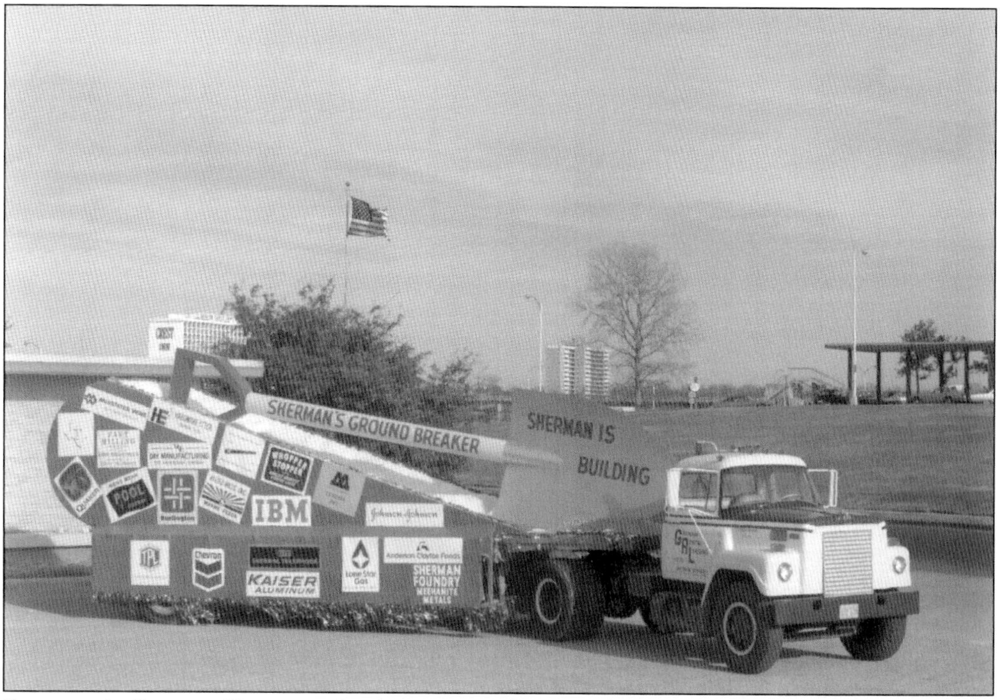

SHERMAN'S GROUND BREAKER. In the 1960s and 1970s, the Sherman Chamber of Commerce advertised, "Sherman Is Building" with their Ground Breaker. The huge shovel was taken to various industry ground breakings to advertise the growth of the community. Men would stand on the cross blade of the shovel during the ground-breaking ceremony for a photo opportunity. (Courtesy of the Sherman Economic Development Corporation.)

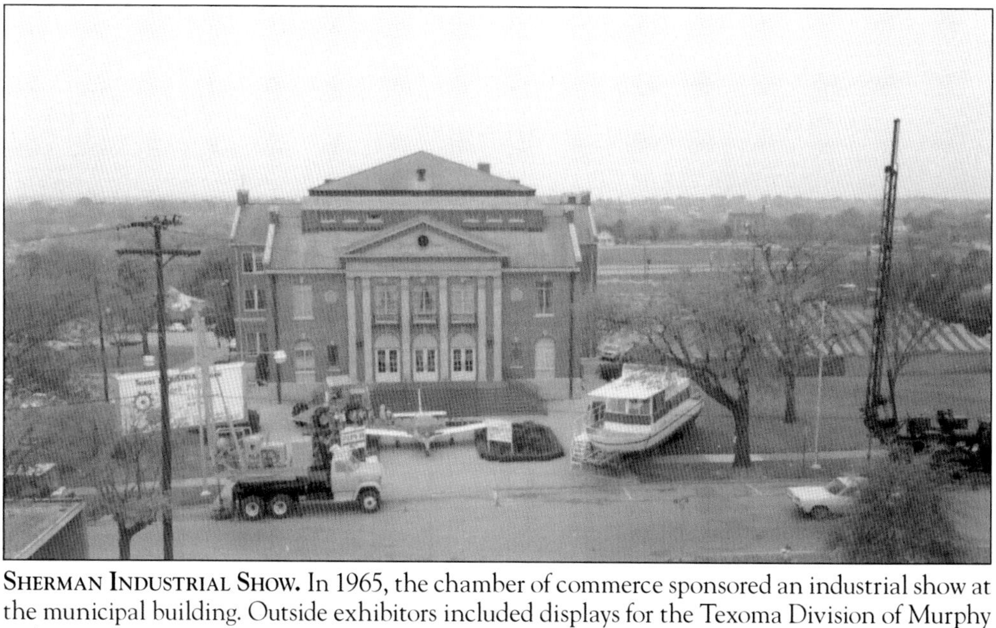

SHERMAN INDUSTRIAL SHOW. In 1965, the chamber of commerce sponsored an industrial show at the municipal building. Outside exhibitors included displays for the Texoma Division of Murphy Industries, Loe's Highport Marina Boat Sales and Manufacturing, Sherman Piper Aircraft Sales, Olson Bodies, and Texas Power and Light Company. (Courtesy of the Sherman Museum.)

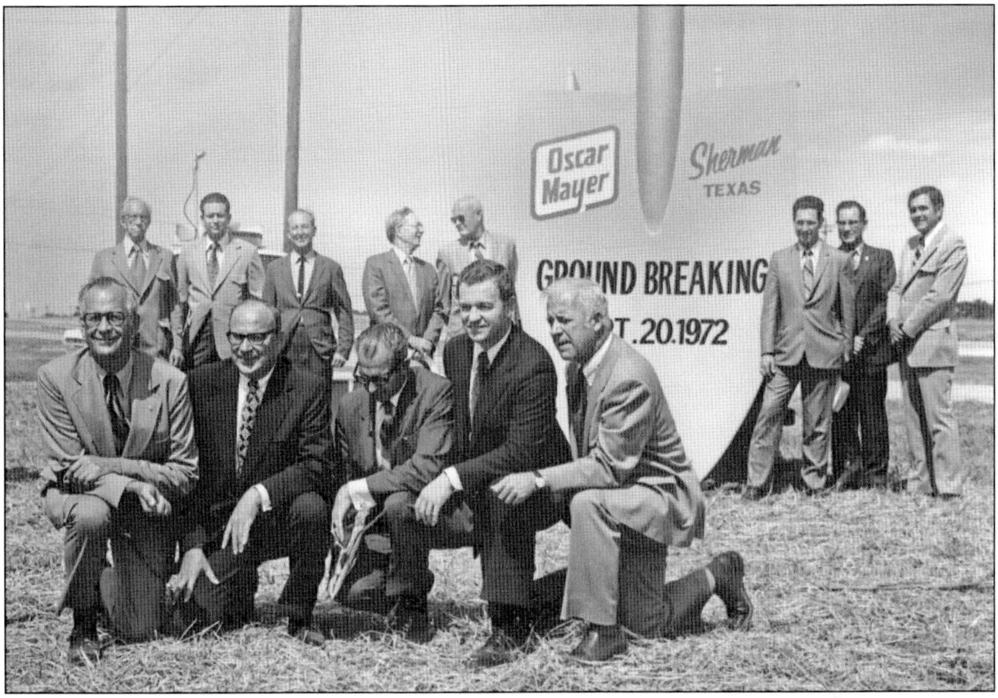

OSCAR MAYER GROUND BREAKING. The ground breaking for the Oscar Mayer plant was held in 1972, and the facility opened in 1976. The $12-million plant was located on a 70-acre site adjoining the Texas Instruments property. The meat processing plant was expected to employ 500 people. (Courtesy of the Sherman Economic Development Corporation.)

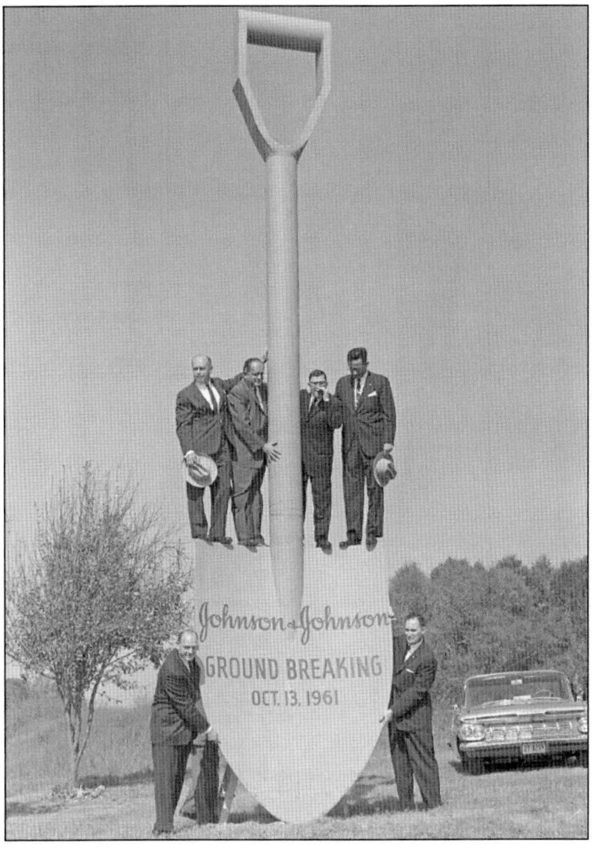

JOHNSON & JOHNSON GROUND BREAKING. On October 13, 1961, civic leaders and company executives gathered to break ground on the new Johnson & Johnson facility that would be located in the Blalock Industrial District. The new $2,500,000 plant was located on a 440-acre tract and in 1963 employed 300 people and manufactured 40 different products. (Courtesy of the Sherman Economic Development Corporation.)